LIBRARY OF PHILOSOPHY AND RELIGION

General Editor: John Hick

Danforth Professor, Claremont Graduate School

Claremont, California

This series of books explores contemporary religious understandings of humanity and the universe. The books contribute to various aspects of the continuing dialogues between religion and philosophy, between scepticism and faith, and between the different religions and ideologies. The authors represent a correspondingly wide range of viewpoints. Some of the books in the series are written for the general educated public and others for a more specialised philosophical or theological readership.

Masao Abe	ZEN AND WESTERN THOUGHT
William H. Austin	THE RELEVANCE OF NATURAL SCIENCE TO THEOLOGY
Paul Badham	CHRISTIAN BELIEFS ABOUT LIFE AFTER DEATH
Paul and Linda Badham	IMMORTALITY OR EXTINCTION?
Daniel E. Bassuk	INCARNATION IN HINDUISM AND CHRISTIANITY
Patrick Burke	THE FRAGILE UNIVERSE
Margaret Chatterjee	GANDHI'S RELIGIOUS THOUGHT
Dan Cohn-Sherbok	ISSUES IN CONTEMPORARY JUDAISM
	ISLAM IN A WORLD OF DIVERSE FAITHS
William Lane Craig	THE *KALÂM* COSMOLOGICAL ARGUMENT
	THE COSMOLOGICAL ARGUMENT FROM PLATO TO LEIBNIZ
Stephen T. Davis	LOGIC AND THE NATURE OF GOD
Lynn A. de Silva	THE PROBLEM OF THE SELF IN BUDDHISM AND CHRISTIANITY
Padmasiri de Silva	AN INTRODUCTION TO BUDDHIST PSYCHOLOGY
Clement Dore	GOD, SUFFERING AND SOLIPSISM
Ramchandra Gandhi	THE AVAILABILITY OF RELIGIOUS IDEAS
J.C.A. Gaskin	HUME'S PHILOSOPHY OF RELIGION
Brian Haymes	THE CONCEPT OF THE KNOWLEDGE OF GOD
John Hick and Edmund S. Meltzer (*editors*)	THREE FAITHS – ONE GOD
H.A. Hodges	GOD BEYOND KNOWLEDGE
J. Kellenberger	THE COGNITIVITY OF RELIGION
	GOD RELATIONSHIPS WITH AND WITHOUT GOD
Jonathan L. Kvanvig	THE POSSIBILITY OF AN ALL-KNOWING GOD
Hywel D. Lewis	PERSONS AND LIFE AFTER DEATH

Julius J. Lipner	THE FACE OF TRUTH
Eric Lott	VEDANTIC APPROACHES TO GOD
Geddes MacGregor	REINCARNATION AS A CHRISTIAN HOPE
Hugo A. Meynell	AN INTRODUCTION TO THE PHILOSOPHY OF BERNARD LONERGAN
F.C.T. Moore	THE PSYCHOLOGICAL BASIS OF MORALITY
Dennis Nineham	THE USE AND ABUSE OF THE BIBLE
Martin Prozesky	RELIGION AND ULTIMATE WELL-BEING
D.Z. Phillips	BELIEF, CHANGE AND FORMS OF LIFE
Bernard M.G. Reardon	HEGEL'S PHILOSOPHY OF RELIGION
	KANT AS PHILOSOPHICAL THEOLOGIAN
Joseph Runzo	REASON, RELATIVISM AND GOD
John J. Shepherd	EXPERIENCE, INFERENCE AND GOD
Patrick Sherry	RELIGION, TRUTH AND LANGUAGE GAMES
	SPIRIT, SAINTS AND IMMORTALITY
Ninian Smart	CONCEPT AND EMPATHY
	RELIGION AND THE WESTERN MIND
Wilfred Cantwell Smith	TOWARDS A WORLD THEOLOGY
Jonathan Sutton	THE RELIGIOUS PHILOSOPHY OF VLADIMIR SOLOVYOV
Linda J. Tessier (*editor*)	CONCEPTS OF THE ULTIMATE
Shivesh Chandra Thakur	RELIGION AND RATIONAL CHOICE
Robert Young	FREEDOM, RESPONSIBILITY AND GOD

Issues in Contemporary Judaism

Dan Cohn-Sherbok

Director
Centre for the Study of Religion and Society
University of Kent, Canterbury

MACMILLAN

First published 1991

Published by
MACMILLAN ACADEMIC & PROFESSIONAL
Houndmills, Basingstoke, Hampshire RG21 2XS
and London
Companies and representatives
throughout the world

Printed in Hong Kong

British Library Cataloguing in Publication Data
Cohn-Sherbok, Dan
Issues in Contemporary Judaism.
1. Judaism
I. Title   II. Series
296

ISBN 0–333–53553–7

For Lavinia, Herod, and Dido

Contents

Acknowledgements   viii

Introduction   ix

 1 Jewish Faith and the Holocaust   1

 2 The Afterlife in Contemporary Jewish Belief   19

 3 The Torah in Modern Judaism   31

 4 Law and Freedom in Reform Judaism   38

 5 Jewish Missionising in Contemporary Society   51

 6 Judaism and the Problems of the Inner City   63

 7 Judaism and Christian Anti-Semitism   84

 8 Obstacles to Jewish-Christian Encounter   91

 9 A New Vision of Jewish-Christian Dialogue   98

10 Judaism and the Theology of Liberation   107

11 Judaism and the Universe of Faiths   128

12 Ranking Judaism and Other Religions   135

Notes   146

Bibliography   155

Index   160

Acknowledgements

Earlier versions of the following chapters in this book have appeared elsewhere: 'The Afterlife in Contemporary Jewish Belief' was published as 'Death and Immortality in the Jewish Tradition' in *Death and Immortality in the Religions of the World* edited by Paul and Linda Badham (Paragon House, New York, 1987); 'The Torah in Modern Judaism' came out as 'The Torah Controversy' in *Religion Today*, Vol. III, No. 1, 1986; 'Jewish Missionizing in Contemporary Society' appeared as 'Jewish Missionizing and Conversion' in *The Journal of Religious Studies*, Vol. VII, No. 1, 1979; 'Judaism and the Problems of the Inner City' was published as 'Faith in the City: A Jewish Response' in *Theology in the City* edited by Anthony Harvey (London: SPCK, 1989); 'Judaism and Christian Anti-Semitism' came out as 'Christianity and Anti-Semitism' in *The Month*, Vol. CCXLVII, No. 1421, 1986; 'Obstacles to Jewish-Christian Encounter' appeared as 'Between Christian and Jew' in *Theology*, Vol. LXXXIII, 1980; 'A New Vision of Jewish-Christian Dialogue' was published as 'Jewish-Christian Dialogue: A New Proposal' in *Kings Theological Review*, Vol. VI, No. 2, 1983; 'Judaism and the Theology of Liberation' came out under the same title in *Modern Theology*, Vol. 3, No. 1, 1986; 'Judaism and the Universe of Faiths' appeared under the same title in *New Blackfriars*, Vol. 65, No. 763, 1984; 'Ranking Judaism and Other Religions' was published as 'Ranking Religions' in *Religious Studies*, Vol. 22.

I would like to thank Sophie Lillington of Macmillan for her help and encouragement, and Mollie Roots for typing the manuscript.

Introduction

Over the last two hundred years Jewry has entered the mainstream
of Western society – such a transformation has profoundly altered
the nature of Jewish existence. In the past Judaism was essentially
a unified structure embracing different interpretations of the same
tradition. This was the case, for example, in Hellenistic times
when the Jewish community was divided into three main parties:
Pharisees, Sadduccees and Essenes. Again, in the early modern
period the Hasidim and traditional rabbis (Mitnagdim) vied with
one another for supremacy. But the modern period has witnessed
an unprecedented fragmentation of the Jewish people into a wide
variety of sub-groups with markedly different orientations.

This development in Jewish life has been largely the result of the
Enlightenment which began at the end of the 18th century. No
longer were Jews insulated from non-Jewish currents of culture and
thought, and this change led many Jews to seek a modernization
of Jewish worship. The earliest reformers engaged in liturgical
revision, but quickly the spirit of reform spread to other areas
of Jewish existence. Eventually modernists convened a succession
of rabbinical conferences in order to formulate a common policy.
Such a radical approach to the Jewish tradition evoked a hostile
response from a number of leading Orthodox rabbis and stimulated
the creation of neo-Orthodoxy. Such opposition, however, did not
stem the tide; the development of the scientific study of Judaism and
the positive-historical school continued to inspire many reformers
who were sympathetic to modern culture and learning.

The fragmentation of the Jewish people was accompanied by
the growth of anti-Semitism which in previous centuries had been
enflamed by Christian hostility. Political conditions in Europe after
1870 brought about considerable disruption – several proud and
independent nations emerged and fought against indigenous minority
groups which threatened their homogeneity. Living in such conditions Jews were regarded as aliens and unassimilable. In Germany
a number of writers criticized the Jews on racist grounds and the
German Christian Social Party was founded on the basis of an
anti-Semitic platform. The Dreyfus affair in France led Jewish
intellectuals to conclude that Jews would never be accepted in

the countries where they lived. Pogroms in Russia at the end of the century had a similar impact on Jewish thinkers. According to these writers the liberation of Jewry could only be secured by the establishment of a Jewish homeland. By the turn of the century the idea of Jewish nationalism had spread to other countries, resulting in the convocation of several Zionist conferences. At the same time waves of settlers had migrated to Palestine; most of these pioneers lived in cities and worked on farm colonies under the control of the Jewish Organization Association.

The rise of Nazism in the 1930s brought about the most traumatic episode in modern Jewish history, the Holocaust. The ideology of the Nazi party was based on German nationalism, anti-communism and anti-Semitism. According to Hitler, the Jews were responsible for Germany's defeat in the First World War as well as the economic and cultural decline of the post-war period. Once the Nazis gained control of the government they were able to put their racist policies into practice. Initially Jews were eliminated from the legal and medical professions and from cultural and educational institutions. Jewish communal bodies were put under the control of the Gestapo. Later in the year the party organized an onslaught against the Jewish population in which Jews were murdered and Jewish property was destroyed. Subsequently death camps were established in Chelmno, Auschwitz, Treblinka, Sobibor, Majdanek and Belzec where millions of Jews from European countries were killed.

For many Jews the decimation of European Jewry in the Second World War highlighted the need for a Jewish state. Though the Balfour Declaration supported the re-establishment of a Jewish homeland in Palestine, the 1939 White Paper policy of the British effectively nullified this proposal. After several years of struggle against the British, the Jewish population in Palestine succeeded in establishing a state. In March 1947 the General Assembly of the UN voted in favour of partitioning Palestine between the Jews and the Arabs, and in the next year, the Jews having accepted the principle and the Arabs having refused, the State of Israel was proclaimed. Over the next few decades Israel and the Arabs fought a series of wars culminating in the Six Day War in 1967. This major victory for Israel did not, however, bring about security for the Jewish state. In 1973 the Israelis suffered serious losses in the Yom Kippur War; in the 1980s the offensive against the Palestinian Liberation Organization in Lebanon also led to numerous Israeli casualties.

These central events of the last two centuries have transformed the nature of Jewish life worldwide. As Jews stand on the threshold of the 21st century, answers must be found to the perplexing problems now facing Jewry as a result of these turbulent events.

First, and arguably most importantly, Jews ask themselves what they should make of the greatest tragedy of modern Jewish history – the destruction of six million of their number by the Nazis. If the God of Israel is an all-powerful, omniscient, benevolent Father who loves His children, how could He have allowed such an event to take place? If there is a divine providential scheme, what is the purpose of this slaughter of those who consider themselves God's chosen people? These haunting questions will not disappear, and even if some theologians wish to suspend judgement about the horrific experiences of the death camps, individual Jews will not find it so easy to escape from this theological dilemma. Some Jews in contemporary society have simply abandoned their belief in God; others have substituted the state of Israel as the source of salvation. Yet whatever the response there is a vitally important theological task to be undertaken if the Jewish faith is to continue as a vibrant force in the future. Within the Biblical and rabbinic heritage, the belief in a merciful and compassionate Deity is of fundamental significance. The Holocaust challenges such a religious commitment: Jewish theologians must grapple with the religious perplexities of the death camps if Judaism is to survive as a coherent religious faith.

Related to the problem of religious belief is the dilemma of legal (halachic) observance. Today Orthodoxy claims the largest number of adherents. Yet the majority of those who profess allegiance to Orthodox Judaism do not live by the halachic system. Instead each individual Jew feels free to write his own *Shulchan Arukh* (Code of Jewish Law). This is so also within the other branches of Judaism. For most Jews the halachic tradition has lost its hold on Jewish consciousness – the bulk of rituals and observances appear anachronistic and burdensome. In previous centuries this was not the case; despite the divisions within the Jewish world – between Sadducees and Pharisees, Rabbinites and Karaites, Hasidim and Mitnagdim – all Jews accepted the binding authority of the law contained in the Torah. The 613 Biblical commandments were universally viewed as given by God to Moses on Mt Sinai and understood as binding for all time. Thus food regulations, stipulations regarding ritual purity, the moral code, as well as all other commandments served as the framework for an authentic Jewish way of life. Throughout Jewish history the validity of the Written Torah was never questioned. In contemporary society, however, most Jews of all religious positions have ceased to regard the legal heritage in this light. Instead individual Jews, including those of the Orthodox persuasion, feel at liberty to choose which laws have a personal spiritual significance. Such an anarchic approach to the halachic tradition highlights the fact that Jewish law no longer serves as a cohesive force for contemporary Jewry. In short, many modern Jews no longer believe in the doctrine of *Torah MiSinai* (Torah from Sinai) which previously served as a cardinal principle of the Jewish faith. Instead they subscribe only to a limited number of legal precepts which for one reason or another they find meaningful. Such a lack of uniformity of Jewish practice means that there is a vast gulf between the requirements of halachic observance and the actual lifestyle of the majority of Jews both in Israel and the diaspora.

In this connection there is also considerable confusion about the status of the Torah. According to Orthodox belief the Five Books of Moses were revealed to Moses on Mt Sinai. This act of revelation provided the basis for the legal system as well as Jewish theology. Many modern Orthodox adherents pay lip-service to this conviction but in their daily lives illustrate that such a belief has little if any relevance. They fail to live up to the halachic requirements as prescribed in Scripture and are agnostic about the nature and activity of God. The gap between traditional belief and contemporary views of the Torah is even greater in the non-Orthodox branches of Judaism. Here there is a general acceptance of the findings of Biblical criticism – the Five Books of Moses are perceived as divinely inspired but at the same time the product of human reflection. Thus, the Torah is viewed as a unified text, combining centuries of tradition, in which a variety of individual sources were woven together by a number of editors. Such a non-fundamentalist approach, which takes account of recent scholarly developments in the field of Biblical studies, rules out the traditional belief in the infallibility of Scripture and in this way provides a rationale for halachic change. Arguably in many cases Jewish law needs to undergo radical transformation. But how is such a departure from tradition to be justified? Frequently Conservative, Reconstructionist and Reform scholars cite various criteria which can be implemented in deciding which laws should be retained, discarded or changed. Yet such decision-making is ultimately subjective, and there are no clear guidelines for altering the legal and theological features of the Biblical narrative. Even more perplexing is the question of what elements of Scripture are of divine origin. By what criteria is one to determine which elements of the Torah were revealed to Moses? The lack of satisfactory answers to this question points to the religious chaos that exists in the various branches of non-Orthodox Judaism. Thus, in contemporary society many Orthodox Jews who express allegiance to the Torah do not live according to the tenets of the tradition, while non-Orthodox Jews are uncertain which aspects of Scripture should be revered. In both cases the Torah has for most Jews ceased to be, in the words of the Psalmist, 'A tree of life to those who hold fast to it'.

Not only is there uncertainty in the Jewish world about practice and belief, there is also a great deal of confusion about Jewish identity. Are the Jews a nation, a civilization or a religious community? In the past it was relatively easy to answer this question – Jewry was united by a common heritage and way of life. Jews constituted an identifiable religious grouping sharing ancient folkways. No longer is this the case. Contemporary Jewish existence is pluralistic and most Jews are secularized and assimilated. This disordered situation is further complicated by the fact that the Reform movement has recently altered the sociological definition of Jewish status. Previously all branches of Judaism held the view that a person was Jewish if he or she had a Jewish mother; in other words, Jewishness was seen as dependent on maternal descent. However, in 1983 the Central Conference of American Reform Rabbis decreed that a child of either a Jewish mother or a Jewish father should be regarded as Jewish. By expanding the definition of Jewishness to include children of both matrilineal and patrilineal descent the Reform movement defined as Jews individuals whom the other branches of Judaism regard as gentiles; this means that neither these persons nor their descendants can be accepted as Jews by the non-Reform religious establishment.

A similar situation applies to Reform converts and their offspring who, according to Orthodox Judaism, are non-Jews. The Orthodox movement has debarred such individuals from access to Jewish privileges, and has exerted pressure on the government of Israel not to allow Reform converts the right to return to the Holy Land as Jewish citizens. A final complication concerning Jewish status concerns the remarriage of Jewish women who, though civilly divorced, have failed to obtain a Jewish bill of divorce (get). Orthodoxy does not recognize their divorces as valid and any subsequent liaison, even when accompanied by a non-Orthodox Jewish marriage ceremony or civil marriage, is regarded as adulterous. Further, the children of such unions are stigmatized as bastards (mamzerim) and barred from marrying other Jews unless they also are mamzerim. These problems, produced by deviations from traditional Jewish practice, present contemporary Jewry with enormous perplexities and highlight the fissures separating the various Jewish religious groupings. How a commitment to Jewish peoplehood (klal Yisrael) can be sustained when religious organizations are so deeply divided about such fundamental aspects of Jewish identity is a deeply troubling question for present and future generations.

Today Jews are also faced with the issue of religious pluralism. What should the relationship be between Judaism and other faiths? In the medieval world the general view of Jewish thinkers was that Islam was not to be classified as idolatry, but there was considerable debate about the status of Christianity. By the time of the Enlightenment it was widely held that Christians and Muslims were in no way to be included in the harsh condemnation of heathens in classical sources, but Far Eastern religions such as Hinduism were regarded as idolatrous. In contemporary society there are some traditionalists who hold an exclusive view of Judaism. The Jewish religion, they believe, is absolutely true since at Mt Sinai God revealed His Holy Torah to Moses. Sinaitic revelation is viewed as a unique, divine act which provides a secure foundation for the sacred traditions of Israel. In this light other religions are regarded as false – such an interpretation assumes that throughout the history of the world other human beings have mistakenly assumed that they have had an encounter with the Divine, while in fact God made Himself known only to His chosen people.

Some progressive Jewish thinkers have criticized this point of view. For these writers God is seen as the providential Lord of history, and they question the conviction that God hid His presence and withheld His revelation from all mankind with the exception of the Jews. To allow humanity to wallow in darkness and ignorance weighed down by false notions of divine disclosure, they argue, is hardly what we would expect from a loving, compassionate and caring God. According to these thinkers, what is much more likely is that in the past God revealed Himself not only to the Jews but to others as well. Some of these theologians desire to preserve the centrality of the Jewish faith while giving credence to the claims of other faiths that they have had an encounter with the Divine. Other more radical thinkers take this position one stage further: they contend that in each and every generation and to all the peoples of the world God has disclosed Himself in numerous ways. Thus neither in Judaism – nor for that matter in any other religion – has God revealed Himself absolutely and completely. Whatever one makes of this view, there is no doubt that the Jewish community will need to respond to the issue of religious pluralism as Jews gain a greater awareness of other faiths. What they learn and experience may well affect their understanding of their own heritage.

All of these dilemmas about the nature of contemporary Judaism are in varying degrees related to the fundamental issue of assimilation. Prior to the Enlightenment Jews did not have full citizenship rights of the countries in which they lived. Nevertheless, they were able to regulate their own affairs through an organized structure of self-government. Within such a context Jewish law served as the basis of communal life, and rabbis were able to exert power and authority in the community. But as a result of political emancipation, Jews entered the mainstream of modern life taking on all the responsibilities of citizenship. The rabbinical establishment thereby lost its status and control, and the halachic system became voluntary. In addition, Jews took advantage of widening social opportunities: they were free to choose where to live, whom to marry, and what career to follow. By gaining access to secular educational institutions, the influence of the surrounding culture also pervaded all aspects of Jewish life. As a consequence Jewry in modern society is fragmented and secularized; intermarriage is on the increase.

Thhe Jewish community is thus in a state of crisis deep-seated and acute. Orthodox Jewish theology, traditional Jewish practice, the divine status of the Torah, the ancient definition of Jewishness, and the primacy of the Jewish faith are all being questioned. The aim of this volume is to explore some of the central issues in these areas and to offer positive suggestions for the future. The writing is on the wall. If the Jewish people are not to become extinct like the Sumerians, Akkadians, and Assyrians of the ancient world these problems must be confronted. What is at stake is nothing less than the survival of Judaism as a viable religious tradition.

1
Jewish Faith and the Holocaust

Throughout their long history suffering has been the hallmark of the Jewish people. Driven from their homeland by Imperial Rome, buffeted from country to country and plagued by persecutions, Jews have been rejected, despised and led as a lamb to the slaughter. The Holocaust is the most recent chapter in this tragic record of events. The Third Reich's system of murder squads, concentration camps and killing centres wiped out nearly six million Jews; though Jewish communities had previously been decimated, such large-scale devastation profoundly affected the Jewish religious consciousness. For many Jews it has seemed impossible to reconcile the concept of a loving, compassionate and merciful God with the terrible events of the Nazi regime. A number of important Jewish thinkers have grappled with traditional beliefs about God in the light of such suffering, but in various ways their responses are inadequate. If the Jewish faith is to survive, Holocaust theology will need to incorporate a belief in the Afterlife in which the righteous of Israel who died in the death camps will receive their due reward.

THEOLOGY OF PROTEST

Prominent among modern Jewish writers who have wrestled with the theological implications of the Holocaust is the novelist Elie Wiesel. At the concentration camp Birkenau, Wiesel came close to death as he marched toward a pit of flaming bodies only to stop a few feet from the edge. 'Never shall I forget those flames which consumed my faith forever',[1] he wrote. For Wiesel the Holocaust is inexplicable with God, but also it cannot be understood without Him. Auschwitz made it impossible for Wiesel to trust God's goodness, but it also made questions about God more important. In this regard Wiesel has been heard to remark: 'If I told you I believed in God, I would be lying; if I told you I did not believe in God, I would be lying'.[2] Wiesel is thus at odds with God because the only way he can be for God after

1

Auschwitz is by being against Him – to embrace God without protest would be to vindicate Him and legitimize evil.

This stance is eloquently portrayed in Wiesel's play, *The Trial of God* which is set in the village of Shamgorod during the season of Purim. Three Jewish actors have lost their way and arrive at the village which they discover is not the place for joyous celebration since it was devastated by a pogrom two years before. Only two Jews survived: Berish the innkeeper who escaped and his daughter who was abused on her wedding night and has now lost touch with the world. In the area of Shamgorod anti-Semitic hatred has flared up once again and a new pogrom appears imminent. The Festival of Purim calls for a play which will enact the trial of God. Yet there is a difficulty. None of the actors wants to speak up for God. Unnoticed, however, a stranger whose name is Sam enters the inn and volunteers to act as a defence attorney for God. It appears that Berish's housekeeper Maria has seen this person before and she cautions Berish to have nothing to do with him. But despite this warning the play commences.

Berish begins his prosecution by contending that God could use his power to save the victims, but He does not. 'So', he asks, 'on whose side is He? Could the killer kill without His blessing – without His complicity?'[3] Berish has no sympathy for the defendant: 'If I am given the choice of feeling sorry for Him or for human beings, I choose the latter anytime. He is big enough, strong enough to take care of Himself; man is not'.[4] In response Sam answers every accusation and urges that emotion should not take the place of evidence. The actors who have formed the court are impressed and inquire who Sam is. As the play concludes, a violent mob approaches the inn. Realizing the end is near, the Jewish actors elect to die wearing their Purim masks. Sam puts on a mask as well, and Maria's premonition is confirmed – the mask he wears is that of Samael, which signifies Satan. As a final candle is extinguished, the inn door opens to the sound of a murderous tumult including Satan's laughter.

Though this play is not directly about the Holocaust, since it is set three centuries previously, it does touch on the central theological dilemma posed by the death camps. As Wiesel explains in the foreword to the play and elsewhere, he witnessed a trial of God at Auschwitz where three rabbis who conducted the proceedings found God guilty and then participated in the daily prayer. The reason they performed this seemingly inconsistent act is related to a story Wiesel tells about a Spanish Jewish family that had been expelled from Spain. Finding no refuge from continual persecution the father, who was the last to survive, prayed:

> Master of the Universe, I know what you want – I understand what you are doing. You want despair to overwhelm me. You want me to cease invoking your name to glorify and sanctify it. Well, I tell you! No, no – a thousand times no! You shall not succeed! In spite of me and in spite of you, I shall shout the Kaddish, which is a song of faith, for You and against You. The song you shall not still, God of Israel.[5]

In stating his case for and against God, Wiesel emphasizes that there was no need for God to allow the Holocaust to occur – it was an event that produced only death and destruction. Yet Wiesel asserts that to be Jewish is 'never to give up – never to yield to despair'.[6] It is in this spirit that Wiesel conducts his dispute with God. As a survivor of the horrors of the death camps, Wiesel refuses to let God go. His struggles serve as a testimony that the religious quest was not incinerated in the gas chambers of the Nazi period. Although Wiesel's literary works dealing with the Holocaust are not intended to provide a systematic theological response to the death camps, he does struggle with central religious questions. As we have seen, his experience does not lead him to atheism, yet he repeatedly casts doubt on the traditional Jewish understanding of God. Unfortunately, in these reflections Weisel does not clarify what position he adopts; his statement that he would be lying if he claimed both to believe in God and not to believe in Him simply highlights his own confusion. Thus, for those who are anxious to find a solution to the theological dilemmas posed by the Holocaust, Wiesel's protest against God simply reinforces their religious perplexity and underscores the urgency of discovering a theodicy in which God's silence during the Second World War can be understood.

A NON-THEISTIC RESPONSE

Unlike Wiesel, some Jewish thinkers have found it impossible to sustain a belief in the traditional understanding of God after the Holocaust. According to Richard Rubenstein – the most eloquent spokesman for this viewpoint – Auschwitz is the utter and decisive refutation of the traditional affirmation of a providential God who acts in history and watches over the Jewish people whom he has chosen from all nations. In *After Auschwitz*, published in 1966, he writes:

> How can Jews believe in an omnipotent, beneficent God after Auschwitz? Traditional Jewish theology maintains that God is the ultimate, omnipotent actor in historical drama. It has interpreted every major catastrophe in Jewish history as God's punishment of a sinful Israel. I fail to see how this position can be maintained without regarding Hitler and the SS as instruments of God's will . . . To see any purpose in the death camps, the traditional believer is forced to regard the most demonic, anti-human explosion of all history as a meaningful expression of God's purposes.[7]

In this study Rubenstein insists that the Auschwitz experience has resulted in a rejection of the traditional theology of history which must be replaced by a positive affirmation of the value of human life in and for itself without any special theological relationship. Joy and fulfillment are to be sought in this life, rather that in a mystical future or eschaton. Thus he maintains that we should attempt to establish contact with those powers of life and death which engendered the ancient Canaanites' feelings about Baal, Astarte and Anith. This would not mean literally a return to the actual worship of these deities, but simply that earth's fruitfulness, its vicissitudes and its engendering power will once again become the central spiritual realities of Jewish life. According to Rubenstein God is the ultimate nothing, and it is to this Divine source that humanity and the world are ultimately to return. There is no hope of salvation; a person's ultimate destiny is to be returned to Divine nothingness. In this context Auschwitz fits into the archaic religious consciousness and observance of the universal cycle of death and rebirth. The Nazi slaughter of European Jewry was followed by the rebirth of the Jewish people in the land of Israel.

Today Rubenstein sees his position as akin to mystical religion. In a recent investigation of the origins of the Holocaust and its consequences on Jewish thought,[8] he notes that his loss of faith and the events of the Second World War caused him to have a bleak view of the world. But at present he would be more apt to adopt an optimistic stance. Yet what has remained the same is his insistence that the traditional conception of God needs to be rejected. Further, he asserts that the Jews are not God's Divinely chosen people; they are a people like any other, whose religion was influenced by cultural and historical events. Some of Rubenstein's critics have asked whether anyone who accepts his view has any reason to remain Jewish, since the Jewish heritage is infused with the belief that the Jews are under the obligation to observe Divinely ordained commandments. What reason could there be to keep the Sabbath, observe dietary laws, practice circumcision, or even marry someone Jewish if the God of the Biblical and rabbinic tradition does not exist?

In an early response to such criticism, Rubenstein pointed out that the elimination of the religious framework of the Jewish faith does not undermine the sociological and psychological functions of Judaism. The ethical content of Judaism can persist even in the absence of religious faith. Judaism, he argued, is not simply a belief system – it is constituted of rituals and customs, which enable adherents of the tradition to celebrate life-cycle events and cope with crises. As Rubenstein explained:

> I do not believe that a theistic God is necessary for Jewish religious life . . . I have suggested that Judaism is the way in which we share the decisive times and crises of life through the traditions of our inherited community. The need for that sharing is not diminished in the time of the death of God.[9]

Yet despite this stance, Rubenstein believed it is nevertheless possible to view the cosmos as the expression of a single, unified and unifying source and ground which we name as God. If human beings are seen as an integral element of the cosmos, which is an expression of the Divine ground, then God is capable of thought, reflection and feeling.

Such a reversion to pantheism parallels the return of the Jewish people to the land of Israel. Referring to traditional liturgy, Rubenstein pointed out that during the period of the diaspora Jews prayed that they be returned to the Holy Land. When this goal was attained, a major phase of Jewish history had in principle come to an end, but since Rubenstein does not embrace polytheism, he argued that after Auschwitz and the return to Israel, the Divine manifested in nature was the God to whom Jews would turn in place of the God of history, especially in Israel. Rejecting the Biblical view of a providential God, Rubenstein thus subscribed to a form of Canaanite nature paganism.

Over the years Rubenstein's earlier paganism lost its importance. He formerly argued that when the Jewish people lived in their own country, they would revert to nature worship. But he eventually came to see that most Jews did not desire to live in Israel and those who settled there had no interest in nature paganism. Those who ceased to believe in God simply became secular Jews. But Rubenstein has parted company with these Jewish secularists; in mysticism he has found the God in whom he can believe after Auschwitz. 'I believe there is a conception of God', he writes, 'which remains meaningful after the death of the God-Who-Acts-in-History. It is a very old conception of God with deep roots in both Western and Oriental mysticism. According to this conception, God is spoken of as the holy nothingness. 'When God is thus designated, He is conceived as the ground and source of all existence . . . God as the nothing is not absence of being but superfluity of being.'[10] Though such a view has affinities with other religions, such as Buddhism, Rubenstein's position is far removed from the traditional understanding of God as the compassionate redeemer of Israel who lovingly watches over his chosen people.

Rubenstein's redefinition of God's nature avoids the dilemma of Divine theodicy, but it is meaningless for Jews who accept the traditional understanding of God. Rubenstein declares that after Auschwitz it is an illusion to believe in such a God and that each of us must accept that the universe is unconcerned with our lives, prayers and hopes. Yet it is just such a view that the theist rejects; what he seeks instead is a justification for God's ways, and that is what Rubenstein contends is impossible. To say that God is Divine nothingness merely confuses the issues. Thus, rather than providing an adequate theodicy in the face of the horrors of the Holocaust, Rubenstein merely plunges the believer deeper into despair.

A DEISTIC ALTERNATIVE

Unlike Wiesel and Rubenstein, a number of Jewish thinkers have attempted to adopt a more positive theological stance. In the *Tremendum* published in 1981 Arthur A. Cohen addressed the religious dilemmas raised by the Holocaust. Previously he had said nothing about the religious perplexities connected with the destruction of six million Jews in the Nazi era. In *The Natural and the Supernatural Jew*, published in 1962, he had constructed a modern theology of Judaism without dealing with evil either in itself or in its horrific manifestation in the concentration camps. But in his later book Cohen uses the term 'tremendum' to designate an event of vast significance. Mindful of Rudolf Otto's characterization of God's holiness as *mysterium tremendum*, Cohen argues that *mysterium tremendum* and *tremendum* convey the aspect of vastness and the resonance of terror. Yet these terms designate different realities. According to Cohen, the Holocaust was the human *tremendum*, 'the enormity of an infinitized man, who no longer seems to fear death or, more to the point, fears it so completely, denies death so mightily, that the only patent of his refutation and denial is to build a mountain of corpses to the divinity of the dead'.[11] For Cohen the death camps were the *tremendum* since they represent an inversion of life to an orgiastic celebration of death. Like Otto's *mysterium tremendum*, Cohen's notion of the *tremendum* is meant to suggest a sense of unfathomable mystery. Cohen believes that the Holocaust was completely irrational and unique, and he doubts whether historians can understand its nature and significance.

Like Rubenstein, Cohen recognizes that the Holocaust presented insurmountable difficulties for classical theism and for the Jewish understanding of God's relationship with the Jewish people. For Cohen post-Holocaust theology must take account of three central elements: (1) God must abide in a universe in which God's presence and evil are both seen as real; (2) the relationship of God to all creation must be seen as meaningful and valuable; and (3) the reality of God is not isolated from God's involvement with creation. In formulating a theological response which embraces these features, he drew on Lurianic kabbalah as well as the philosophy of Franz Rosenzweig. According to Cohen, initially God was all-in-all and there was nothing else. But God overflowed absolute self-containment in a moment of love. For Cohen the world is God's created other, lovingly formed by the Divine word without the surrender of human freedom. Humanity is essential because without it the world would be unable to respond to God's love or personality.

Human beings, Cohen asserts, have the capacity to respond to God since they partake of God's speech and freedom. According to Cohen, such freedom was intended to be tempered by reason, but this did not occur and therefore human freedom became the basis of the horrific events of the Holocaust. In advancing this view, Cohen criticizes those who complain that God was silent during the events of the Holocaust. Such an assessment, Cohen notes, is a mistaken yearning for a non-existent interruptive God who is expected to interfere with earthly life. But if there were such a God, the created order would be an extension of the Divine realm, and there would be no opportunity for freedom. 'God is not the strategist of our particularities or our historical condition', he writes, 'but rather mystery of futurity, always our *posse*, never our acts. If we can begin to see God less as the interferer whose insertion is welcome (when it accords with our needs) and more as the immensity whose reality is our prefiguration . . . we shall have won a sense of God whom we may love and honour, but whom we no longer fear and from whom we no longer demand.'[12]

Since Cohen does not believe that God acts in history, he dismisses the view that God was responsible for Auschwitz. Instead he asserts that God acts in the future. The Divine Life is 'a filament within the historical, but never the filament that we can identify and ignite according to our requirements'. Human beings, he believes, have the capacity to 'obscure, eclipse, burn out the Divine filament'.[13] God's role is not to act as a direct agent in human affairs, but as a teacher; His intention is to instruct human beings so as to limit their destructive impulses. For Cohen, Divine teaching is manifest in the halachah; in this way human freedom is granted within the framework of Jewish law. Given this conception of Divine action, God is in no way responsible for the horrors of the death camps – Auschwitz was the work of human beings who exercised their freedom for destruction and murder. According to Cohen such license to act against God's will raises serious doubts about the viability of the State of Israel to protect the Jewish community from future disasters. The return to a homeland may prove more threatening even than genocide for, 'in no way is the Jew allowed any longer . . . to repeat his exile amid the nations, to disperse himself in order to survive'.[14] Further, Cohen asserts that dedication to the Holy Land devoid of a belief in a transcendent Diety can become a form of paganism. The founding of a Jewish state is thus not an adequate response to the religious perplexities posed by the Holocaust.

Although Cohen's redefinition of God's nature avoids the difficulties of seeing God as responsible for the events of the Holocaust, he has eliminated a fundamental aspect of Divine activity which is presupposed by Biblical and rabbinical Judaism. Throughout Jewish sources, God is understood as both transcendent and immanent – He created the universe and continuously sustains it. The God of the Jewish faith is the Lord of History. He guided His chosen people out of Egypt, revealed Himself on Mt Sinai, delivered them up to the Promised Land, and providentially directs human history to its ultimate fulfillment in the world to come. Within this eschatological endeavour, God intervenes in history; He is a God who is present in everyday life. Conceiving God as a Divine filament in no sense corresponds with this traditional conception. Thus, Cohen's solution to the problem of the Holocaust deprives the faith of a view of God which is central to the Jewish heritage. His response to the horrors of the death camps is unsatisfactory for those who seek to explain how a benevolent God could have permitted the slaughter of six million innocent victims.

TRADITIONAL JEWISH THEOLOGY

A number of theologians have been unwilling to alter the traditional understanding of God in attempting to make sense of the Holocaust. According to Eliezer Berkovits in *Faith after the Holocaust*, the modern Jewish response to the destruction of six million Jews should be modelled on Job's example. We must believe in God, he contends, because Job believed. If there is no answer to the quest for an understanding of God's silence in the face of Nazi genocide, 'it is better to be without it than in the sham of . . . the humbug of a disbelief encouraged by people who have eaten their fill at the tables of a satiated society'.[15] At Auschwitz God was hidden, yet according to Berkovits in His hiddenness He was actually present. As hidden God, He is Saviour; in the apparent void He is the redeemer of Israel. How this is to be understood is shrouded in mystery. Berkovits writes that if Jewish faith is to be meaningful in the post-Holocaust age, the Jew must make room for the inpenetrable darkness of the death camps within religious belief: 'The darkness will remain, but in its "light" he will make his affirmations. The inexplicable will not be explained, yet it will become a positive influence in the formulation of that which is to be acknowledged . . . perhaps in the awful misery of man will be revealed to us the awesome mystery of God'.[16] The Holocaust is thus part of God's incomprehensible plan, defying rational justification and transcending human understanding.

Such an argument is obviously not a solution to the problem of the Holocaust; rather it is a challenge to believe in God despite overwhelming obstacles. This evasion of the theological difficulties, while leaving room for blind faith, in no way explains how God could have allowed the Holocaust to take place. Berkovits claims that in His hiddenness, the hidden God is revealed and that He was both saviour and redeemer in the death camps. But how can this be so? For some Jews such an appeal to God's inscrutable plan merely aggravates and caricatures the horrors of the Nazi regime and deprives them of any firm foundation for religious belief. Thus Berkovits offers no help for those who are unable to follow Job's example, and instead seek a viable Jewish theodicy, in which the justice and righteousness of God are defended in the face of evil and suffering.

Another attempt to provide a Biblically-based explanation for God's activity during the Nazi regime was proposed by Ignaz Maybaum in *The Face of God After Auschwitz*. In this study Maybaum argues that God has an enduring covenantal relationship with Israel, that He continues to act in history and that Israel has a Divinely sanctioned mission to enlighten other nations. According to Maybaum the Holocaust is a result of God's intervention, but not as a Divine punishment. In explaining this view, he uses the crucifixion of Jesus as a model for understanding Jewish suffering during the Holocaust. Just as Jesus was an innocent victim whose death provides a means of salvation for humanity, so the deaths of the victims of the Holocaust were sacrificial offerings. Maybaum asserts that the Jews were murdered by the Nazis because they were chosen by God for this sacrifice. In this way God's purposes can be fulfilled. 'The Golgotha of modern mankind is Auschwitz', he asserts. 'The cross, the Roman gallows, was replaced by the gas chamber.'[17]

Maybaum contends that Jewish history was scarred by three major disasters which he designates by the Hebrew word *churban* – a term referring to an event of massive destructiveness. For Maybaum each *churban* was a Divine intervention which had decisive significance for the course of history. The first of these cataclysmic occurances was the destruction of Jerusalem in 586 BCE, which resulted in the diaspora of the Jewish community. This uprooting of the population was a catastrophe for the nation, but it did inaugurate the Jewish mission to bring a knowledge of God and His laws to other peoples outside Israel's borders. In this respect the first *churban* was a manifestation of 'creative destructiveness'. The second *churban* was the Roman devastation of the second Temple in Jerusalem, which inaugurated the establishment of the synagogue as the major focus of dispersed Jewish life where study and prayer replaced sacrifice.

According to Maybaum, such activity is of a higher order than the sacrificial system of the Biblical period – this transformation of religious life was possible only through an act of destruction. Such an interpretation of the Jewish past runs counter to the traditional understanding of these events as Divine punishment for the sinfulness of the nation.

The final *churban* was the Holocaust, an event in which the Jewish people were sacrificial victims in an event of creative destructiveness. In Maybaum's view God used the Holocaust to bring about the end of the Middle Ages, and usher in a new era of modernity. The sin for which the Jews died was the retention of remnants of the medieval European feudal structure. After the First World War the West could have transformed Eastern European society, but it did not act. As a result the devastation of the war served no purpose and Hitler was sent by God to bring about unknowingly what the progressives had failed to do deliberately. According to Maybaum, God used the Holocaust as a means to bring about the modern world. In this tragedy all that was medieval in character – including the majority of Eastern European Jews who lived in ghettos – had to perish. The murder of six million Jews was thus an act of creative destruction. With the elimination of the traditional Jewish community of Eastern Europe, the focus of world Jewry shifted to the United States, Western Europe, Russia, and Israel. In these countries Jews were able to live in an emancipated environment which celebrated rationality and progress. Jews therefore suffer in order to bring about the rule of God over the world and its peoples; their God-appointed mission is to serve the course of historical progress and bring mankind into a new era. Only a part, though admittedly a traumatically large part of the Jewish people, was exterminated. The planned genocide of the Jewish people did not succeed, and Maybaum emphasizes that the remnant that was saved has been selected by God as a perennial witness to His presence in the world and in the historical process. Of the sacrificial victims of Auschwitz he states categorically: 'Their death purged western civilization so that it can again become a place where man can live, do justly, love mercy, and walk humbly with God'.[18]

Though this justification of the Holocaust is based on Biblical concepts, Maybaum's explanation will no doubt strike many as offensive. If God is benevolent, merciful and just in his dealings with mankind, how could He have intentionally planned the destruction of six million Jews? Surely through His omnipotence God could have brought about the redemption of the world without decimating His chosen people. Furthermore, the image of Hitler as God's instrument is a terrible and grotesque picture; to see God as a surgeon operating on the body of Israel, lacking pity for those who died in the process, is to make a mockery of God's eternal love. Unlike the ancient Israelites, whom God punished for their sins through the military intervention of Nebuchadnezzar, Jews who lost their lives in the camps were simply innocent victims of Nazi persecution. Thus Maybaum's conception of God as slayer and saviour is hardly an adequate justification for God's apparent indifference to mass death, injustice, and suffering in the concentration camps.

THE HOLOCAUST AND REVELATION

Another traditional approach to the Holocaust is to see in the death camps a manifestation of God's will that His chosen people survive. Such a paradoxical view is most eloquently expressed by Emil Fackenheim in a series of publications in which he contends that God revealed Himself to Israel out of the furnaces of Auschwitz. For Fackenheim the Holocaust was the most disorienting event in Jewish history – a crisis which requires from the Jewish community a reassessment of God's presence in history. Through the Holocaust, he believes, God issued the 614th commandment: Jews are forbidden to grant posthumous victories to Hitler. According to Fackenheim, Jews are here instructed to survive as Jews. They are commanded to remember in their very guts and bowels the martyrs of the Holocaust, lest their memory perish: Jews are forbidden, furthermore, to deny or despair of God, however much they may have to contend with Him or with belief in Him. They are forbidden finally to despair of the world as the place which is to become the kingdom of God lest we help make it a meaningless place. 'We help make it a meaningless place in which God is dead or irrelevant and everything is permitted . . . to abandon any of these imperatives, in response to Hitler's victory at Auschwitz, would be to hand him yet other posthumous victories . . .'[19] For Fackenheim, it is a betrayal of the Jewish heritage to question whether the traditional Jewish conception of God can be sustained after the Holocaust.

In his later work, Fackenheim stresses that the Holocaust represents a catastrophic rupture with previously accepted views of Judaism, Christianity and Western philosophy.[20] According to Fackenheim, the process of mending this rupture (*tikkun* –

restoration) must take place in the scheme of life rather than of thought. The resistance to the destructive logic of the death camps constitutes the beginning of such repair. As Fackenheim explains: some camp inmates were unwilling to become 'muselmann', (those who were dead while still alive). Such resistance was exhibited by pregnant mothers who refused to abort their pregnancies, hoping that their offspring would survive and frustrate the plans of the National Socialist Party to eliminate every Jew. Again, other Jewish partisans took to the woods to fight the Nazis, and Hasidic Jews prayed even though they were forbidden to do so. Though the number of those who resisted the Nazis was small, they did exhibit that the logic of destruction could be overcome. These acts of resistance are of primary importance. It is not enough to understand the Holocaust – it must be resisted in flesh-and-blood action. In this connection, Fackenheim stresses that only as a consequence of the deed of resistance can reflective thought have any significance. The Holocaust was intended to give its victims no possibility of escaping the fate of becoming the living dead and subsequently dying in the gas chambers. The first act of resistance was the determination to survive or to die as a human being. The second step was to resist the nature of the logic of destruction. In the case of those victims who did resist, thought and action were interconnected: their recognition of the Nazi logic of destruction helped produce resistance to it – a life-and-death struggle that went on day and night.

Such resistance was more than self-protection. Since the Holocaust was a *novum* in history, this resistance was also a *novum*. As emphasised by Pelgia Levinska, a Polish Roman Catholic, 'They had condemned us to die in our own filth', she wrote, 'to drown in mud, in our own excrement. They wished to abuse us, to destroy our human dignity. From the instant when I grasped the motivating principle . . . it was as if I had been awakened from a dream. . . . I felt under orders to live and if I did die in Auschwitz, it would be as a human being, I would hold on to my dignity'.[21] Fackenheim views this statement as evidence of the ontological dimension of resistance and of a commanding voice. In the past when Jews were threatened, they bore witness to God through martyrdom but Fackenheim believes that such an act would have made no sense in the concentration camps. Such death was what the Nazis hoped to accomplish. This resistance served as a new kind of sanctification; the refusal to die was a holy act. For Fackenheim those who heard God's command during the Holocaust were the inmates of the camps who felt under an obligation to resist the logic of destruction. The rupture between the pre-Holocaust and post-Holocaust world must be mended by such resistance. Among the most significant Jewish acts of *tikkun* in the post-Holocaust world was the decision of the survivors of the Nazi period to make their homeland in Israel. Though Israel is continually endangered, the founding of a Jewish state represents a monumental attempt to overcome the Holocaust. For the first time in nearly two thousand years Jews have assumed responsibility for their own future. Furthermore, the rebirth of a Jewish state is the precondition of a post-Holocaust *tikkun* of Jewish-Christian relations. Before the Holocaust Jews depended on the majority for their welfare, but after the Holocaust Jews became the majority in their own country. In Israel the Jews became independent and produced weapons with which they could defend themselves. This transformation of Jewish life offers hope for the continuation of Jewishness after the tragic events of the Holocaust.

The difficulty with Fackenheim's view is that he does not attempt to justify his claim that Auschwitz was a revelation-event bearing Torah to 20th-century Jews. This is simply asserted, yet it is not at all clear why this should be so. On the contrary, for many Jews the Holocaust has made it impossible to believe in the traditional Jewish picture of God as a Lord of history who has revealed His will to the Jewish people. For such Jews the world is a tragic and meaningless place where human beings have no basis for hope in Divine aid or in any ultimate solution to the ills that beset them. Though they might agree that the lesson of the Holocaust is that the Jewish people must survive against all odds, this would not be because of God's revelation in the death camps. Further, it is hard to see how Fackenheim's admonition to believe in God 'lest Judaism perish' could actually sustain religious belief. Trust in God – the leap of faith – is of a different order altogether from commitment to the Jewish people, and it is regrettable that Fackenheim fails to see this distinction.

JEWISH SUFFERING AND THE AFTERLIFE

These varied attempts to come to terms with the Holocaust all suffer from serious defects. As we have seen, Rubenstein rejects the traditional Jewish understanding of God's nature and activity and argues for a concept of Divine reality far-removed from the Jewish heritage. For Jewish traditionalists seeking to make sense of the horrors of the Holocaust such a suggestion offers no consolation or promise of hope. Cohen's conception of deism is also so remote from mainstream Jewish thought that it cannot resolve the religious perplexities posed by the deaths of six million Jews in the camps. Wiesel's agonizing struggle with religious doubt illuminates the theological problems connected with the events of the Nazi period but plunges the believer deeper into despair. At the other end of the spectrum the views of writers who have attempted to defend the Biblical and rabbinic concept of God are beset with difficulties. Maybaum's view that God used Hitler as an instrument for the redemption of mankind is a monstrous conception. Fackenheim's assertion that God issued the 614th commandment through the ashes of the death camps will no doubt strike many as wishful thinking. Finally, Berkovits' view that God was hidden during the Nazi period offers no theological solution to the problem of suffering. These major Holocaust theologians have therefore not provided satisfactory answers to the dilemmas posed by the death camps. Contemporary Jewish theology is thus in a state of crisis, both serious and fundamental: for the first time in history Jews seem unable to account for God's ways.

One element is missing from all these justifications of Jewish suffering; there is no appeal to the Hereafter. Though the Bible only contains faint references to the realm of the dead, the doctrine of Life after Death came into prominence during the Maccabean period (2nd century BCE) when righteous individuals were dying for their faith. Subsequently the belief in the World to Come was regarded as one of the central tenets of the Jewish faith. According to rabbinic scholars, it was inconceivable that life would end at death: God's justice demanded that the righteous of Israel enter into a realm of eternal bliss where they would be compensated for their earthly travail. Because of this belief generations of Jews have been able to reconcile their belief in a benevolent and merciful God with the terrible tragedies they have endured. Through the centuries the conviction that the righteous would inherit eternal life has sustained generations of Jewish martyrs who suffered persecution and death. As Jews were slaughtered, they glorified God through dedication to the Jewish faith – such an act is referred to as *Kiddush ha-Shem* (Sanctification of the Divine Name). These heroic Jews who remained steadfast in their faith did not question the ways of God; rather their deaths testify to their firm belief in a providential Lord of history who would reserve a place for them in the Hereafter.

In Judaism this act of sanctification was a task for all Jews if tragic circumstances arose. Thus through centuries of oppression *Kiddush ha-Shem* gave meaning to the struggle of Jewish warriors, strength of endurance under cruel torture, and a way out of slavery and conversion, through suicide. In the Middle Ages repeated outbreaks of Christian persecution strengthened the Jewish determination to profess their faith. *Kiddush ha-Shem* became a common way of confronting missionary coercion – if Jews were not permitted to live openly as Jews, they were determined not to live at all. When confronted by force, Jews attempted to defend themselves, but chose death if this proved impossible. Thousands of Jews in the Middle Ages lost their lives. Some fell in battle, but the majority committed suicide for their faith. In the chronicles of this slaughter *Kiddush ha-Shem* was the dominant motif; Jews endeavoured to fight their assailants, but when their efforts failed they died as martyrs.

During the medieval period Jews also suffered because of the accusation that they performed ritual murders of Christian children, defamed Christianity in the Talmud, desecrated the Host, and brought about the Black Death. As they endured trials and massacres, they were fortified by the belief that God would redeem them in a future life. Repeatedly they proclaimed their faith in God and witnessed to the tradition of their ancestors. In later centuries *Kiddush-ha-Shem* also became part of the history of Spanish Jewry. Under the fire and torture of the Inquisition chambers and tribunals Jews remained committed to their faith. The principles of *Kiddush-ha-Shem* supported multitudes of Jews as they faced calamity and death. The reality of their sacrifice and the image of their martyrdom became a dominant element in the Jewish consciousness. Due to the belief in divine reward, the Jewish community escaped disillusionment and despair in the face of tragedy: the courage of those who gave their lives to sanctify God's name became an inspiration to all those who faced similar circumstances. The history of the Jewish people thus bears eloquent testimony to the heroic martyrs who were convinced that reward in Heaven would be vouchsafed to them if they remained faithful to God in their life on earth.

In the concentration camps as well a number of religious Jews remained loyal to the tradition of *Kiddush-ha-Shem*. Joining the ranks of generations of martyrs, they sanctified God with unshakeable faith. As they awaited the final sentence, they drew strength from one another to witness to the God of Israel. In the camps many

Jews faced death silently. When their last moments arrived they died without fear. They neither grovelled nor pleaded for mercy since they believed it was God's judgement to take their lives. With love and trust they awaited the death sentence. As they prepared to surrender themselves to God, they thought only of the purity of their souls. The martyrs of the concentration camps were convinced that their deaths would serve as a prelude to redemption. In Heaven they would receive their just reward.

CONCLUSION

On the basis of the belief in eternal salvation which sustained the Jewish people through centuries of persecution, it might be expected that Holocaust theologians would attempt to explain the events of the Nazi period in the context of a future life. As we have seen, this has not occurred. Instead, these writers have set aside doctrines concerning messianic redemption, resurrection and final judgement. This shift in orientation is in part due to the fact that the views expressed in rabbinic literature are not binding. All Jews are obliged to accept the Divine origin of the Law but this is not so with regard to theological concepts and theories expounded by the rabbis. Thus it is possible for a Jew to be religiously pious without accepting all the central beliefs of mainstream Judaism.

Given that there is no authoritative bedrock of Jewish theology, Holocaust theologians will no doubt have felt fully justified in ignoring various elements of traditional rabbinic eschatology which have ceased to retain their hold on Jewish consciousness in the 20th century. Due to a shift in emphasis in Jewish thought, Jewish Holocaust theologians have simply refrained from appealing to the traditional belief in other-wordly reward and punishment in formulating their responses to the horrors of the death camps. Yet without this belief, it is simply impossible to make sense of the world as the creation of an all-good and all-powerful God. Without the eventual vindication of the righteous in Paradise, there is no way to sustain the belief in a providential God who watches over His chosen people. The essence of the Jewish understanding of God is that He loves His chosen people. If death means extinction, there is no way to make sense of the claim that He loves and cherishes all those who died in the concentration camps – suffering and death would ultimately triumph over each of those who perished. But if there is eternal life in a World to Come, then there is hope that the righteous will share in a Divine life. Moreover, the Divine attribute of justice demands that the righteous of Israel who met their death as innocent victims of the Nazis will reap an everlasting reward. Here then is an answer to the religious perplexities of the Holocaust. The promise of immortality offers a way of reconciling the belief in a loving and just God with the nightmare of the death camps. As we have seen, this hope sustained the Jewish people through centuries of suffering and martyrdom. Now that Jewry stands on the threshold of the 21st century, it must again serve as the fulcrum of religious belief. Only in this way will the Jewish people who have experienced the Valley of the Shadow of Death be able to say in the ancient words of the Psalmist: 'I shall fear no evil for thou art with me'.

2
The Afterlife in Contemporary Jewish Belief

Until long after the exile, the Jewish people shared the view of the entire ancient world that the dead continue to exist in a shadowy realm of the nether world where they live a dull, ghostly existence. According to K. Kohler, 'throughout the Biblical period no ethical idea yet permeated this conception, and no attempt was made to transform the nether world into a place of Divine judgement, of recompense for the good and evil deeds accomplished on earth'.[1] This was so because Biblical Judaism stressed the importance of attaining a complete and blissful life with God during earthly life; there was no need to transfer the purpose of existence to the Hereafter. In the words of R.H. Charles, 'So long indeed as Yahweh's jurisdiction was conceived as limited to this life, a Yahwistic eschatology of the individual could not exist; but when at last Israel reached the great truth of monotheism, the way was prepared for the moralisation of the future no less than that of the present'.[2] It was only then under social, economic and political oppression that pious Jews looked beyond their bitter disappointment with this world to a future beyond the grave when virtue would receive its due reward and vice its befitting punishment.[3] In the modern world, however, this traditional view has lost its hold on Jewish consciousness.

THE BIBLICAL VIEW OF THE AFTERLIFE

Though there is no explicit reference to the Hereafter in the Old Testament, a number of expressions are used to refer to the realm of the dead. In Psalms 28:1 and 88:5, *bor* refers to a pit. In Psalm 6:6 as well as in Job 28:22 and 30:23, *mavet* is used in a similar sense. In Psalm 22:16 the expression *afar mavet* refers to the dust of death; in Exodus 15:2 and Jonah 2:7 the earth (*eretz*) is described as swallowing up the dead, and in Ezekiel 31:14 the

19

expression *eretz tachtit* refers to the nether parts of the earth where the dead dwell. Finally, the word *she'ol* is frequently used to refer to the dwelling of the dead in the nether world.[4] In addition, the words *ge ben hinnom*,[5] *ge hinnom*[6] and *ge*[7] are used to refer to a cursed valley associated with fire and death where, according to Jeremiah, children were sacrificed as burnt offerings to Moloch and Baal.[8] In later rabbinic literature the word ordinarily used for 'Hell' (*Gehinnom*) is derived from these names.

Though these passages point to a Biblical conception of an after-life, there is no indication of a clearly defined concept; it is only later in the Graeco-Roman world that such a notion began to take shape. The notion of a future world in which the righteous would be compensated for the ills they suffered in this life was prompted by a failure to justify the ways of God by any other means. According to Biblical theodicy men were promised rewards for obeying God's law and punishments were threatened for disobedience. Rewards included health, children, rainfall, a good harvest, peace and prosperity; punishments consisted of disease, war, pestilence, failure of crops, poverty and slavery. As time passed, however, it became clear that life did not operate in accordance with such a tidy scheme. In response to this dilemma the rabbis developed a doctrine of reward and punishment in the Hereafter. Such a belief helped Jews to cope with suffering in this life, and it also explained, if not the presence of evil in the world, then at least the worthwhileness of creation despite the world's ills.[9]

THE HEREAFTER IN RABBINIC THOUGHT

Given that there is no explicit belief in eternal salvation in the Bible,[10] the rabbis of the post-Biblical period were faced with the difficulty of proving that the doctrine of resurrection of the dead is contained in Scripture, which they regarded as authoritative. To do this they employed certain principles of exegesis which are based on the assumption that every word in the Pentateuch was transmitted by God to Moses. Thus, for example, R. Elezar, the son of R. Jose, claimed to have refuted the Sectarians who maintained that resurrection is not a Biblical doctrine: 'I said to them: You have falsified your Torah . . . For ye maintain that resurrection is not a Biblical doctrine, but it is written (in Num. 15.31ff), 'Because he hath despised the word of the Lord, and hath broken his commandments, that soul shall utterly be cut off, his iniquity shall be upon him. Now, seeing that he shall utterly be cut off in this world, when shall his iniquity be upon him? Surely in the next world'.[11]

Again, R. Meir asked, 'Whence do we know resurrection from the Torah?'. From the verse, 'Then shall Moses and the children of Israel sing this song unto the Lord' (Ex. 15.1). Not 'sang', but 'sing' is written. Since Moses and the children of Israel did not sing a second time in this life, the text must mean that they will sing after resurrection. Likewise it is written, 'Then shall Joshua build an altar unto the Lord God of Israel' (Joshua 8.30). Not 'build' but 'shall build' is stated. Thus resurrection is intimated in the Torah.[12] Similarly, R. Joshua b. Levi said: 'Where is resurrection derived from the Torah? From the verse, 'Blessed are they that dwell in thy house; they shall ever praise thee.' (Ps.84.5). The text does not say 'praised thee' but 'shall praise thee'. Thus we learn resurrection from the Torah'.[13]

The principle qualification for entrance to Heaven (Gan Eden) is to lead a good life in accordance with God's law. Conversely, the rabbis point out that by disobeying God's law one forfeits a share in the World to Come and is doomed to eternal punishment in Hell (Gehinnom).[14] According to the Mishnah there are various categories of sinners who will be damned: (1) He who says there is no resurrection of the dead prescribed in the Torah; (2) He who says that the Torah is not from Heaven; (3) A heretic; (4) A reader of heretical books and one that utters a charm over a wound; (5) He who pronounces God's name by supplying vowels; (6) The generation of the flood; (7) The generation of Babel; (8) The men of Sodom; (9) The 12 spies; (10) The ten lost tribes; (13) The children of the wicked; (14) The people of an apostate city; (15) Those who have been executed by a rabbinical court unless they confessed their sins before death.[15] On the basis of the discussion of these categories in the Babylonian Talmud and the remarks of sages elsewhere in rabbinic literature, Maimonides in his *Guide to the Perplexed* drew up a different list of those who have no share in Heaven which has been regarded by many as authoritative.[16]

THE NATURE OF THE HEREAFTER

The World to Come is itself divided into several stages: first, there is the time of the Messianic redemption. According to the Babylonian Talmud the Messianic Age (Yemot Hamashiah) is to take place on earth after a period of decline and calamity and will result in a complete fulfillment of every human wish. Peace will reign throughout nature; Jerusalem will be rebuilt; and at the close of this era, the dead will be resurrected and rejoined with their souls, and a final judgement will come upon all mankind. Those who are judged righteous will enter into Heaven (Gan Eden) which is portrayed in various ways in Rabbinic literature.[17] One of the earliest descriptions is found in Midrash Konen, and the following extract is a representative sample of the type of elaboration in rabbinic sources:

> The Gan Eden at the east measures 800 000 years (at ten miles per day or 3650 miles per year.). There are five chambers for various classes of the righteous. The first is built of cedar, with a ceiling of transparent crystal. This is the habitation of non-Jews who become true and devoted converts to Judaism. They are headed by Obadiah the prophet and Onkelos the proselyte, who teach them the Law. The second is built of cedar, with a ceiling of fine silver. This is the habitation of the penitents, headed by Manasseh, King of Israel, who teaches them the Law.
>
> The third chamber is built of silver and gold, ornamented with pearls. It is very spacious, and contains the best of heaven and of earth, with spices, fragrance, and sweet odours. In the centre of this chamber stands the Tree of Life, 500 years high. Under its shadow rest Abraham, Isaac and Jacob, the tribes, those of the Egyptian exodus, and those who died in the wilderness, headed by Moses and Aaron. There are also David and Solomon, crowned, and Chileab, as if living, attending on his father, David. Every generation of Israel is represented except that of Absalom and his confederates. Moses teaches them the Law, and Aaron gives instruction to the priests. The Tree of Life is like a ladder on which the souls of the righteous may ascend and descend. In a conclave above are seated the Patriarchs, the Ten Martyrs, and those who sacrificed their lives for the cause of His Sacred Name. These souls descend daily to the Gan Eden, to join their families and tribes, where they lounge on soft cathedrals studded with jewels. Everyone, according to his excellence, is received in audience to praise and thank the Ever-living God; and all enjoy the brilliant light of the Shekinah. The flaming sword, changing from intense heat to icy cold, and from ice to glowing coals, guards the entrance against living mortals. The size of the sword is ten years. The souls on entering paradise are bathed in the 248 rivulets of balsam and attar.

The fourth chamber is made of olive-wood and is inhabited by those who have suffered for the sake of their religion. Olives typify bitterness in taste and brilliancy in light (olive-oil), symbolizing persecution and its reward.

The fifth chamber is built of precious stones, gold and silver, surrounded by myrrh and aloes. In front of the chamber runs the river Gihon, on whose banks are planted shrubs affording perfume and aromatic incense. There are couches of gold and silver and fine drapery. This chamber is inhabited by the Messiah of David, Elijah, and the Messiah of Ephraim. In the centre are a canopy made of the cedars of Lebanon, in the style of the Tabernacle, with posts and vessels of silver; and a settee of Lebanon wood with pillars of silver and a seat of gold, the covering thereof of purple. Within rests the Messiah, son of David, 'a man of sorrows and acquainted with grief' suffering, and waiting to release Israel from the Exile. Elijah comforts and encourages him to be patient. Every Monday and Thursday, and Sabbath and on holy days the Patriarchs, Moses, Aaron, and others, call on the Messiah and condole with him, in the hope of the fast-approaching end.[18]

As with Heaven, we also find extensive and detailed descriptions of Hell in Jewish literature. In the Babylonian Talmud, R. Joshua b. Levi deduces the divisions of Hell from Biblical quotations: *she'ol*, *abaddon*, *be'er shahat*, *bor sha'on*, *tit ha-yawen*, *zel mawet* and *erez ha-tahtit*. This Talmudic concept of the seven-fold structure of Hell is greatly elaborated in midrashic literature. According to one source it requires 300 years to traverse the height or width or the depth of each division, and it would take 6300 years to go over a tract of land equal in extent to the seven divisions.[19] Each of these seven divisions of Hell is in turn divided into seven subdivisions and in each compartment there are seven rivers of fire, and seven of hail. The width of each is 1000 ells, its depth 1000, and its length 300; they flow from each other and are supervised by the Angels of Destruction. Besides, in each compartment there are 7000 caves, and in each cave there are 7000 crevices, and in every crevice there are 7000 scorpions. Every scorpion has 300 rings, and in every ring 7000 pouches of venom from which flow seven rivers of deadly poison. If a man handles it, he immediately bursts, every limb is torn from his body, his bowels are cleft, and he falls upon his face.[20]

Confinement to Hell is the result of disobeying God's Torah as is illustrated by the midrash concerning the evening visit of the soul to

Hell before it is implanted in an individual. There it sees the Angels of Destruction smiting with fiery scourges; the sinners all the while crying out, but no mercy is shown to them. The angel guides the soul and then asks: 'Do you know who these are?' Unable to respond the soul listens as the angel continues: 'Those who are consumed with fire were created like you. When they were put into the world, they did not observe God's Torah and His commandments. Therefore they have come to this disgrace which you see them suffer. Know, your destiny is also to depart from the world. Be just, therefore, and not wicked, that you may gain the future world'.[21]

The soul was not alone in being able to see Hell; a number of Biblical personages entered into its midst. Moses, for example, was guided through Hell by an angel, and his journey there gives us the most complete picture of its torments:

> When Moses and the Angel of Hell entered Hell together, they saw men being tortured by the Angels of Destruction. Some sinners were suspended by their eyelids, some by their ears, some by their hands, and some by their tongues. In addition, women were suspended by their hair and their breasts by chains of fire. Such punishments were inflicted on the basis of the sins that were committed: those who hung by their eyes had looked lustfully upon their neighbours' wives and possessions; those who hung by their ears had listened to empty and vain speech and did not listen to the Torah; those who hung by their tongues had spoken foolishly and slanderously; those who hung by their hands had robbed and murdered their neighbours. The women who hung by their hair and breasts had uncovered them in the presence of young men in order to seduce them.[22]

In another place, called Alukah, Moses saw sinners suspended by their feet with their heads downward and their bodies covered with long black worms. These sinners were punished in this way because they swore falsely, profaned the Sabbath and the Holy Days, despised the sages, called their neighbours by unseemly nicknames, wronged the orphan and the widow, and bore false witness.

In another section Moses saw sinners prone on their faces with 2000 scorpions lashing, stinging, and tormenting them. Each of these scorpions had 70 000 heads, each head 70 000 mouths, each mouth 70 000 stings, and each sting 70 000 pouches of poison and venom. So great was the pain they inflicted that the eyes of the sinners melted in their sockets. These sinners were punished in this way because they had robbed other Jews, were arrogant in the community, put their neighbours to shame in public, delivered their fellow Jews into the hands of the gentiles, denied the Torah, and maintained that God is not the creator of the world.

In another place, called Tit ha-Yawen, sinners stood in mud up to their navels while Angels of Destruction lashed them with fiery chains, and broke their teeth with fiery stones. These sinners were punished in this way because they had eaten forbidden food, lent their money at usury, had written the name of God on amulets for gentiles, used false weights, stolen money from fellow Jews, eaten on the Day of Atonement, and drank blood.

Finally, after seeing these tortures, Moses observed how sinners were burnt in the section of Hell called Abaddon. There one-half of their bodies were immersed in fire and the other half in snow while worms bred in their own flesh crawled over them and the Angels of Destruction beat them incessantly. By stealth these sinners took snow and put it in their armpits to relieve the pain inflicted by the scorching fire. These sinners were punished because they had committed incest, murder, idolatry, called themselves gods, and cursed their parents and teachers.

From this description it might appear that Hell is reserved for those Jews who have disobeyed the Mosaic law. Such exclusivism, however, was refuted throughout rabbinic literature. For example, in *Midr. Prov.* R. Joshua explained that gentiles are doomed to eternal punishment unless they are righteous.[23] Asked how a man can escape the judgement of Hell, he replied, 'Let him occupy himself with good deeds', and he pointed out that this applies to gentiles as well as Jews.

Of course, gentiles were not expected to keep all of Jewish law in order to escape Hell; they were simply required to keep the Noachide Laws, that is, those laws which Noah and his descendants took upon themselves. The violation of such laws was regarded by the rabbis as repugnant to fundamental human morality, quite apart from revelation, and was a basis for confinement to Hell. However, there was some disagreement as to the laws themselves. In Gen. R., Noah 34:8, for example, we read that 'The sons of Noah were given seven commands: in respect of (1) idolatry, (2) incest, (3) shedding of blood, (4) profanation of the Name of God, (5) justice, (6) robbery, (7) cutting off flesh or limb from a living animal. R. Hanina said: Also about taking blood from a living animal. R. Elazar said: Also about "diverse kinds" and mixtures (Lev.19:19). R. Simeon said:

Also about witchcraft. R. Johanan b. Baroka said: Also about castration (of animals). R. Assi said: Everything forbidden in Deut. 18:10,11 was also forbidden to the sons of Noah, because it says, "whoever does these things is an abomination unto the Lord".' Nevertheless, despite this disagreement, a gentile who lived a sinful life by violating the Noachide laws was destined to be punished in Hell, and conversely, if he lived in accordance with them, he could gain entry into the World to Come.[24]

This eschatological scheme, which was formulated over the centuries by innumerable rabbis, should not be seen as a flight of fancy. It was a serious attempt to explain God's ways to man. Israel was God's chosen people and had received God's promise of reward for keeping his law. Since this did not happen on earth in this life, the rabbis believed it must occur in the World to Come. Never did the rabbis relinquish the belief that God would justify Israel by destroying the power of the oppressing nations. This would come about in the Messianic Age. The individual who had died without seeing the justification of God would be resurrected to see the ultimate victory of the Jewish people. And just as the nations would be judged in the period of Messianic redemption, so would each individual. In this way the vindication of the righteous was assured in the Hereafter.

THE DECLINE OF RABBINIC ESCHATOLOGY

On the basis of this scheme of eternal salvation and damnation – which was at the heart of rabbinic theology throughout the centuries – it might be expected that modern Jewish theologians of all shades of religious observance and opinion would attempt to explain contemporary Jewish history in the context of traditional eschatology. This, however, has not happened: instead many Jewish writers have set aside doctrines concerning Messianic redemption, resurrection, final judgement, and reward for the righteous and punishment for the wicked. This shift in emphasis is in part due to the fact that the views expressed in the narrative sections of the midrashim and the Talmud are not binding. As mentioned, all Jews are obliged to accept the Divine origin of the Law but this is not so with regard to theological concepts and theories expounded by the rabbis. Thus it is possible for a Jew to be religiously pious without accepting all the central beliefs of mainstream Judaism. Indeed throughout Jewish history there has been widespread confusion as to what these beliefs are. In the first century BCE, for example, the sage Hillel stated that the quintessence of Judaism could be formulated in a single principle: 'That which is hateful to you, do not do to your neighbour. This is the whole of the Law; all the rest is commentary'.[25] Similarly in the second century CE, the Council of Lydda ruled that under certain circumstances the laws of the Torah may be transgressed in order to save one's life, with the exception of idolatry, murder and unchastity.[26]

In both these cases the centre of gravity was in the ethical rather than the religious sphere. However, in the medieval period Maimonides formulated what he considered to be the 13 principles of the Jewish faith.[27] Other thinkers though challenged this formulation. Hasdai Crescas, Simon ben Zemah Duran, Joseph Albo and Isaac Arami elaborated different creeds, and some thinkers, like David ben Solomon Ibn Abi Zimrah argued that it is impossible to isolate from the whole Torah essential principles of the Jewish faith. He wrote: 'I do not agree that it is right to make any part of the perfect Torah into a "principle" since the whole Torah is a "principle" from the mouth of the Almighty'.[28] Thus when formulations of the central theological tenets of Judaism were propounded, they were not universally accepted since they were simply the opinions of individual teachers. Without a central authority whose opinion in theological matters was binding on all Jews, it has been impossible to determine the correct theological beliefs in Judaism. In the words of Solomon Schechter 'any attempt at an orderly and complete system of rabbinic theology is an impossible task'.[29]

Given that there is no authoritative bedrock of Jewish theology, many modern Jewish thinkers have felt fully justified in abandoning the various elements of traditional rabbinic eschatology which they regard as untenable. The doctrine of Messianic redemption, for example, has been radically modified. In the last century Reform Jews tended to interpret the new liberation in the Western world as the first step towards the realization of the Messianic dream. But the Messianic redemption was understood in this-worldly terms. No longer, according to this view, was it necessary for Jews to pray for a restoration in Eretz Israel (Palestine); rather they should view their own countries as Zion and their political leaders as bringing about the Messianic age. Secular Zionists, on the other hand, saw the return to Israel as the legitimate conclusion to be drawn from the realities of Jewish life in Western countries, thereby viewing the State of Israel as a substitute for the Messiah himself. As L. Jacobs notes, 'most modern Jews prefer to interpret the Messianic hope in naturalistic terms, abandoning the belief in a personal Messiah, the restoration of the sacrificial system, and to a greater or lesser degree, the idea of direct Divine intervention'.[30]

Similarly, the doctrine of the resurrection of the dead has in modern times been largely replaced in both Orthodox and non-Orthodox Judaism by the belief in the immortality of the soul. The original belief in resurrection was an eschatological hope bound up with the rebirth of the nation in the Days of the Messiah, but as this Messianic concept faded into the background so also did this doctrine. For most Jews physical resurrection is simply inconceivable in the light of a scientific understanding of the nature of the world. The late Chief Rabbi, Dr J.H. Hertz, for example, argued that what really matters is the doctrine of the immortality of the soul. Thus he wrote: 'Many and various are the folk beliefs and poetical fancies in the rabbinical writings concerning Heaven, *Gan Eden*, and Hell, *Gehinnom*. Our most authoritative religious guides, however, proclaim that no eye hath seen, nor can mortal fathom, what awaiteth us in the Hereafter; but that even the tarnished soul will not forever be denied spiritual bliss'.[31]

In the Reform community a similar attitude prevails. In a well-known statement of the beliefs of Reform Judaism it is stated that Reform Jews 'reassert the doctrine of Judaism that the soul is immortal, grounding this belief on the Divine nature of the human spirit, which forever finds bliss in righteousness and misery in wickedness. We reject as ideas not rooted in Judaism the belief in bodily resurrection and in Gehenna and Eden (Hell and Paradise) as abodes for eternal punishment or reward'.[32] The point to note about the conception of the immortal soul in both Orthodox and Reform Judaism is that it is dissociated from traditional notions of Messianic redemption and Divine judgement.

The belief in eternal punishment has also been discarded by a large number of Jews partly because of the interest in penal reform during the past century. Punishment as retaliation in a vindictive sense has been generally rejected. Thus Jacobs writes, 'the value of punishment as a deterrent and for the protection of society is widely recognised. But all the stress today is on the reformatory aspects of punishment. Against such a background the whole question of reward and punishment in the theological sphere is approached in a more questioning spirit'.[33] Further, the rabbinic view of Hell is seen by many as morally repugnant. Jewish theologians have stressed that it is a delusion to believe that a God of love could have created a place of eternal punishment. In his commentary on the prayerbook, Chief Rabbi Hertz categorically declared, 'Judaism rejects the doctrine of eternal damnation'.[34] And in *Jewish Theology* the Reform Rabbi, K. Kohler, argued that the question whether the tortures of Hell are reconcilable with Divine mercy 'is for us superfluous and superseded. Our modern conceptions of time and space admit neither a place or a world-period for the reward and punishment of souls, nor the intolerable conception of eternal joy without useful action and eternal agony without any moral purpose'.[35]

Traditional rabbinic eschatology has thus lost its force for a large number of Jews in the modern period, and in consequence there has been a gradual this-worldly emphasis in Jewish thought. Significantly, this has been accompanied by a powerful attachment to the State of Israel. For many Jews the founding of the Jewish State is the central focus of their religious and cultural identity. Jews throughout the world have deep admiration for the astonishing achievements of Israelis in reclaiming the desert and building a viable society, and great respect for the heroism of Israel's soldiers and statesmen. As a result it is not uncommon for Jews to equate Jewishness with Zionism, and to see Judaism as fundamentally nationalistic in character – this is a far cry from the rabbinic view of history which placed the doctrine of the Hereafter at the centre of Jewish life and thought.

CONCLUSION

We can see therefore that the wheel has swung full circle from the faint allusions to immortality in the Biblical period which led to an elaborate development of the concept of the Hereafter in rabbinic Judaism. Whereas the rabbis put the belief in an Afterlife at the centre of their religious system, modern Jewish thinkers, both Orthodox and Reform, have abandoned such an other-worldly outlook, even to the point of denying the existence of such doctrines. It may be that these concepts are outmoded and should be abandoned in the light of contemporary thought, but there is no doubt that such a development raises major problems for Judaism in the modern age. The belief in the Hereafter has helped Jews make sense of the world as a creation of a good and all-powerful God and provided a source of great consolation for their travail on earth. Without the promise of Messianic redemption, resurrection and the eventual vindication of the righteous in Paradise, Jews will face great difficulties reconciling the belief in a providential God who watches over his chosen people with the terrible events of modern Jewish history. If there is no eschatological unfolding of a Divine drama in which Jewish victims will ultimately triumph, what hope can there be for the Righteous of Israel who have suffered for their convictions?

3
The Torah
in Modern Judaism

For centuries Jews have maintained that the Torah was revealed by God to Moses on Mt Sinai. Such belief 'guarantees' that the Five Books of Moses including history, theology, and legal precepts are of Divine origin and have absolute authority. In consequence Orthodoxy refuses to accept any modernist interpretation of the Pentateuch. As Zwi Werblowsky explains: 'Jewish Orthodoxy has . . . always staunchly upheld the theory of verbal inspiration in its extremist form – at least so far as the Pentateuch is concerned. Higher Criticism of the Pentateuch is flatly rejected and is considered a major heresy. The underlying assumption is that the whole fabric of traditional Judaism would crumble if its foundation, the notion of Divine legislation to Moses, were to be exchanged for modernist ideas about historical growth and the composite nature of sacred texts'.[1] This clash between the Orthodox understanding of scripture and the modern liberal perspective has been and continues to be the central theological stumbling-block to inter-Jewish unity. Recently this irreconcilable conflict was highlighted in a notorious debate between Rabbi Dr Jonathan Sacks, the designate Chief Rabbi of the UK, and the distinguished scholar, Rabbi Dr Louis Jacobs. Their disagreement and the subsequent public reaction illustrate that the traditional and liberal conceptions of Torah inevitably preclude the possibility of religious reconciliation.

NEO-ORTHODOX FUNDAMENTALISM

In 'The Origin of Torah' in the 2 November 1984 issue of the *Jewish Chronicle*[2] Sacks presents his view of Torah in a lengthy review of a recent book by Jacobs – *The Tree of Life*. According to Jacobs, the Torah was not revealed in its totality at Mt Sinai; it grew slowly as the accretion of documents and decisions. (This view, Sacks notes, was originally propounded by Jacobs in *We Have Reason To Believe* published nearly 30 years ago.) Jacobs' view is invalid,

Sacks believes, since it contains several errors. First, Sacks attacks Jacobs' contention that the Torah is a collaboration between God and man. What sort of collaboration could this be? Sacks asks. 'He [Jacobs] has told us; men make up the words. What then did the Almighty contribute? The theme? The plot? The rough idea? How are we to tell? The only evidence we have is the words themselves. And the words, says Jacobs, are human, all too human!'[3] Thus Sacks concludes that throughout Jacobs' work there is a persistent confusion between the historical and the metaphysical. On the one hand, there is an acceptance of historical scholarship; on the other hand, Jacobs argues that revelation is a matter of faith rather than historical scholarship. Sacks contends it is inconsistent for Jacobs to employ the criterion of historical scholarship in evaluating the veracity of the Orthodox claim that God revealed the Torah to Moses on Mt Sinai.

Sacks' second criticism concerns Jacobs' use of the term 'fundamentalist' to describe the rabbinic approach to Torah and halachah. Fundamentalism, he points out, is an approach to the Bible which sets primacy on the literal reading of the text and sees the main function of the Torah as conveying information of a factual nature. But, Sacks continues, the rabbinic tradition gave supremacy to the Oral Law which frequently departed from the apparent plain meaning and saw the Torah's function as establishing communal obligations. Here there is a confusion between the Bible as a document and the Torah as the constitution of the covenant between God and His people. To ask of the Bible if it is true is to view the Torah as a document – this would be a fundamentalistic approach. But when the Torah is correctly seen as an halachic constitution, such a question is irrelevant. Sacks concludes that in arguing for a 'non-fundamentalistic halachah' Jacobs has misunderstood this distinction and has thereby coined a phrase which is devoid of meaning.

Related to this criticism is what Sacks sees as a further important error: Jacobs mistakenly believes in halachic change since Jewish law is man-made and occasionally wrong. However, Sacks argues that laws are not an individual's private code but rules which govern a community. No law can be changed by an individual will or a sub-group unless they have authority over the community. 'A group of Jews', he writes, 'could constitute themselves as a *beth din* and issue rulings designed at a stroke to remedy every religious grievance, but they would not have changed the law; rather they would have unilaterally declared independence from it.'[4] Sacks contends that

Jacobs fails to grapple with the question of halachic authority and his opinions therefore lack any communal basis. Jacobs asserts that halachic authorities have not addressed themselves to the issues of our time. Sacks disagrees – he thinks they have done so but have given answers which Jacobs simply does not like. These halachists who issued non-concessive rulings were not evading the present, but responding to it in a way that recognizes idealism as a more potent spring of action than compromise. They sensed the need to re-establish the fundamentals of faith after the Holocaust.

The final criticism of Jacobs' position concerns the role of the modern halachists. Jacobs states that they should take account of the history of halachic change: Sacks argues that it would be a mistake for them to become historians. Why, Sacks asks, should halachists have a methodology that negates time? The answer is that the Torah is an eternal covenant, a mutually binding constitution between God and Israel. Such a covenant does not change; it resists time: 'The eternity of the Torah is the eternity of the Jewish people, an island in the stream of time'.[5] This conception has important consequences. When a rabbi decides an issue in Jewish law, he is bound by the decrees of previous rabbinic authorities. Even when the issue is topical he must bring to bear the halachah's cumulative verdicts. According to Sacks, Jacobs' analysis does not take into account this timeless quality of the tradition. Thus Sacks concludes: 'in taking too rough a hold on the Tree of Life, he has pulled it, roots and all, from the soil in which it grows'.[6]

A NON-PROPOSITIONAL VIEW OF REVELATION

In the 16 November issue of the *Jewish Chronicle*, Jacobs presents his defence. In 'The Origin of the Torah: A Response' he attempts to answer Sacks' claim that there is a contradiction between accepting Divine revelation and the conclusions of historical scholarship. Jacobs asserts that this is in no way inconsistent: revelation is an event or series of events in which there is a meeting between God and man – a matter of faith. Biblical criticism examines the accounts of such encounters. It asks how they came about, who wrote them down, and when and whether our present texts are completely accurate in all their details. Jacobs grants that if revelation is understood as verbal inspiration, Biblical scholarship is impossible. But it is Jacobs' view that such scholarship renders the notion of verbal inspiration untenable. Here he invokes the example of Abraham Ibn

Ezra's contention that the final section of Deuteronomy describing Moses' ascent on the mountain to die could not have been written by Moses. If, Jacobs asks, the claim is made on the grounds of faith that Moses did write it, on what is such faith based? The issue, Jacobs believes, can be settled by human investigation. Invoking faith is unnecessary. Thus Jacobs believes that both faith and historical criticism have separate roles and can harmoniously combine in a true understanding of God's relation to man.

Concerning Sacks' criticism of his use of the term 'fundamentalist' to describe the rabbinic approach to Torah and halachah, Jacobs disputes Sacks' understanding of the concept. Fundamentalism is concerned primarily with inerrancy rather than the literal reading of the text. 'Non-fundamentalist halachah' is therefore not a confusion but a legitimate notion of halachah based on tenable premises. Jacobs continues by examining Sacks' claim that he (Jacobs) believes that the law can be changed by an individual or sub-group. 'I have never argued for such a position', Jacobs writes. 'Where a change in the law is required it must be brought about by the acknowledged authorities of the whole observant community.'[7] Jacobs points out that in the past halachists conceived of the law as dynamic in character; this should provide the basis for a creative interpretive approach. Yet such a change is inhibited by the present climate of Orthodox opinion. The obstacle to such a dynamic perspective is the Orthodox adherence to a rigid fundamentalist understanding of the origin of Torah.

Such fundamentalism, Jacobs believes, cannot be sustained in the face of critical research. Let us ask Sacks, he writes, 'whether he believes that the Masoretic text is always accurate and all the versions always wrong; whether he rejects any suggestion that the Pentateuch is a composite work; whether the massive researches of Krochmal, Ginzberg, Finkelstein, Buchler, I.H. Weiss, Lieberman and many other historians of the Talmudic period, into the way the doctrine of the Oral Torah has developed, are so much hot air'.[8] Jacobs notes that Sacks gives the appearance of accepting the results of modern scholarship – even where they are at variance with traditional views. But if so, it would have been helpful to have a clear exposition of his position. In response to Sacks' final criticism concerning his views about halachah and history, Jacobs emphasises that he does not wish that halachists become historians. What he urges is that they should have a better knowledge of the past, and not think Judaism is beyond space and time. 'If new knowledge in medicine, science, and technology is allowed a voice in the halachic process, where is the logic in denying increased historical knowledge a voice?'[9] What Jacobs seeks to show is that the Law is not unyielding and lifeless; it can grow as it has in the past.

IRRECONCILABLE DIFFERENCES

In this debate there is clearly no possibility of agreement; in the letters to the editor printed in subsequent issues of the *Jewish Chronicle* similarly irreconcilable views were expressed. Supporting Rabbi Sacks, the Rev. Chaim Ingram declared: 'the vast majority, ever growing legions of yeshiva-oriented Jewish young men and women . . . espouse the very so-called "fundamentalist" approach to Torah which Rabbi Sacks defends. They have realised that the middle-of-the-road is an indecisive and potentially dangerous place to be'.[10] Again, Rabbi Alan Kimche writes: 'It is common knowledge that from father to son for over 3,000 years the Jewish people have lived with God by total acceptance of the historical and textual authenticity of the Torah. Those who left this position rarely lasted to the third generation within the Jewish nation. By subjecting the Torah and Sinai to historical and textual criticism, Jacobs has placed himself fair and square outside the national Talmudic heritage'.[11] In praise of Sacks, Dr Tali Lowental asserts that the Torah is supra-rational in the life of the Jewish people. Is this supra-rational force relevant to the rational man of today's world? he asks. 'Rabbi Sacks in his commendable article is clearly saying "yes". Halachah takes note of reality – continuously – and at the same time gives guidance which ultimately is Divine.'[12]

Supporters of Jacobs, however, contend that Sacks is mistaken in his criticisms. Michael Milston, for example, writes: 'It is unfortunate that Rabbi Jonathan Sacks has joined the mountainous ranks of Anglo-Jewish thinkers who have failed to understand the point which Rabbi Jacobs is making. It is agreed amongst all Jewish thinkers that God is infinite but it is also agreed amongst everyone that language is finite. Therefore, language must, *ipso facto*, contain only part of God's revelation. In that sense language is finite man's attempt to understand the infinity of God'.[13] Isaac Newman emphasizes the importance of historical criticism: 'As one who studied under the illustrious teachers of Jew's College', he writes, 'I cannot today dispense with the tools of their historical and critical methodology in the study of Judaism – with the hopeful possibility of applying its findings to the contemporary world of thought and practice where it is so badly needed. To do so would be not the Way Ahead but the Way to Regress'.[14]

At the heart of this disagreement between Sacks and Jacobs and their respective supporters is an unbridgeable gulf between fundamentally differing conceptions of the nature of revelation. For Sacks and his followers, the doctrine of *Torah MiSinai* entails a notion of verbal inspiration in which God is conceived as communicating His will clearly and directly to Moses. The Torah thus consists of propositions dictated word by word and letter by letter. Though there are different views in rabbinic sources about the process of this communication, there is nonetheless the conviction that the Five Books of Moses are infallible because they were transmitted by God – the source of truth. Jacobs, however, thinks that such a traditional view is no longer tenable; scholarly research, he argues, has demonstrated that Judaism is a developing faith: the sciences of geology, zoology, botany, astronomy, anthropology and archaeology all demonstrate that the Torah is a composite work reflecting different social and cultural conditions in the history of Ancient Israel. Yet what Jacobs fails to recognize is that the traditional conception of revelation is unassailable because it is ultimately grounded on an act of faith. For those who are committed to the religious belief that God revealed the Torah to Moses on Mt Sinai, contrary evidence of whatever kind is utterly irrelevant.

Similarly, there is simply no way the Orthodox could convince Jacobs and his followers that their view of revelation is invalid. In place of verbal inspiration Jacobs conceives of revelation as a form of Divine encounter in which human inspiration plays a vital role. In a recent study of Jewish theology, he explains what he means by such Divine self-disclosure: 'On this view revelation does not mean that God conveys to man detailed propositions at all but rather that He enables men to have an encounter with Him of a specially intense form. It is God Himself who is disclosed in revelation. Revelation is an event not a series of propositions about God and His demands'.[15] Such a conception enables Jacobs to see the Bible as a record of how the Jews were confronted by God. The Genesis narrative, for example, is about the covenant – a generous God finding Israel and Israel finding God and bringing Him to all mankind. Yet for all the human colouring of the story, it is in this book of the Bible that God is revealed. This religious conviction and theological conception is as unassailable as that of the Orthodox view of revelation on Mt

Sinai. Jacobs' belief that revelation is the disclosure of God Himself
rather than of statements on Mt Sinai is grounded in an act of faith.
Thus, like Sacks' view, Jacobs' position cannot be contradicted by
counter-argument and evidence.

CONCLUSION

Here then is an unbridgeable theological impass that separates Orthodox from non-Orthodox Judaism. Arguments deployed by either side
inevitably fall on deaf ears – there can be no meeting of minds when
such fundamental religious beliefs stand in conflict. For the Orthodox
what is at stake is the whole fabric of Judaism as it developed through
the ages. It is not surprising therefore that religious unity has been,
presently is, and no doubt will continue to be an impossibility for the
different branches of the Jewish faith. As the Sacks-Jacobs debate
eloquently illustrates, religious cohesion among Jews cannot feasibly
be a reality in modern society despite the fact that Jews worldwide
are bound together by feelings of community and peoplehood.

4

Law and Freedom in Reform Judaism

Recently a number of leading Reform rabbis have criticised the Progressive Judaism of the past for its emphasis on individual decision-making, and they strongly advocate formulating a new approach to the legal system.[1] What is needed, they argue, is a modern code of law for Reform Jews which is rooted in the Jewish heritage. Such a legal system would differ from Orthodoxy in that it would be based on a thorough examination and critical analysis of traditional Law and would be open to revision in the future. Yet, as in Orthodoxy, it would give coherence and structure to the Reform movement and provide a basis for discipline to law.

CRITERIA FOR A REFORM CODE OF LAW

A contemporary code of Jewish Law for Reform Judaism would require explicit criteria for deciding which traditional laws should be eliminated and which retained. Thus, in a variety of publications Reform rabbis give a great deal of thought to the principles they believe could be employed.[2] One common suggestion is that Reform Jews should attempt to ascertain what God's will is. In this way they would be able to establish an ultimate, absolute authority for their adherence to tradition. But what has God revealed? Reform Jews believe that the Bible contains God's revelation, but where is it to be found? In the Pentateuch? Or the Prophetic books? Or the rest of Scripture? Is God truly concerned if Jews eat lobster? Does He care whether they wear fringes, or seethe the kid in its's mother's milk? Is He annoyed if they go out to work, drive a car to synagogue, or smoke on the Sabbath? Is He angry if they commit adultery or steal? Perhaps He does concern Himself with such things, but if so, does He care about all these things equally? Reform Jews in the past have been anxious to distinguish between ritual and moral law, but is this distinction valid as far as God is concerned? These are unanswerable questions for one reason: there is no basis for knowing what God's intention is. Some Reform rabbis have stated categorically that they have some sort of knowledge of God's revelation; but any examination of the wide diversity of opinion among these rabbis illustrates that such claims are nothing more than subjective beliefs based on personal disposition and judgement.

If there is disagreement as to what constitutes revelation, what can be said about the claims of conscience? Perhaps conscience is a reliable guide in formulating a modern system of law? This is a view frequently expressed by Reform rabbis, but it too is beset with difficulties. No doubt many Reform Jews do follow their consciences, but how can they be sure that what they are doing is right? The dictates of one person's conscience often differ from someone else's. To take a simple example: one person's conscience might urge him to see euthanasia as an inalienable human right, whereas another person might well condemn it as utterly sinful. Here there is a direct conflict, yet there is no way to discover which person's conscience is on the right track. And if in trying to decide who was right, some external standard, like humaneness is invoked, then conscience ceases to be the final criterion for moral action.

Conscience then, like revelation, is undependable. But what if we ask whether particular laws are relevant for our time. This is an approach frequently advocated by Reform rabbis, but the notion of relevance is equally problematic. It is obvious that what one person considers relevant is an ambiguous concept. So too is the notion of contemporary appeal. How is one to decide what is really of value when change is so constant? Most people have enough difficulty keeping up with modern ideas, much less employing them as criteria for deciding which traditional laws should be retained.

The same applies to such standards as ethical propriety, justice, and aesthetic value which have been recommended as well. From everyday experience it is clear that what is offensive to one person can be totally acceptable to another. Recently there was an interesting case of just this sort of disagreement. In a recent issue of Debretts' *Etiquette and Modern Manners*[3] the authors state that it is a courtesy to put visiting unmarried couples who ordinarily live together in the same bedroom. In a letter to *The Times* the Dean of Durham objected to this on religious and moral grounds[4]; no doubt some Reform Jews would raise the same protest. One could cite innumerable similar cases such as the current debates about abortion, nuclear disarmament or genetic engineering. There is no concensus in society generally, or in the Jewish community in particular, about a very wide range of moral issues.

The concept of justice is equally unclear. Is it *just* that one individual receives higher wages than someone who works equally hard but at a different sort of task? Is it *just* that some people have great wealth, or a larger house, or more material possessions than others? Is it *just* that certain children receive a privileged education at expensive independent schools? Is it *just* that a limited number of people have private medicine? Or are able to hire expensive lawyers? In all these cases some Jews think it is just and some do not. The concept of justice is thus as nebulous and ill-defined a notion as moral propriety.

Aesthetic sensitivity too does not provide the answer. Some laws, like ritual immersion, might commend themselves on such grounds. Indeed, there are English Reform rabbis today who maintain that converts crave for just such ritualism and symbolism to give meaning to the conversion ceremony. Other Liberal rabbis, however, believe that ritual immersion is aesthetically offensive because it involves the personal indignity of the convert who must be interrogated naked. This is just one example but it illustrates that taste, like so many other things, varies from person to person.

Some Reform rabbis have suggested that psychological considerations should be taken into account. On this basis certain laws could be ruled out because of a modern understanding of human psychology. But here again there is widespread disagreement. An interesting case concerns homosexuality, which is explicitly forbidden in the Bible. On humane and psychological grounds it is possible to take a lenient view of homosexual behaviour, but in a well-known statement, Rabbi Solomon Freehof, an American Reform rabbi who is an expert on legal matters declared: 'Homosexuality runs counter to the sancta of Jewish life. There is no sidestepping the fact that from the point of view of Judaism, men who practice homosexuality are to be deemed sinners'.[5]

What then about common sense? A number of Reform rabbis have argued that it is important to consider whether traditional Jewish law legislates beyond such limits. For example: some Liberal rabbis have stated that the laws governing Sabbath observance transcend the boundary of common sense and that more room should be made for individual spontaneity. Yet there are other rabbis, especially in the English Reform and American Conservative movements, who advocate a strict observance of Sabbath law. It is common sense, they believe, for Jews to differentiate themselves in just this way so as to perpetuate Judaism as a civilization and to establish their identity as Jews in the increasingly secularized Western world.

In this connection it is equally hopeless appealing to the notion of reasonableness as a criterion. How could Jewish ritual and practice be regarded as reasonable? Is it *reasonable* for a secular man in the modern world to wear a prayer shawl and hat in synagogue, blow the shofar (ram's horn) on Rosh Hoshanah (the New Year), eat matzot (unleavened bread) on Passover, light candles on the Sabbath, fast on the Day of Atonement, build a succah (tabernacle) and so forth? Such traditional observances have become part of Reform Judaism not because of their reasonableness, but because some Reform Jews find them meaningful.

Another standard of selection is what has been termed by various rabbis as 'the good of the community'. Here what is important is the significance of traditional Jewish laws for Progressive Jewry. But who is to say what is good for the Reform Jewish community as a whole? A disagreement among English Reform Jews illustrates this point. Rabbi Dow Marmur argued the case for ritual immersion for converts, yet he stressed that the decision of the Reform Synagogues of Great Britain was not welcomed by many English Reform Jews.[6] Due to 'failure of communication', he notes, 'the decision of the Reform rabbinate was badly received in the movement. So far most of the arguments among the laymen have been primarily about the rabbis' right to decide, and not about the intrinsic merits of the decision made'.[7] Rabbi Marmur believes that the lay leadership will in the end endorse the rabbinic decision, but they may not. Thus here is a case of a rabbinic body laying down law for Reform Jewry despite the wishes of a large segment of the community. Such a lack of agreement about what is best for Reform Jews exemplifies the extreme difficulty of deciding which elements of Jewish law are applicable to the movement.

Finally, it has been suggested that certain traditional laws should be retained because of commitment to the wider Jewish community. Thus, for example, Rabbi Marmur in his defence of circumcision and ritual immersion for converts as well as for the issuing of a bill of divorce by the Reform rabbinical court contends that concern for the entire Jewish community 'is not a matter of expediency but a religious principle . . . (We) are, therefore, prepared to act to further the unity of the Jewish people, out of a sense of responsibility and concern . . . out of our concern for the people of Israel we are able to provide an acceptable forum, which, at some future time, may really become the authentic rabbinical court of Anglo-Jewry'.[8] Yet, given this commitment to the unity of the Jewish community, where is one to draw the line? If ritual immersion, circumcision and Jewish divorce are mandatory, why not the food regulations? Or the laws of ritual purification? Or the Sabbath observances? Or the wearing of teffilin and tzizis? Why indeed not all the law in the *Code of Jewish Law*? Furthermore, is not the ordination of women a public declaration of Reform unwillingness to join together with the Orthodox?

What can be seen therefore is that there seems to be no way to decide which traditional laws ought to be included in a contemporary system of law for Reform Judaism. Revelation, conscience, relevance, contemporary appeal, ethical propriety, justice, aesthetic value, psychological considerations, common sense, reasonableness, the good of the Reform Jewish community, the peoplehood of Israel – all these criteria which have been prescribed by leaders of the Reform movement are so nebulous and contentious as to be of little if any use. All that we can say is that although Reform Jews are heirs to a vast legal tradition, they lack any well-defined, coherent and consistent method for sorting out those traditional laws they should adopt for themselves. This is not a temporary difficulty which can be resolved in the future; it is rather an inevitable consequence of the rejection of the Divine authority of the legal system.

REFORM PRACTICE IN AMERICAN JUDAISM

On a theoretical level then it can be seen that there is no way to establish a modern code of Jewish law. Nevertheless, from the very beginning of the Reform movement in the 19the century various rabbis and rabbinical synods were anxious to regulate Reform Jewish practice on the basis of traditional law.[9] And more recently in the writings of the eminent American rabbi Solomon Freehof there has been an attempt to systematize law within Reform Judaism. Rabbi Freehof, who is the Rabbi Emeritus of Temple Rodeph Shalom in Pittsburgh, Pennsylvania, is the leading expert on Jewish law within Reform Judaism on both sides of the Atlantic. In a number of studies of Reform Jewish observance in the light of its rabbinic background, he has developed a legal framework which in the eyes of many Reform rabbis is tantamount to a system of law for Reform Jews.[10]

Yet, as might be expected, Freehof's recommendations are often internally inconsistent because he lacks a clear set of criteria for deciding which traditional laws should be retained. His work, which is the most comprehensive approach to Jewish law ever attempted in the Reform movement, is a concrete illustration of Reform Judaism's inevitable inability to establish a sound legal basis. To take several examples from his work:

Freehof frequently asserts that there are a number of traditional laws which should be rigorously followed. Concerning circumcision of Jewish babies, for example, he writes: 'The ancient practice of circumcising a male child at the age of eight days, the first commandment given to Abraham our father is strictly observed.'[11] Similarly, Freehof argues that Reform Judaism should adopt the same position as Orthodoxy regarding intermarriage. 'The attitude of Reform Judaism', he states, 'became exactly the same as that of all of Judaism, namely, that while marriage of a Jew and a converted gentile is considered a perfect marriage in every respect, marriage between a Jew and an unconverted gentile cannot be considered a Jewish marriage and a rabbi cannot officiate'.[12] Yet, in other instances, Freehof asserts that Orthodox law should be overturned without explaining why. For example, concerning the Orthodox custom of leaving some blades of grass or pebbles on the tombstones after visiting the grave, Freedhof decrees: 'The custom of leaving pebbles on tombstones is not observed by Reform Jews'.[13] In the absence of any criteria to distinguish between these laws such judgements seem arbitrary and contradictory.

In other cases Freehof argues that Reform Jewish practice should run counter to Orthodoxy where ordinances are based on custom rather than law. For example, he states that the popular custom of turning mirrors to the wall or covering them in the room where a corpse lies has no basis in Jewish law and in fact is part of general folklore. Thus, he contends, there is no reason to observe it in Reform Judaism.[14] Again, in response to the question whether one ought to fast if the Torah is dropped, he writes: 'Fasting if the Torah is dropped is not a legal requirement . . . since this custom has no real legal status, nothing should be done by the entire congregation'.[15] In other instances, however, he maintains that Jewish customs should be practised by Reform Jews. For example, concerning the question whether a marriage can take place without a rabbi and without Hebrew, Freehof writes that though these customs are not based on legal requirements, they should be adhered to.[16]

At times Freehof argues that traditional law, while providing general guidelines for Reform Judaism, should be extended. Concerning autopsy, for example, Freehof points out that in general autopsy and dissection are forbidden by Jewish law, but there are some Orthodox authorities who permit autopsy when there is in the same locality a person suffering from the same disease. Thus autopsy is permitted if it could save a life; this accords with the Orthodox ruling that in order to save life all the laws of the Torah, except those relating to idolatry, incest and murder, may be violated. Extending this principle Freehof states that since 'Nowadays the discoveries made by one physician are broadcast all over the world and may result in the saving of innumerable lives; it is in line with this Orthodox ruling to allow all autopsies to take place'.[17] But Freehof is not always willing to extend Orthodox rulings. For example, in the case of the traditional ruling that marriages are not to be held during the first month of mourning except in certain circumstances Freehof does not extend this leniency in the law to allow all Reform rabbis to perform such marriages during that month.[18]

In some circumstances Freehof asserts that a particular law should be incorporated into Reform Judaism if it is Biblically-based, even if it runs counter to present-day Orthodoxy. Many Reform synagogues, particularly in the United States, for example, celebrate only one day of various festivals rather than two because, as Freehof notes, 'Progressive Judaism reverted to the Biblical observance of the length of the festivals'.[19] On other occasions, however, Freehof advocates following the rulings of the rabbis rather than Biblical law. Thus, in answer to the question whether wearing costumes on Halloween is forbidden by Jewish law, he states, 'There is a Biblical basis upon which an objection could well be raised. The Bible, in Deut. 22.5, clearly prohibits men from putting on women's garments and women from putting on men's garments'. Nevertheless, Freehof believes that one should follow the ruling of the great Orthodox rabbi Judah Minz who decreed that it was permissible to wear masks and costumes on Purim. Though this decision relates specifically to a Jewish festival, Freehof argues that it should apply as well to Halloween since this holiday has no Christian associations.[20]

Again, in some cases Freehof argues that Reform Jews should follow the spirit rather than the letter of the law, whereas in other cases he thinks the letter of the law is all-important. Thus, in answer to the question whether there is any legal justification for the practice of accepting adult converts without circumcision, Freehof points out that although Maimonides, the great medieval Jewish scholar, and the Code of Jewish Law have circumcision as a firmly established law, 'it seems contrary to the spiritual and ethical spirit of Judaism to insist upon this ritual'.[21] In other examples, however, he maintains that traditional law should be upheld. In the case of a married gentile couple where the man wishes to convert to Judaism, Freehof argues that if we convert the husband he would be a Jew under the yoke of the law married to a gentile: 'He was a righteous Christian before we converted him', he writes. 'Now, if he is the head of a gentile family he becomes a sinful Jew . . . we have no right to convert him.'[22]

On other occasions Freehof recommends that traditional law should be abandoned if it discriminates against women. Progressive Judaism, he states, proclaimed from the very beginning the religious equality of men and women, and this notion of equality also applies to the religious status of all Jews. Yet, at times questions concerning sexual and religious equality are answered by Freehof in a way inconsistent with this principle. For example, in reply to the query whether the children of a widow who are adopted by the second husband who is a priest are to be considered priests, Freehof appeals to a number of distinctions in the law about Jewish status: 'If a woman's first husband was a priest', he writes, 'then the children remain priests, no matter how many times or whom she marries. If her first husband was not a priest and her second husband is a priest, this marriage does not affect the status of the children of a previous marriage'.[23] In this instance he completely omits mentioning that the category of priesthood has been abolished in Reform Judaism. In another case Freehof declares that if a Jewish man is living together sexually with a non-Jewish woman who eventually converts to Judaism, he may never marry her. Yet he states that if a gentile man lives sexually with a Jewish woman 'perhaps it would be right to convert the gentile so that they may be able to marry in accordance with Jewish law and custom'.[24] Here it is clear that Freehof undermines the view that men and women should be treated equally.

In other cases Freehof asserts that traditional law should be abandoned if it is not well-adapted to modern life. For example, Freehof writes: 'Since in modern times it was difficult to obtain the close attention and the uninterrupted decorum of the service during the lengthy reading of the entire weekly portion, the custom arose in Reform congregations to shorten the reading'.[25] Neverthe-less, in other instances Freehof advocates following laws which are unquestionably ill-adapted to modern life. For example, in response to the question whether anaesthetics should be used for circumcision Freehof states: 'We should not institute the use of anaesthetics as a regular procedure, but should permit them when the surgeon or the patient asks that they may be given'.[26] Yet given that Jewish law does not insist that pain be experienced in circumcision, there is every reason for Reform Judaism to adopt this scientific advance.

Finally, another argument Freehof frequently employs is that certain laws should be eliminated on humane grounds. Where a husband has disappeared, for example, Freehof writes that 'there is tragic hardship involved in Jewish law of divorce which the best rabbinic minds have been unable to remove, namely the case of the Agunah (the woman chained to marriage even though her husband has disappeared). . . . countless women whose husbands have disappeared have no way of being freed from the bonds of matrimony'. For reasons of humanity, he states, the Reform movement has abolished the traditional law of divorce.[27] Yet in his discussion of euthanasia he follows traditional law which maintains that it is forbidden to take life.[28] On humane grounds, however, it is possible to defend euthanasia, given the mental and physical agony of some patients in the face of long, useless and incurable illness. Or again, in answer to the question whether a doctor should be permitted to inform a patient that he is dying, Freehof declares that 'in the light of Jewish law and tradition, it is clearly wrong to tell a patient that his case is hopeless and he is dying.[29] Yet there are patients who desire to know the truth about their illness so that they are better able to cope with death; to deny them such information could be a heartless act. Thus, it is not clear why Freehof accepts that the law should be more in line with principles of humanity in some cases, but by no means all.

From this survey we can see that Freehof has an ambiguous and inconsistent attitude to Jewish law. When deciding which traditional observances should be retained in Reform Judaism, he frequently does not follow his own principles of selection. Sometimes his judge-ments seem to be based simply on expediency, while at other times they seem motivated by an unjustified prejudice for traditional ways.

This confusion no doubt results from a lack of clearly delineated criteria for accepting Orthodox practice. The entire approach is thus disorganised and unmethodical, thereby illustrating the great uncertainty in the movement about Reform Judaism's relation to tradition.

THE ENGLISH REFORM MOVEMENT AND JEWISH LAW

The same confused attitude to Jewish law exists within the English Reform movement. In a number of articles Rabbi Marmur has defended the increasingly conservative stance of the Reform Synagogues of Great Britain. 'We believe', he writes, 'that the traditional criteria for the acceptance of converts and issuing of bills of divorce makes it possible, in principle, for our converts to be accepted by all communities and our divorcees married in all synagogues'.[30] But the facts are that the British Orthodox establishment will not accept them. And in Israel, despite Reform Judaism's insistence on meticulously following legal procedures, the Orthodox ruling party still rejects Reform converts out of hand simply because they are Reform Jews. Aware of this intransigence, Marmur states, 'If spokesmen for Orthodoxy still refuse to accept our documentation, it is a reflection on them – not on us'.[31] But this is clearly illogical since he is arguing on two mutually incompatible planes at once: on the one hand he says that more stringent procedures will make Reform converts and divorcees acceptable to the Orthodox; on the other hand he states that if it does not make them acceptable, this is not important since this is the fault of the Orthodox.

But why are the Orthodox so inflexible given that English Reform Judaism has adopted traditional conversion and divorce procedures? The answer is obvious: Orthodox Judaism is unwilling to acknowledge the legitimacy of any version of Judaism other than its own. Reform Judaism is seen by Orthodox Jews as heretical because of its rejection of the Divine sanction and authority of the Written and Oral Law. A movement which permits not only its members, but also its rabbis, to violate the laws of ritual purity, food regulations, Sabbath and Festival observance, and so forth is in the eyes of Orthodoxy an unholy scandal and a perversion of God's covenant. It is not surprising, therefore, that the Orthodox refuse to recognize Reform Jewish divorce procedures and grant acceptance into the peoplehood of Israel to Reform Jewish converts. To think, as Marmur does, [32] that the Orthodox establishment will change its mind in the future is a serious delusion based on a total misunderstanding of traditional Judaism as well as a profound misreading of the course of modern Jewish history.

At times, however, Marmur appears to be unconcerned with the reaction of the Orthodox community. Traditional conversion and divorce procedures are, he believes, intrinsically valuable and truly authentic. To justify this claim he appeals to the writings of anthropologists and sociologists who emphasize the importance of ritual and symbolism in religion.[33] But if external forms are of such importance, why does Marmur restrict his attention to conversion and divorce? If Reform Judaism should draw closer to traditional Jewish law, as he recommends, why is this principle not extended to other areas as well? Surely by his argument all Reform Jews should keep kosher, lay tefillin (phylacteries), abstain from working on the Sabbath, and cover their heads at all times. These are surely all equally meaningful rituals. The answer to this question is all too clear: proselytes and divorcees are the most vulnerable members of the Jewish community. Unlike ordinary dues-paying members of the synagogue who regard their rabbi as an employee, proselytes and divorcees come to the rabbi in pursuit of a conversion certificate or a bill of divorce. They must conform to the rabbi's recommendations if they wish to attain their goal and this places the rabbi in a position of real power and control. The rabbi is thereby free to impose rules. But over the ordinary members of his congregation he has no such authority. Because he is paid a salary by his congregants, he cannot legislate about their activities lest he find himself without a job. In other words, the conditions of rabbinical employment make it virtually impossible for the rabbi to compel the members of his congregation to follow Jewish law. He can suggest, but he cannot insist as he can with proselytes and converts.

Further it is nonsense for Marmur to think that having accepted the desirability of a legal framework, British Reform has 'in no way abandoned the principles of concern for the individual over the system'.[34] By adopting traditional procedures, the dictates of individual conscience are of no importance whatsoever. Indeed, conformity to the system is now such an important principle in British Reform that the Reform Assembly of Rabbis has decreed that any of its members who wish to officiate at or bless a mixed marriage will in all likelihood be expelled from the movement. In this case the Reform establishment is clearly refusing to allow the individual minister to follow his own conscience.

Finally, there is no reason to believe, as Marmur insists, that the decisions of the English Reform movement will influence Reform Judaism throughout the world.[35] At a meeting of the Central Conference of American Rabbis, the major Reform Jewish rabbinic association where Marmur defended the stand of British Reform, several important spokesmen for American Reform Judaism strongly criticized these initiatives. Rabbi Samuel Karff, for example, formerly the editor of the *Journal of Reform Judaism*, stated: 'To be legally acceptable in the eyes of Orthodoxy and at the same time retain a liberal sense of values is as practical as posing for a Marlboro man's cigarette commercial and working for the American Cancer Society. In trying to serve two masters (a liberal approach to Jewish law and traditional legal authority) one ends up being true to neither and endangering one's own integrity'.[36]

CONCLUSION

Progressive Judaism thus seems to be in confusion. Reform rabbis lack criteria for distinguishing between the traditional observances which should be retained and those which should be eliminated. They are illogical and inconsistent when they actually do lay down the law, and they discriminate against the most vulnerable members of the community. Given these difficulties, what should their relationship be to Jewish law? There is only one answer: they must free themselves from the legal system. As has been shown, it is impossible to evolve a new modern code of law for Reform Judaism. What they need instead is a new understanding of the legal tradition within the Reform movement. They should admit that they cannot be legalistic in their approach to Jewish life. Reform Judaism must allow all individuals the freedom to practice those observances which they find meaningful. This, of course, is not an innovation; it has always been a central tenet of Reform Judaism that individuals have the right to select those elements from the Jewish heritage which ar- personally significant. But this principle must be carried to its logical conclusion. Reform Jews must be fee to make up their own minds in all spheres. No one – no rabbi, nor rabbinical body – should be allowed to decide what observances are acceptable for the Reform community as a whole. In other words, there can be no law nor legislators in the movement. Instead what is needed is a declaration of personal liberty and freedom. In this context Reform rabbis have a duty to inform their congregations about Jewish law, but they must be descriptive rather than prescriptive. All should be free to choose for themselves which provisions of the traditional law are helpful in promoting their own spiritual development. Any return to centralized rules and regulations laid down by small self-appointed groups of rabbis is merely a new Orthodoxy in disguise. This is intolerable to the liberating spirit of Reform Judaism to which Reform Jews have always been committed.

5

Jewish Missionizing in Contemporary Society

During the past few years several Reform rabbis have argued that Judaism should actively seek converts to replace the large number of Jews in modern society who have left Judaism through indifference or intermarriage. In a study of mixed marriage, for example, Rabbi Allen Malter writes that 'Jews have an obligation to teach all men and to welcome them into the Jewish people . . . There can be no reason to prefer an assimilated Jew who has no desire to be Jewish to an interested gentile'.[1] Similarly, in a study of conversion, Rabbi B. Martin asserts that 'already several thousand persons in the United States are converted to Judaism each year in contemplation of marriage. There seems to be little reason why that number should not be doubled or trebled. All that may be required is a more positive and encouraging attitude on the part of the rabbis whom they seek out for help toward both the Jewish and non-Jewish parties to an impending marriage'.[2] Again, in a study of conversion to Judaism from the Biblical period to the present, Rabbi J. Rosenbloom argues that today great numbers of people feel a lack in their lives which they vaguely describe as spiritual. To fill this gap, he writes, 'Judaism must take a few steps forward from the closed mediaevalism it still retains, and which produces its enclavist and ghetto outlook on life, and several steps backward to those ancient attitudes which were outward-looking in their encouragement for seeking and winning converts'.[3]

It is important to explore the process of conversion to Reform Judaism in the light of this recent interest in Jewish missionizing. On the basis of a comparison between conversion procedures in traditional and Reform Judaism, it will be seen that Reform Judaism is inconsistent in emphasising the convert's personal religious conviction rather than willingness to join the Jewish community. Given that a significant segment of the Reform community, including rabbis, is agnostic or atheistic, it is illogical to debar candidates for

51

conversion because they lack religious belief. If Jewish missionizing is important, as these rabbis suggest, then the Reform conversion procedure should be revised so as to cater for those converts who find belief in God difficult, if not impossible, to accept.

CONVERSION TO TRADITIONAL JUDAISM

Although there is no formal term for the process of conversion in the Hebrew Bible, there are several Biblical terms which are suggestive of such an act: *Hityahed* (Esther 8:17) is used to describe the Persians who are said to have converted to Judaism for fear of the Jews; *amilam* (Ps 118:10–12) may well refer to the circumcision of foreign nations; *nilvah* (Is 56:3) refers to the alien who has joined himself to the Lord. Such terms as these illustrate that conversion was practised during the Biblical period in order to assimilate conquered peoples as well as those who came to live within the Israelite community.

During the rabbinic period (100–600 AD) conversion was frequently extolled by various rabbinic authorities. According to Rabbi Elazar, for example, conversion was viewed as part of God's salvationist scheme: 'The Holy One, blessed be He, dispersed the people of Israel among the nations in order that they might acquire proselytes' (Pes. 87b). According to Rabbi Hoshiah, God acted righteously towards Israel when He scattered them among the nations (Pes. 87b). In another passage it is asserted that the proselyte is dearer to God than the Israelite since he has come of his own accord while the Israelites are believers as a result of the miracles exhibited on Mount Sinai (Tanh. B., Lek leka, 6, f.32a). Resh Lakish noted that the person who oppresses the convert is as one who oppresses God (Hag.5a). In Tannh. B. (Lek leka, f.40b.) it is maintained that it is never too late to convert; to teach this Abraham did not enter the covenant until he was 99 when he was circumcised. As with Abraham, so every Israelite has the obligation to bring men under God's wings. In Num. R (Naso. 8, 2–4.), we read that God loves proselytes exceedingly: 'So spoke the Holy One: "I owe great things to the stranger in that he has left his family and his father's house, and has come to dwell among us; therefore I order in the Law: Love the stranger".'

This positive attitude to proselytes is echoed by the historian Josephus who, in *Against Apion* (210), describes the openness of Hellenistic Judaism to converts: 'The consideration given by our legislator (Moses) to the equitable treatment of aliens also merits attention. To all who desire to come and live under the same laws as us he gives a gracious welcome . . .'⁴

As a result of such openness to converts, a number of gentiles converted to Judaism during the early rabbinic period. However, the rise of Christianity led to the cessation of Jewish missionizing. Nevertheless, during the Talmudic and post-Talmudic period occasional conversions did take place in accordance with rabbinic law. Eventually the regulations governing conversion were drawn together and edited by Joseph Karo, the compiler of the *Shulchan Aruch*, which, since its publication in 1565, has served as the authoritative code of Jewish Law. In Chapter 268 of Yoreh Deah, one of the four major divisions of the work, the requirements for conversion, as laid down in the Talmud as well as in other codes, are outlined in detail: 'When one presents himself as a candidate for conversion he is asked: "What motivates you? Do you know that, in these days, Jews are subject to persecution and discrimination, that they are hounded and troubled?" If he replies: "I know this and yet I regard myself as unworthy of being joined to them", he is accepted immediately' (Yeb 47a). 'The root principles of our faith, namely, the unity of God and the prohibition of idol worship, are expounded to him at considerable length' (Maimonides, *Hilchot Issurey Biah*, Ch. 14). 'He is taught, too, some of the simpler and some of the more difficult commandments; and he is informed of the punishment involved in violating the commandments, so too is he told of the rewards for observing them, particularly that by virtue of keeping the commandments, he will merit the life of the world to come' (Yeb 47a). 'He is told that no one is considered wholly righteous except those who understand and fulfil the commandments. He is also told that the world to come is only intended for the righteous' (Yeb 47a). 'If he finds these doctrines acceptable, he is circumcised immediately. After his circumcision has completely healed, he undergoes ritual immersion' (Yeb 47a). 'Three learned Jews stand by while he is in the water and instruct him in some of the easy and some of the difficult commandments. In the case of a female proselyte, Jewish women accompany her and immerse her up to her neck. The three learned male Jews remain outside the baptismal chamber and give the convert instruction while she is in the water' (Asheri).

Concerning the candidate's motives, the *Shulchan Aruch* states: 'When the would-be proselyte presents himself, he should be examined lest he be motivated to enter the congregation of Israel by hope of financial gain or social advantage or by fear. A man is examined lest his sole motive be to marry a Jewish woman and a woman is questioned lest she have similar desires toward some Jewish man' (Maimonides). 'If no unethical motive is found, the candidate is told of the heaviness of the yoke of the Torah and how difficult it is for the average person to live up to the commandments of the Torah. This is done to give the candidate a chance to withdraw if he so desires. If the candidate goes through all this and is not dissuaded and it is apparent that his motives are of the best, he is accepted. Once a person is circumcised and ritually immersed, he is no longer a non-Jew, although he continues to be under suspicion until he proves by his righteous living that he is worthy of respect.'

The point to note about these regulations governing the traditional conversion procedure is that their emphasis is on joining the Jewish community and accepting the law, not on the candidate's personal religious convictions. For this reason the convert is told of the persecution and discrimination that Jews have endured because, as a member of the Jewish community, he will no doubt suffer similar indignities. Further, the candidate is made aware of the legal obligations he must assume as a Jew. Thus, in traditional Judaism conversion is viewed as a legal rite of passage through which the convert takes his place within the Jewish community.

CONVERSION TO REFORM JUDAISM

In the second half of the nineteenth century a number of Reform rabbis in the United States voiced the same positive attitude to converts as expressed by rabbis in the Tannaitic period. Rabbi David Einhorn, for example, believed that Judaism was destined to become a universal religion. Leading his congregation in the closing service on the Day of Atonement, he prayed: 'This evening, so full of light, reminds us still of that glorious evening promised by Thee, on which Thy light will break for all the children of men and the progeny of Israel will be as numerous as the stars of heaven. Arm us, O our Keeper and Guardian, with strength and love for that high mission. May Israel prize as his highest treasure the conviction that both to bear witness to the One God and to battle for the one Humanity he was sent into the world'.[5]

Emphasizing this belief in the Jewish mission, Rabbi I.M. Wise wrote in *A Defence of Judaism Versus Proselytizing Christianity*: 'I can show in my books the names of thirty-seven Christian-born persons who embraced Judaism without any solicitations on my part . . .

Of the hundreds of covenrts from Christianity to Judaism . . . which we have made, we have advertised none, because we consider it a private affair, too holy to be drummed to the curious news seekers'.[6] Similarly Rabbi A. Moses declared in a graduation sermon at the Reform rabbinical seminary that 'For the first time in many centuries an arena has been opened, in this country and in our age, for pure Yahvism to unfold its universal nature, to accomplish its mission as a religion of many races and nations, to gather into its fold those gentiles whose reason cannot accept the peculiar tenets of Christianity, who are separated from us only by name'.[7]

In addition to such statements made by Reform rabbis several Reform Rabbinical Conferences issued pronouncements in the latter half of the nineteenth century encouraging conversion to Judaism. In November 1869, for example, a Conference of Reform Rabbis in Philadelphia affirmed that the destruction of the Jewish commonwealth and the dispersion of Jews throughout the world are not to be regarded as a punishment for sins but rather an opportunity for true knowledge and worship of God.

Sixteen years later the Pittsburgh Conference of American Reform Rabbis declared: 'We hold that Judaism presents the conception of the God-idea as taught in our Holy Scriptures and spiritualised by the Jewish teachers, in accordance with the moral and philosophical progress of their respective ages. We maintain that Judaism preserved and defended . . . this God-idea as the central religious truth for the human race . . . We acknowledge that the spirit of broad humanity of our age is our ally in the fulfillment of our mission . . .'[8]

These proclamations by rabbinic conferences were used as guidelines by Reform religious leaders in their attitude to conversion. Emphasizing the universalistic mission of Judaism, the Reform movement very early in its history abrogated the necessity of ritual immersion for converts. On the question of circumcision opinion was at first divided. In 1869 the Pittsburgh Conference took no definite stand, but a particular case of conversion without circumcision brought this question to the forefront of rabbinic debate. In 1890 a non-Jew petitioned Rabbi H. Berkowitz of Kansas City to be admitted into the Jewish fold without undergoing circumcision. Rabbi Berkowitz requested an opinion from leading American Reform rabbis. Moses Meilziner, Professor of Talmud at the Hebrew Union College, replied that circumcision was necessary; ten other rabbis, including such renowned leaders as I.M. Wise, K. Kohler and E.G. Hirsh disagreed. In the light of this majority decision, Rabbi Berkowitz admitted the young man without requiring that he be circumcised.

This case and the discussions which it caused convinced the Reform rabbinate that they needed to reach a consensus. Thus, in 1892 the Central Conference of American Rabbis concluded that any rabbi with the concurrence of two associates, could accept into the Jewish faith any 'honourable and intelligent person, without any initiating rite'. The only requirements were that the person freely seek membership, that the candidate be of good character, and be sufficiently acquainted with the faith and practices of Judaism. In addition the candidate was required to give evidence of sincere desire: (a) to worship only the God of Judaism; (b) to live by God's laws; and (c) to adhere in life and death to the sacred cause of Israel.

In 1927 the Central Conference of American Rabbis published a handbook entitled *Judaism, a Manual for the Instruction of Proselytes*, which included a conversion ceremony along these lines. Among the questions asked the candidate were queries about his voluntary acceptance of the Jewish faith, his pledge of loyalty to Judaism, his determination to cast his lot with that of the Jewish people, his promise to lead a Jewish life, and to rear his children as Jews.

In an effort to look more carefully into the subject of conversion, the Central Conference of American Rabbis in 1950 established a committee to study practical means of extending the influence and acceptance of the Jewish religion. During the next year a committee on the unaffiliated was appointed; six years later a call was made for the preparation of literature, radio and television programmes as well as congregational preaching missions. Despite the fact that nothing came of this proposal numerous non-Jews converted to Judaism during this period.

In 1961 the Central Conference of American Rabbis issued a revised version of the Conversion service paralleling the 1927 format, which is structured as follows:[9]

(1) Two persons representative of the congregation should be witnesses of the ceremony which should be conducted in the synagogue, preferably before the open ark.

(2) The rabbi opens the service by saying, 'Blessed be you who come in the name of the Lord; we bless you from the house of the Lord.'

(3) The rabbi continues with the following prayer, filling in the name of the convert: 'Our God and Father, with grateful hearts we thank Thee for many blessings. We thank Thee that Thou didst reveal Thy truth to mankind. Above all we praise Thee for the gift of the Torah, which has ever been a lamp unto our feet and a light unto our path. We recall with reverence and gratitude all those of the seed of Abraham who have been faithful unto Thee, and those who of their own free will have sought to serve Thee in the faith and fellowship of Israel. Be near us in this solemn hour. Grant, O God, Thy loving favour to . . . . , as in this holy place we welcome him (her) into Jewish life. Help him (her) to live in fidelity to the decision he (she) has made, and to the promise he (she) is about to utter. May he (she) always find joy in the fulfillment of the Torah and enduring satisfaction in the practice of Judaism. Vouchsafe unto him (her) many years of strength and happiness as a worthy son (daughter) of the Synagogue. Blessed art Thou, O Lord, in whose presence is fulness of joy. Amen.'

(4) The rabbi then delivers a brief sermon to the convert and asks the following questions:

(a) Do you of your own free will seek admission to the Jewish faith?

(b) Have you given up your former faith and severed all other religious affiliations?

(c) Do you pledge your loyalty to Judaism and to the Jewish people amid all circumstances and conditions?

(d) Do you promise to establish a Jewish home and to participate actively in the life of the Synagogue and of the Jewish community?

(e) If you should be blessed with children, do you promise to rear them in the Jewish faith?

(5) When the convert has answered Yes to all these questions the rabbi asks the convert to recite the *Shema*: ('Hear O Israel, the Lord our God, the Lord is One.')

(6) The rabbi has the option of including Biblical readings (Deut. 6:5–9; Ruth 1:16–17), and concludes the service with a prayer of adoration of God and the priestly benediction: ('May the Lord bless thee and keep thee; May the Lord cause His countenance to shine upon thee and be gracious unto thee; May the Lord lift up His countenance unto thee and give thee peace.')

Unlike the traditional conversion procedure, the Reform service indicates that definite religious commitment is necessary in order to be accepted. The convert must state that he seeks admittance to the

Jewish faith. While he is not under an obligation to profess that he worships 'only the One and Eternal God' as in the 1892 procedure, the service in the 1961 *Rabbis Manual* makes it clear that conversion to Judaism essentially entails the acceptance of religious belief. For this reason the service is conducted in the Synagogue, and throughout the service the convert is told that conversion to Judaism is a religious act performed in God's presence. Thus, both explicitly and implicitly, conversion in Reform Judaism is construed as primarily a religious ceremony expressing the convert's particular religious convictions.

THE PROBLEM OF REFORM CONVERSION

Comparing the conversion procedure in traditional Judaism with that in Reform Judaism, it is evident that there are striking differences. First, since 1892 Reform Judaism has abandoned circumcision and immersion as the primary rituals connected with conversion.[10] Secondly, though converts in Reform Judaism are obligated to 'establish a Jewish home and to participate actively in the life of the Synagogue and of the Jewish community', they are free to decide for themselves which of the Jewish laws they wish to observe. Unlike converts to traditional Judaism, they are not under any obligation to keep all the commandments. Indeed, it has always been a central tenet of Reform Judaism since its beginnings in the nineteenth century that Reform Jews should be liberated from the heavy yoke of rabbinic and Mosaic law. In the Declaration of Principles adopted by Reform rabbis in Pittsburgh in 1885, for example, it was declared that: 'We recognise in the Mosaic legislation a system of training the Jewish people for its mission during its natural life in Palestine, and today we accept as binding only its moral laws and maintain only such ceremonials as elevate and sanctify our lives, but reject all such as are not adapted to the views and habits of modern civilisation'.[11]

Though Reform Judaism has undergone innumerable changes since this declaration was formulated, there is still a general recognition among Reform rabbis that Jewish law is not authoritative in the same way that it is in traditional Judaism. For example, in *Reform Judaism* Rabbi Charles Berg writes; 'We must be careful not to accept uncritically every law which previous generations regarded as of a moral character . . . We must of necessity be selective when it comes to ritual laws . . . The final decision on whether to comply with a traditional observance lies, in our time, with the individual Jew. Under the conditions in which we live compulsion of any kind is impossible . . .'[12] This selective approach is clearly the proper attitude for converts to Reform Judaism to adopt.

The third difference between traditional and Reform conversion concerns religious belief. Unlike the traditional procedure, Reform conversion focusses on theological commitment. Though converts are obligated to pledge their loyalty to the Jewish people, promising to support Jews 'amid all circumstances and conditions', the conversion ceremony explicitly and implicitly demands that the convert evince religious belief and places the entire ritual in a religious context.

What is obvious therefore is that Reform Judaism has radically shifted the emphasis of conversion. In place of dedication and willingness to accept the entire body of Mosaic and rabbinic law, which includes circumcision and/or immersion, Reform Judaism has substituted religious commitment. The question we must ask is whether this shift is consistent with the nature of the contemporary Reform movement. In other words, we must ask whether it is logical to demand specific religious belief from converts given the state of religious belief in the Reform community as a whole.

An answer to this question is provided by a study of the rabbi and synagogue in American society,[13] which is based on the responses of 620 Reform rabbis, 58 Reform rabbinical students, 948 Reform congregants and 264 young Reform Jews. According to this study religious motivation was not the dominant factor which led the majority of rabbis questioned to pursue a rabbinical career: rather 61 per cent identified with the following: 'As an occupation it offered me the most opportunity to "do my own thing" in terms of my interests, needs and general fulfillment'. This lack of religious incentive is echoed in the survey of religious belief among Reform rabbis. Only one in ten stated that they adhere to a belief in God 'in the more or less traditional sense'. Some 62 per cent qualified their belief in God by adding, 'in terms of my own views of what God is and what He stands for'. More than one in four (28 per cent) see themselves as either non-traditionalists (14 per cent), agnostics (13 per cent), or atheists (1 per cent). Looking at these statistics in terms of the age of the rabbis questioned, the following pattern emerges: of the 162 rabbis ordained before 1942, 13 per cent are traditionalists, 70 per cent are qualified traditionalists, 6 per cent are non-traditionalists, 11 per cent are agnostics and none are atheists. Of the 39 rabbis ordained between 1942 and 1946, 13 per cent are traditionalists, 72 per cent qualified traditionalists, 3 per cent non-traditionalists, 9 per cent agnostics, and 3 per cent atheists. Of the 52 rabbis ordained between 1947 and 1951, 13 per cent are traditionalists, 67 per cent qualified traditionalists, 13 per cent non-traditionalists, 7 per cent agnostic and 0 per cent atheists. Of the 60 rabbis ordained between 1952 and 1956, 13 per cent are traditionalists, 63 per cent qualified traditionalists, 10 per cent non-traditionalists, 11 per cent agnostics and 3 per cent atheists. Of the 87 rabbis ordained between 1957 and 1961, 11 per cent are traditionalists, 53 per cent qualified traditionalists, 16 per cent non-traditionalists, 20 per cent agnostics, and 0 per cent atheists. Of the 105 rabbis ordained between 1962 and 1966, 7 per cent are traditionalists, 58 per cent qualified traditionalists, 23 per cent non-traditionalists, 11 per cent agnostics and 1 per cent atheists. Of the 101 rabbis ordained between 1967 and 1971, 3 per cent are traditionalists, 55 per cent qualified traditionalists, 21 per cent non-traditionalists, 10 per cent agnostics and 1 per cent atheists. From these statistics we can see that there is an unmistakeable trend; traditional religious belief in Reform Judaism is on the decline. Thus, as Lenn reports, there is now 'a situation where an increasing number of Reform rabbis reject or question the central religious tenets of Judaism'.

This movement away from traditional belief is also evidenced by rabbinical students. According to Lenn, 'belief even in a qualified version of God is much lower among seminarians, much lower even than among rabbis who were ordained in the last five years. The slack is not taken up, it should be noted, by a *non*-traditional belief in God either. Instead virtually all the shift has been in the direction of agnosticism'. Among the comments noted by Lenn are the following: 'Being an agnostic is not being an atheist . . . and it is not contrary to Judaism to search one's soul. Agnosticism means searching'. Another rabbinical student declared, 'If I had faith in God before I came here (to the rabbinical seminary), and I'm not sure if I did or not . . . I was never confronted with it . . . I lost it here soon enough. When a rabbi-relative of mine once asked me if my professors believe in God, I couldn't honestly answer him'.

This disenchantment with traditional belief in God is reflected in Reform congregations as well. About 17 per cent of those questioned stated that they believe in God 'in the more or less traditional Judaic sense'. An additional 49 per cent claim to hold this belief, but qualify the statement by adding 'as modified in terms of my own views of what God is and what He stands for'. Some 8 per cent stated that they are non-traditionalists, bringing the total believers in some sense of the word to 74 per cent. One out of four congregants identify themselves as either agnostics (21 per cent) or atheists (4 per cent). Among the comments from this segment of the community as quoted by Lenn are the following: 'I am an atheist. I lost my belief in God many years ago, but I believe that the study of Torah and Midrash and other works are helpful'. Another congregant asserted: 'Religion is something that I accept now only for its moral, ethical and cultural teaching. The prayers and the gods should disappear as most superstitions do. Truth and enlightenment are the true guiding lights'.

Turning to the young congregational Jews surveyed, the same trend away from traditional religious belief is manifest. Some 51 per cent believe in a more or less traditional view of God as against 66 per cent of the adults; 12 per cent as compared with 8 per cent of the adults have a rather radical view of God; 33 per cent are agnostic as compared with 21 per cent of adults, while 4 per cent, the same percentage as adults, declare that they are atheists.

Assuming that Lenn's study is an accurate survey of religious belief in Reform Judaism, it is clear that there is not a consensus of conviction. Given such a confused state of affairs, it seems absurd to demand religious commitment from converts. It might of course be argued that in spite of the lack of conviction in the community, higher standards should be set for converts. There are several flaws, however, in this point of view. First such a double standard is conspicuously unfair to the convert who, like many Reform Jews born of Jewish parents, may wish to identify as a Jew but finds belief in God difficult to accept. To debar such individuals from the Jewish fold simply because of the accident of birth is hypocritical and unjust, since those born of Jewish parents who likewise have no religious belief are regarded as Jews. Secondly, such a religious requirement can cause a profound crisis of conscience to those gentiles without conviction who wish to marry a Jew, become members of the Jewish community and rear their children as Jews. Since the Reform movement accepts conversion for the purpose of marriage as legitimate,[14] such a religious impediment is unnecessary. Thirdly, the stipulation that belief in God is a requirement can easily give the convert a false impression of today's Reform Jewish community in which, according to Lenn's survey, one out of every four congregational members is either an agnostic or an atheist.

The obvious solution to this problem is to revise the present Reform conversion service, or, alternatively, provide another service for those converts who do not believe in God. The procedure of conversion in this revised form might well resemble traditional conversion with circumcision and/or immersion depending on the inclinations of the rabbi. The convert would simply be asked if he or she wished to join the Jewish community despite any worldly disadvantage before the ritual act. In this way the problem of Reform conversion would be removed.

CONCLUSION

Ever since the early rabbinic period, when Jewish missionising reached its zenith, Jews have been reluctant to engage in active proselytizing. Recently, however, some Reform rabbis have advocated a return to the ancient universalistic outlook of Judaism which sought and won converts. However, in order for such missionising to succeed, Reform Judaism should critically evaluate its current regulations governing conversion. Given that approximately one out of every four congregational members is either an agnostic or an atheist, it is nonsensical to demand belief in God as a necessary condition for acceptance in the Reform Jewish fold. There are, of course, converts who do believe in God, but for those who find belief difficult if not impossible to accept, alternative requirements should be set. Possibly what is needed is some sort of modification of the traditional conversion procedure which is essentially a ritualistic process through which the convert takes his place in the Jewish community. If conversion were viewed in this way, those unbelieving converts who wished to become Jews for the purpose of marriage as well as to rear their children as Jews, or in order to share in the cultural and ethical heritage of Judaism, would be spared a serious crisis of conscience.

6
Judaism and the Problems
of the Inner City

Faith in the City (the report of the Archbishop of Canterbury's Commission on Inner City Deprivation published in 1985) has evoked considerable reaction from various quarters of society – it has even touched a sensitive nerve in the English Jewish community. In an article in the *Jewish Chronicle*[1] the Chief Rabbi, Lord Jakobovits, criticized its findings at several points and offered a Jewish alternative for combatting the hardships of inner city life. The experience of the Jewish community, he argues, can serve as a model for those who are deprived in modern society. According to the Chief Rabbi, it was not by preaching Jewish power or non-violence that Jews were able to break out of the ghettos. Rather it was through ambition, education and hard work. But is such a policy of self-help the only response that the Jewish community can make to the Archbishop's Report? The purpose of this study is to present an alternative view – to find within the Jewish tradition spiritual resources which reinforce the Report's commitment to empathize with the suffering of those who are poor and oppressed and to side with them in their struggle for a better life.

THE CHIEF RABBI'S RESPONSE

In his response to *Faith in the City*, the Chief Rabbi emphasizes that Judaism is in complete agreement with the basic assumption underlying the study, namely that religious leaders and organizations should address themselves to important social problems. In this regard he notes that the Biblical prophets were history's supreme leaders of opposition. Yet for the Chief Rabbi there are important reasons why Jews are unable to accept many of the conclusions of the Archbishop's Commission.

First, the historical experience of Jewry has been entirely different from that of Christians. Until very recent times Jews have been a small minority, subject to discrimination and persecution. For centuries Jews were forced to live in crowded ghettos in the most adverse conditions. Yet such experience, Lord Jakobovits argues, should provide instructive lessons for those presently enduring similar circumstances. Quoting from a farewell speech he gave in America in the 1960s, he offers advice to today's black community:

> How did we break out of our ghettos and enter the mainstream of society and its privileges . . . we worked on ourselves, not on others. We gave a better education to our children than anybody else had. We hallowed our home life. We channelled the ambition of our youngsters to academic excellence . . . we rooted out crime and indolence from our midst, by making every Jew feel responsible for the fate of all Jews.[2]

On the basis of such experience, the Chief Rabbi prescribes a similar course of action for blacks who suffer similar disabilities in the modern world:

> Let them give two or three hours' extra schooling every day to their children, as we gave to ours; let them build up by charitable endeavours great federations of social welfare, as we did for our poor; let them instil in all negroes a feeling of shame for any crime committed by a negro . . . let them encourage ambition and excellence in every negro child, as Jewish parents encouraged in their children – and they will pull down their ghetto walls as surely as we demolished ours.[3]

In connection with this policy of self-improvement, Lord Jakobovits points out that though the Jewish community was anxious to preserve its own identity, British Jews never demanded that British society change its character and assume a new multi-ethnic form. There was never a demand that there be public allowance for varying ethnic traditions, whether in policing policies or in family counselling under local authority auspices. 'We were quite content', he writes, 'for Britain to remain "ethnocentrically" British'.[4] Jews thus did not insist on public help, nor on changes in official policies; instead the Jewish community created its own educational and social institutions designed to preserve and transmit the Jewish heritage in a contemporary context. Such social objectives took time to attain; it was only after several generations that Jews were able to integrate fully into British society. Agitation and social unrest were never considered the proper course of action. From such an experience it may be salutory, the Chief Rabbi states, to remind those presently enduring much hardship and despair that others have faced similar trials before them, and that self-reliant efforts and perseverance eventually pay off, turning humiliation into dignity and depression into hope and fulfillment.

The Chief Rabbi continues his defence of self-help by illustrating that such a policy is based on Jewish religious teaching which extols the virtues of work. The Jewish work ethic, he declares, is positive and demanding. Human history begins with God's command to Adam in the Garden of Eden: 'to till it and to keep it' (Gen. 2.15). According to the Talmud no work is too menial to compromise human dignity and self-respect. The path to true contentment is through diligent work, as the Psalmist declared: 'You shall eat the fruit of the labour of your hands, you shall be happy, and it shall be well with you' (Ps. 128.2). Conversely, idleness is viewed in the Jewish tradition as a waste of human resources. Furthermore, Judaism does not frown on gaining wealth, nor does it demand that wealth should be shared or distributed to equalize rich and poor. On the contrary, riches (assuming they are honestly accumulated) are seen as a sign of Divine grace to be enjoyed in moderation.

According to the Chief Rabbi the operative words in the Jewish vocabulary concerning relief for the poor are neither entitlement nor compensation. When the Bible demands of the haves to stretch out a helping arm to the have-nots (using the words 'You shall open your hand', Deut. 15.8) the 'open hand' is not the beggar's asserting his entitlement to receive, but the giver's acknowledging his duty not to be tight-fisted. When the concept of compensation appears in the Jewish tradition, it has a specialized meaning. The Talmud states that 'more than the wealthy man gives to the poor, the poor gives to the wealthy'. The poor man ennobles the giver and is compensated by the knowledge that he gives more than he receives; the rich man is compensated for the diminution of his wealth knowing that in giving he has gained more than he has lost. Here is found the Jewish solution to the problem of humiliation felt by those who are impoverished. Self-respect derives from a feeling that one is contributing to the needs of others. Jewish law therefore stipulates that even the poor man is required to donate some of his proceeds from charity for the relief of others. 'There is a double benefit in this', the Chief Rabbi writes: 'Even the deprived person must learn to part with some of what he receives, thus training him in the art and satisfaction of giving; and his dignity is to be restored by letting him experience a sense of equality with the rich in supporting others in need. In this connection, Judaism defines the highest kind of charity as a form of self-help – the giver is to assist the poor man to rehabilitate himself by lending him money, taking him into partnership, employing him, or giving him work'.[5]

In the light of such theological views as well as the Jewish experience, the Chief Rabbi concludes that Judaism pre-eminently urges the building up of self-respect by encouraging ambition and enterprise through a work-ethic designed to eliminate idleness and to nurture pride in human labour. Though Lord Jakobovits believes that the affluent section of society should provide more social agencies and counselling services and capital for prudent enterprises in the inner cities, he notes that these areas are now denuded of Jewish communities. Thus they have neither the Jewish spiritual nor social workers who would be required to operate such projects, nor the financial assets under Jewish religious control which would be required. But even more important for the recovery of the health of the inner cities than such a programme is the repair of home life as the bastion of love, care, decency and every social virtue. In a Jewish blueprint for the regeneration of the inner cities, the Chief Rabbi maintains that the family would feature prominently: 'For when the family breaks down, the most essential conditions for raising happy, law abiding and creatively ambitious citizens are frustrated. . . . through a dedication to hard-work, self-help, and the rebuilding of family life, the new ghettos can be transformed as were the old, and the resources of the nation can be shared by all'.[6]

There is no doubt the Chief Rabbi's description of self-help in the Jewish community is correct; for centuries Jews have been able to free themselves from disabilities through hard-work and dedication. Further, there are ample sources within the Biblical and rabbinic tradition to support his contention that the Jewish faith extols work and cherishes family life. Nevertheless, these themes do not exhaust Jewish teaching about religion and society – the Jewish heritage is rich in resources which deal directly with social deprivation. By focussing simply on those aspects of the Jewish heritage which support his vision of labour and family life, the Chief Rabbi has given too narrow a vision of social concern within the Jewish faith. What is required instead is a more comprehensive account of social ethics than that given by Lord Jakobovits in his response to *Faith in the City*.

THE EXODUS EXPERIENCE

For the Jewish people, social concern grows out of the experiences of their ancestors in Egypt. There the Jewish people were exploited and oppressed: the Egyptians overwhelmed the Hebrew slaves with work; they 'made their lives bitter with hard service, in mortar and brick, and in all kinds of work in the field' (Exod. 1.14). Such affliction caused the people to cry out to God for liberation, and in response God decreed; 'I have seen the affliction of my people who are in Egypt, and have heard their cry because of their taskmasters; I know their sufferings, and I have come down to deliver them out of the hand of the Egyptians' (Exod. 3.7–8).

To the Jewish mind the Exodus was a pivotal event in the history of the nation – it is the salvation experience par excellence. In the unfolding of the Divine plan of deliverance, God revealed Himself through Moses, and nowhere is this act of liberation celebrated more than in the Festival of Passover. The Passover Seder envisages the Exodus experience as a symbol of freedom from oppression, and the whole of the Haggadah is pervaded by the image of God as the Saviour of mankind. For this reason, the Passover service[7] begins with an ancient formulaic invitation to those who hunger or are in need to participate in the Festival: 'This is the bread of affliction that our fathers ate in the Land of Egypt. All who hunger, let them come and eat: all who are in need, let them come and celebrate the Passover. Now we are here – next year we shall be free men'. Any Jew who sits down to the Passover meal, oblivious of the call of those who are in want, has missed the meaning of the celebration.

During the service the leader displays the unleavened bread to stimulate the curiosity of youngsters at the meal. It is then the turn of the youngest child to ask about the nature of the Passover festivities – the entire ritual of the Seder hinges on these inquiries. In reply the leader recites the narrative of the Exodus, stressing the themes of liberation and freedom from oppression: 'We were Pharoah's slaves in Egypt; and the Lord our God brought us out thereof with a mighty hand and an outstretched arm. Now, had not the Holy One brought out our fathers from Egypt, then we and our children and our children's children would be enslaved to Pharaoh in Egypt. Wherefore, even were we all wise men, all men of understanding, all advanced in years, all men with knowledge of the Torah, it would yet be our duty to recount the story of the coming forth from Egypt; and all who recount at length the story of the coming forth from Egypt are verily to be praised'.

This response implies that the Passover does not simply commemorate a triumph of remote antiquity. Rather, the Passover ceremony is a celebration of the emancipation of each Jew in every generation, for had it not been for the Exodus, Jews would still be slaves in Egypt. Historical continuity is at the heart of this understanding, and is illustrated further by the response made to the wicked son who asks 'What mean ye by this service?' In response the leader states:

> He infers 'ye'; not himself. By shutting himself off from the general body, it is as though he denies the existence of God. Therefore thou shouldst distress him, too, replying: 'This is done because of that which the Lord did unto me when I came forth out of Egypt' – Unto 'me', not him; for if he had been there he would not have been delivered.

The keynote of the Haggadah is enshrined in a central pledge of the Seder: 'It is this Divine pledge that hath stood by our fathers and by us also. Not only one man hath risen against us to destroy us, but in every generation men have risen against us to destroy us: But the Holy One delivereth us always from their hand'. Here Pharaoh's action is seen as a paradigm of all attempts by Israel's enemies to destroy the Jewish people. Echoes of centuries of persecution are evoked by these words, yet it is made clear that God has been, and will continue to be on the side of His oppressed people. In the symbols of the Passover meal, such deliverance is re-enacted. Explaining this symbolism the leader states with regard to the shank-bone:

> The Passover Lamb that our fathers used to eat when the Temple was still standing – what is the reason? It is because the Holy One, Blessed be He, passed over the house of our fathers in Egypt, as it is said; 'Ye shall say, It is the sacrifice of the Lord's Passover, who passed over the houses of the children of Israel in Egypt, when He smote the Egyptians and delivered our houses'. And the people bowed the head and worshipped.

The unleavened bread is the bread of affliction, the historical emblem of the Exodus. The leader declares that it is the symbol of sympathy for the enslaved as well as of freedom from oppression:

> This unleavened bread that we eat – what is the reason? It is because there was no time for our ancestors' dough to become

leavened, before the King, King of all Kings, the Holy One, revealed Himself to them and redeemed them, as it is said; 'And they baked unleavened cakes of the dough which they brought forth out of Egypt, for it was not leavened: because they were thrust out of Egypt, and could not tarry, neither had they prepared for themselves any victual.'

The bitter herbs are the symbol of bitterness and servitude which serves as a reminder to the Jew that it is his duty as a descendant of slaves to lighten the stranger's burden:

'This bitter herb that we eat – what is its reason? It is because the Egyptians embittered the life of our ancestors in Egypt, as it is said: "And they made their lives bitter with hard bondage, in mortar and brick, and in all manner of service in the field, all their service, when they made them serve, was with rigour"'.

The lesson of the Passover service – deeply engraved on the hearts of the Jewish nation – is that persecution and Divine deliverance are realities of the past as well as the present. In each generation, Jews must think of themselves as delivered from a perpetual enemy and should assume the responsibility of rescuing those who suffer under oppression. 'In each and every generation', the Haggadah states, 'it is a man's duty to regard himself as though he went forth out of Egypt, as it is said, "And thou shalt tell thy son in that day saying, 'This is done because of that which the Lord did unto me when I came forth out of Egypt.'" Not our fathers only did the Holy One redeem, but us too. He redeemed them, as it is said, "And He brought us out from thence, that He might bring us in, to give us the Land which He swore into our fathers."' The Passover celebration is thus a symbolic exaltation of freedom; each Jew is to rejoice in God's liberation of his ancestors in which he has taken part. Throughout the history of the Jewish people this Festival has awakened the spirit of the people to the significance of human liberation.

This Jewish understanding of the Exodus event has much in common with contemporary Christian liberation theology which influenced much of the theological reflection contained in the Archbishop's Report. Like liberation theologians, the Jews have found renewed strength and hope in the message of the Exodus. The Passover ceremony unites the Jewish people with their ancestors who endured slavery and oppression in Egyptian bondage. Despite the persecution of centuries, the Jewish nation is confident of eventual deliverance and the ultimate redemption of humankind.

The message of the Exodus calls the Jewish people to hold steadfast to their conviction that justice and freedom will prevail throughout the world. The Passover, by symbolizing the primal act of liberation, points to a future and ultimate redemption of the human family.

THE PROPHETIC MESSAGE

Another central dimension of Biblical theology linked with human liberation and freedom is the message of the prophets. According to Scripture, the role of the prophet was to be the social conscience of the nation. The Hebrew prophets' experience was of a God so concerned with social justice that they perpetually struggled to rescue the nation from its iniquity and draw the people back to the faith of their ancestors. Amos, for example – the earliest of the classical Hebrew prophets – inveighed against the people because of oppression, bribery and injustice. Several decades after Amos began his ministry in Israel, Isaiah began his prophetic mission in Judah. God had chosen Israel to produce justice, he proclaimed, but instead it created bloodshed. Like Amos, he protested against the indifference of the rich to the poor and oppressed and he condemned the offering of sacrifice without a concomitant quest for righteousness.

According to Isaiah, Israel was a sinful nation – a band of wrong-doers; the nation had turned away from God. Thus he condemned the women of Jerusalem who arrogantly and wantonly strolled through the streets, the priests and false prophets who drunkenly proclaimed their messages, and the judges who issued tyrannical judgements, cheated the poor, widows and orphans so as to grow wealthy on bribes. These classical prophets – as well as other prophets who carried on their message – became the conscience of the nation: they attacked the exploitation of the poor by the rich and the people's iniquity. Their words have echoed down the centuries as a call for justice and righteousness for all people.

THE KINGDOM OF GOD AND RABBINIC ETHICS

For the Jews the prophetic tradition amplified the Exodus experience – God is conceived as demanding compassion, justice and righteousness for all those who suffer under the yoke of oppression and exploitation. This concern for those who endure hardship continued throughout the rabbinic period. According to the rabbis, God is a supreme ruler who calls all men to join Him in bringing about this

Kingdom on earth. This Kingdom consists in the reign of trust, righteousness and holiness among all nations. The fulfillment of this conception ultimately rests on the coming of the Messiah; nevertheless, it is man's duty to participate in the creation of a better world in anticipation of the Messianic redemption. In the words of the rabbis: 'Man is a co-worker with God in the work of creation' (Shab. 119b).

According to rabbinic theology, man is the centre of creation, for it is only he among all created beings who through righteousness can make the Kingdom glorious. In rabbinic midrash, the view is expressed that God's Kingship did not come into question until man was created: 'When the Holy One, blessed be He, consulted the Torah as to the creation of the world, he answered, "Master of the world, if there be no host, over whom will the King reign, and if there be no peoples praising him, where is the glory of the King?"' (Pirke Rabbi Eliezer, 3). It is only man then who can make the Kingdom glorious; God wants to reign over free agents who can act as his co-partners in perfecting the world. What God requires is obedience to his ways of righteousness and justice: 'You are my lovers and friends. You walk in my ways', God declares to Israel. 'As the Omnipotent is merciful and gracious, long-suffering and abundant in goodness so be ye . . . feeding the hungry, giving drink to the thirsty, clothing the naked, ransoming the captives, and marrying the orphans' (Agadoth Shir HaShirim 18, 61).

The idea of the Kingdom is conceived by the rabbis as ethical in character. In the words of the distinguished scholar, Solomon Schechter: 'If, then, the Kingdom of God was thus originally intended to be in the midst of men and for men at large (as represented by Adam), if its first preachers were, like Abraham, ex-heathens, who addressed themselves to heathens, if, again, the essence of their preaching was righteousness and justice, and if, lastly, the kingdom does not mean a hierarchy, but any form of government conducted on the principles of righteousness, holiness, justice, and charitableness, then we may safely maintain that the Kingdom of God, as taught by Judaism in one of its aspects, is universal in its aims.'[8]

JEWISH MORALITY

According to the Hebrew Scriptures, God's identification with morality is absolute. In the prophetic writings, as we have seen, the primacy of ethical behaviour is asserted, and this emphasis continues throughout rabbinic literature. Believing themselves to possess an authentic oral tradition as to the meaning of Scripture, the rabbis expounded and amplified the Biblical ethical injunctions. Thus throughout rabbinic literature, the rabbis sought to ensure that God's moral precepts were upheld. In this light the Jewish people are acceptable to God only when they fulfil the commandments of the Torah. Hence we read in the midrash: 'It is like a King who said to his wife, "Deck yourself with all your ornaments that you may be acceptable to me." So God says to Israel, "Be distinguished by the commandments that you may be acceptable to me"' (Sifre Deut., Wa'ethanan §36 fin., f75b).

For the rabbis, morality and religion form a single whole, inseparable from one another. Faith in God entails the obligation to be good, for God has commanded that his people follow his moral dictates. This view is eloquently illustrated in rabbinic lore: 'It happened once that R. Reuben was in Tiberius on the Sabbath, and a philosopher asked him: "Who is the most hateful man in the world?" He replied, "The man who denies his Creator." "How so?", said the philosopher. R. Reuben answered, "Honour thy father and thy mother, thou shalt do no murder, thou shalt not commit adultery, thou shalt not steal, thou shalt not bear false witness against thy neighbour, thou shalt not covet." "No man denies the derivative (that is, the separate commandments) until he has previously denied the Root (namely, God), and no man sins unless he has denied Him who commanded him not to commit that sin"' (T.Shebu'ot III, 6).

Moral precepts are grounded in the will of God; in this light the Torah serves as the blueprint for moral action, and it is through the admonitions of the rabbis in midrashic and Talmudic sources that the Jewish people are encouraged to put the teachings of the Law into effect in their everyday life. In the hierarchy of values, the rabbis declared that justice is of fundamental importance. R. Simeon b. Gamliel, for example, remarked: 'Do not sneer at justice, for it is one of the three feet of the world, for the sages taught that the world stands on three things: justice, truth and peace' (Deut.R.Shofetim, V, 1 and 3). According to R. Elazar; 'The whole Torah depends upon justice. Therefore God gave enactments about justice immediately after the Ten Commandments, because men transgress justice, and God punishes them, and He teaches the inhabitants of the world. Sodom was not overthrown till the men of Sodom neglected justice, and the men of Jerusalem were not banished till they disregarded justice'(Ezek. 16:49; Isa. 1:23) (Ex.R., Mishpatim, 30, 19).

In explaining what is entailed in the principle of justice, the rabbis explained what is required in a court of law. With reference to the Deuteronomic injunction 'Thou shalt not take a bribe, for a bribe blinds the eyes of the wise', R. Hama b. Osha'ya stated: 'If a man suffers from his eyes, he pays much money to a doctor, but it is doubtful whether he will be healed or not. But he who takes a bribe, overturns justice, blinds his eyes, brings Israel into exile, and hunger into the world (Tanh.B., Shofetim, 15b fin.). Regarding the statement in Leviticus, 'In righteousness shall thou judge thy neighbour' the Sifra proclaims: 'You must not let one litigant speak as much as he wants, and then say to the other, "shorten thy speech". You must not let one stand and the other sit' (Sifre 89a). Simeon b. Shetach said: 'When you are judging, and there come before you two men, of whom one is rich and the other poor, do not say, "the poor man's words are to be believed, but not the rich man's". But just as you listen to the words of the poor man, listen to the words of the rich man, for it is said, "Ye shall not respect persons in judgement"(Deut. 1:17) (Ab.R.N. vers.II), XX, 22a. Thus according to rabbinic literature, the Kingdom of God is inextricably linked to the establishment of a moral order on earth.

THE DISTINCTIVE NATURE OF JEWISH SOCIAL ETHICS

According to Rabbinic literature, the Kingdom of God is inextricably linked with the establishment of a moral order on earth. For the Jewish people the Kingdom of God is inconsistent with injustice and social misery; the effort to bring about the perfection of the world so that God will reign in majesty is a human responsibility. Jewish ethics as enshrined in the Bible and in rabbinic literature are inextricably related to the coming of God's Kingdom. In this context a number of distinctive characteristics of Jewish morality are expressed in the Jewish tradition.

First, as we have seen in connection with the prophets, there was an intensity of passion about the moral demands made upon human beings. For sins of personal greed, social inequity and deceit, the prophet in God's name denounced the people and threatened horrific catastrophes. The voice of the prophet was continually charged with agony and agitation. Habbakuk, for example, declared:

> Woe to him who heaps up what is not his own . . . .
> Woe to him who gets evil gain for his house . . .
> For the stone will cry out from the wall,

And the beam from the woodwork respond.
Woe to him who builds a town with blood,
And founds a city on iniquity! [Hab. 2:6, 9, 11–12]

Such shrill denunciations of iniquity were the result of the prophetic conviction that people must be stirred from their spiritual slumber. 'The prophet's word is a scream in the night . . . while the world is at ease and asleep, the prophet feels the blast from heaven'.[9]

Second, Jewish ethics required that each person be treated equally. Biblical and rabbinic sources show a constant concern to eliminate arbitrary distinctions between individuals so as to establish proper balance between competing claims. On the basis of the Biblical view that everyone is created in the image of God, the Torah declared that false and irrelevant distinctions must not be introduced to disqualify human beings from the right to justice. The fatherhood and motherhood of God implied human solidarity; the Torah rejected the idea of different codes of morality for oneself and others, for the great and the humbled, for rulers and ruled, for individuals and nations, for private and public citizens. Given this understanding of the equality of all people, the Torah singled out the underprivileged and the defenceless in society for consideration: 'You shall not afflict any widow or orphan' (Exod. 22.22). 'Thou shalt not be partial to the poor or defer to the great' (Lev. 19.15).

Since all of humanity is created in the image of God, Judaism maintains that there is no fundamental difference between Jew and non-Jew: God's ethical demands apply to all. In the midrash we read:

> This is the gate of the Lord into which the righteous shall enter: not priests, Levites, or Israelites, but the righteous, though they be non–Jews (Sifra, Acharei mot, 13).

Indeed, according to the Talmud, the righteous non-Jew was accorded a place in the hereafter: 'The pious of all nations have a share in the world to come' (San. 105a). In this light, the rabbis emphasized that Jews must treat their non-Jewish neighbours with loving-kindness. One of the most authoritative rabbis of the last century declared:

> It is well known that the early as well as the later geonim wrote that we must abide by the law of the land and refrain from dealing unjustly with a non-Jew . . . Therefore, my brethren, listen to my voice and live. Study in our Torah to love the Almighty and love people regardless of faith or nationality. Follow justice and do

righteousness with Jew and non-Jew alike. The people of my community know that I always caution them in my talks and warn them that there is absolutely no difference whether one does evil to a Jew or a non-Jew. It is a well-known fact that when people come to me to settle a dispute, I do not differentiate between Jew and non-Jew. For that is the law according to our holy Torah.[10]

A third characteristic of Jewish morality is its emphasis on human motivation. The Jewish faith is not solely concerned with actions and their consequences; it also demands right intention. The rabbis explained: 'The Merciful One requires the heart' (San. 106b). It is true that Judaism emphasized the importance of moral action, but the Jewish faith also focusses attention on right-mindedness: inner experiences – motives, feelings, dispositions, and attitudes – are of supreme moral significance. For this reason the rabbis identified a group of negative commandments in the Torah involving thought. The following are representative examples:

Thou shalt not take vengeance, nor bear any grudge against the children of they people (Lev. 19.18).

There are six things which the Lord hateth . . . a heart that deviseth wicked plans. (Pr 6:16, 18).

Take heed lest there be a base thought in thy heart (Dt 15:9).

In the Mishnah the rabbis elaborated on this concern for the human heart:

Rabbi Eliezer said, '. . . be not easily moved to anger' (Avot 2.15).

Rabbi Joshua said, 'The evil eye, the evil inclination, and hatred of his fellow creatures drives a man out of the world' (Avot 2.16).

Rabbi Levitas of Yavneh said, 'Be exceedingly lowly of spirit' (Avot 2.16).

Connected with right thought is the Jewish emphasis on right speech. Jewish sources insist that individuals are morally responsible for the words they utter. Proverbs declared: 'Death and life are in the power of the tongue' (Prov. 18:21). Evil words spoken about one person by another could arouse hatred and enmity and destroy human relations. The rabbis considered slander to be a particular evil:

Whoever speaks slander is as though he denied the fundamental principle [existence of God]. The Holy One, blessed be He, says of such a person who speaks slander, 'I and he cannot dwell together in the world' (Pe'ah 15d, Areakh in 15b).

There was also a positive aspect to this emphasis on human speech. Just as the rabbis condemned false utterances, they urged their disciples to offer cheerful greetings (Avot 1.15, 3.16, 12). On the other hand anger could be soothed with gentle words and reconciliation brought about.

A fourth dimension of Jewish morality concerns the traditional attitude toward animals. Since God's mercy and goodness extend to all creatures (Ps. 145.9), 'a righteous man has regard for the life of his beast' (Prov. 12:10). According to Jewish tradition, human beings are morally obliged to refrain from inflicting pain on animals. The Pentateuch stipulated that assistance be given to animals in distress even on the Sabbath: 'You shall not see your brother's ass or his ox fallen down by the way, and withold you help from them; you shall help him to lift them up again' (Dt 22:4). In rabbinic Judaism, this same theme was reflected in various midrashim. We read, for example, concerning Rabbi Judah Ha Nasi:

> Rabbi Judah was sitting studying the Torah in front of the Babylonian synagogue in Sepphoris, when a calf passed before him on its way to the slaughter and began to cry out as though pleading, 'Save me!' Said he to it 'What can I do for you? For this you were created'. As a punishment for his heartlessness, he suffered toothache for thirteen years. One day, a weasel ran past his daughter, who was about to kill it, when he said to her, 'My daughter, let it be, for it is written, "and His tender mercies are over all His works". Because the Rabbi prevented an act of cruelty, he was once again restored to health (Baba Metzia, 85a).

A final aspect of Jewish ethics is their concern for human dignity; Judaism puts a strong emphasis on the respect due to all individuals. This concept was found in various laws in the Pentateuch and was developed by the rabbis who cautioned that one must be careful not to humiliate or embarrass others. Maimonides, for example, wrote:

> A man ought to be especially heedful of his behaviour towards widows and orphans, for their souls are exceedingly depressed and their spirits low, even if they are wealthy. How are we to conduct

ourselves toward them? One must not speak to them otherwise than tenderly. One must show them unvarying courtesy; not hurt them physically with hard toil nor wound their feelings with harsh speech. [Hilchot De'ot 6.10]

The Torah's concern for human dignity even included thieves. Rabbi Yochanan ben Zakai pointed out that according to the Law whoever stole a sheep should pay a fine of four times the value of the sheep; whoever stole an ox must pay five times its value. 'Those who stole sheep had to undergo the embarrassment of carrying the sheep off in their arms and the Torah compensated them for this indignity, but those who stole oxen were spared such embarrassment because they could simply lead the ox by its tether' (Baba Kamma 99b).

These specific qualities of Jewish ethics illustrate their humane orientation to all of God's creatures. Throughout Biblical and rabbinic literature, Jews were encouraged to strive for the highest conception of life, in which the rule of truth, righteousness and holiness would be established among humankind. Such a desire is the eternal hope of all God's people.

THE FOCUS ON MORAL ACTION

As we have seen, the Jewish hope for the future lies in God's sovereign rule on earth. From ancient times the synagogue liturgy concluded with a prayer in which this hope was expressed:

May we speedily behold the glory of Thy might,
when Thou wilt remove the abomination from the earth,
and the idols will be utterly cut off;
when the world will be perfected under the kingdom of the Almighty,
and all the children of flesh will call upon Thy name;
when Thou wilt turn unto Thyself all the wicked of the earth.

This is the goal of the history of the world in which God's chosen people have a central role. In this context the people of Israel have a historical mission to be a light to the nations. Through Moses God addressed the people and declared:

You have seen what I did to the Egyptians, and how I bore you on eagles' wings, and brought you to myself. Now therefore, if you will obey my voice and keep my covenant, you shall be my own possession among all peoples; for all the earth is mine, and you shall be to me a kingdom of priests and a holy nation. [Ex 19:4–6]

Election meant to be a servant of the Lord, to proclaim God's truth and righteousness throughout the world. Being chosen meant duty and responsibility; it was

> a Divine call persisting through all ages and encompassing all lands, a continuous activity of the spirit which has ever summoned for itself new heralds and heroes to testify to truth, justice and sublime faith.[11]

Judaism did not separate religion from life; instead Jews were called to action, to turn humankind away from violence, wickedness and falsehood. It was not the hope of bliss in a future life but the establishment of the kingdom of justice and peace that was central to the Jewish faith. Moral praxis was at the heart of the religious tradition. The people of Israel as a light to the nations reflected the moral nature of God; each Jew was to be like the Creator, mirroring the Divine qualities revealed to Moses: 'The Lord, the Lord, a God merciful and gracious, slow to anger, and abounding in steadfast love and faithfulness, keeping steadfast love for thousands, forgiving iniquity and transgression and sin' (Ex 34:6–7).

God as a moral being demanded righteous living, as the Psalms declared: 'The Lord is righteous; He loves righteous deeds' (Ps 11:7). 'Righteousness and justice are the foundation of His throne' (Ps 97:2). 'Thou hast established equity; thou hast executed justice and righteousness' (Ps 99:4). Given this theological framework, Jews were directed to obey the revealed will of God, which was the basis of the covenantal relationship between God and the Jewish nation. Orthopraxis, rather than conceptual reflection, served as the foundation of the religion of Israel.

In the Bible, deeds and events involving moral issues could be found in abundance: the punishment of Cain for murdering his brother, the violence of the generation that brought on the flood, the early prohibition against murder, the hospitality of Abraham and his pleading for the people of Sodom, the praise of Abraham for his moral attitudes, the condemnation of Joseph's brothers, Joseph's self-restraint in the house of Potiphar, Moses' intercessions on the side of the exploited.[12]

But it is pre-eminently in the legal codes of the Pentateuch that we encounter moral guidelines formulated in specific rules. The

ACTION /
PRACTICE.

Decalogue in particular illustrates the centrality of moral praxis in the life of the Jew. The first four commandments are theological in character, but the last six deal with relationships between human beings. The first commandments describe God as one who redeemed the Jews from Egypt, the one who forbade the worship of other deities and demanded respect for the Sabbath and the Divine name. These commandments were expressions of the love and fear of God; the remaining injunctions provided a means of expressing love of other human beings. The Decalogue made it clear that moral rules were fundamental to the Jewish faith.

Such ethical standards were repeated in the prophetic books. The teachings of the prophets were rooted in the Torah of Moses. The prophets saw themselves as messengers of the Divine word; their special task was to denounce the people for their transgressions and call them to repentance. In all this they pointed to concrete action – moral praxis – as the only means of sustaining the covenantal relationship with God. The essential theme of their message was that God demanded righteousness and justice.

Emphasis on the moral life was reflected in the prophetic condemnation of cultic practices that were not accompanied by ethical concern. These passages illustrated that ritual commandments were of instrumental value; morality was intrinsic and absolute. The primacy of morality was also reflected in the prophetic warning that righteous action was the determining factor in the destiny of the Jewish nation. Moral transgressions referred to in such contexts concerned exploitation, oppression and the perversion of justice. These sins had the potential to being about the downfall of the nation.

The Book of Proverbs reinforced the teaching of the Torah and the prophets; wisdom was conceived here as the capacity to act morally; it was a skill that could be learned. Throughout Proverbs dispositional traits and moral types were listed. This suggests that moral virtue or vice is to be achieved not by concentrating on individual moral acts but rather by learning to recognise and emulate certain good personality types. Thus here, as in the rest of the Bible, the moral life was seen as the foundation of the Jewish faith. Theology was defined in relation to practical activity; it was through ethical praxis that humanity encountered the Divine.

Rabbinic literature continued this emphasis on action. Convinced they were the authentic expositors of Scripture, the rabbis amplified Biblical law. In their expansion of the commandments, rabbinic exegetes differentiated between the laws governing human relationships to God (*bain adam la makom*) and those that concerned human relationships to others (*bain adam le chavero*). As in the Biblical period, rabbinic teachings reflected the same sense of the primacy of morality. Such texts as the following indicated rabbinic priority:

> He who acts honestly and is popular with his fellow creatures, it is imputed to him as though he had fulfilled the entire Torah. (Mekhilta on Exodus 15.26)

> Hillel said: 'What is hateful to yourself, do not do to your fellow man. This is the entire Torah, the rest is commentary'. (Shabbat 31a)

> Better is one hour of repentance and good deeds in this world than the whole life of the world-to-come. (Avot. 4.22)

In the classic texts of Judaism then moral behaviour was the predominant theme. By choosing the moral life, the Jew could help to complete God's work of creation. To accomplish this task the rabbis formulated an elaborate system of traditions, which were written down in the Mishnah, subsequently expanded in the Talmud, and eventually codified in the *Code of Jewish Law*. According to traditional Judaism, this expansion of the Pentateuchal Law was part of God's revelation. Both the Written Law (*Torah Shebikthav*) and the Oral Law (*Torah Shebe-'alpe*) were binding on Jews for all time:

> The Torah has been revealed from Heaven. This implies our belief that the whole of the Torah found in our hands this day is the Torah that was handed down by Moses and that it is all of Divine origin. By this I mean that the whole of the Torah came unto him from before God in a manner which is metaphorically called speaking.[13]

Since the Torah embraced the interpretations as well as the Pentateuch, Orthodoxy maintained that God gave to Moses the explanations as well as the original laws in the Pentateuch.

> The verse: 'And I will give thee the tables of stone, and the Law and the commandment, which I have written that thou mayest teach them' (Ex. 24:12) means as follows: 'The tables of stone' are the ten commandments; 'the law' is the Pentateuch; 'the commandment' is the Mishnah; 'which I have written' are the

Prophets and the Hagiographa; 'that thou mayest teach them' is the Gemara (Talmud). This teaches that all these things were given on Sinai. (R. Levi b. Hama in the name of R. Simeon b. Laquish)[14]

Given this view of the Torah, Jews regarded the moral law as absolute and binding. In all cases the law was precise and specific; it was God's word made concrete in the daily life of the Jew. The commandment to love one's neighbours embraced all humanity. In the *Code of Jewish Law* the virtues of justice, honesty and humane concern were regarded as central virtues of community life; hatred, vengeance, deceit, cruelty and anger were condemned as anti-social. The Jew was instructed to exercise loving-kindness towards all: to clothe the naked, to feed the hungry, to care for the sick, and to comfort the mourner. By fulfilling these ethical demands, the Jewish people could bring about God's kingdom on earth, in which exploitation, oppression and injustice would be eliminated. What was required in this task was a commitment to ethical praxis as a policy.

THE JEWISH RESPONSE TO MODERN INNER CITY PROBLEMS

These aspects of the Jewish heritage – the Exodus experience, the prophetic message, the doctrine of the Kingdom of God, the nature of Jewish ethics, and the focus on moral action – point the way to a sympathetic appreciation of the plight of those who are afflicted in modern society. The Biblical and rabbinic traditions portray God's reign on earth as the goal of mankind – a world in which all people shall turn away from iniquity, injustice and oppression. This is not the hope of bliss in a future life, but the building up of the Divine Kingdom of truth and peace for all. By putting themselves in the shoes of the disadvantaged – thereby recalling their own history of suffering – the Jewish community can envisage what life must be for the underprivileged.

Such a policy of caring and sharing based on Biblical and rabbinic sources transcends the much narrower prescriptions of the Chief Rabbi. Lord Jakobovits is correct when he declares that Judaism recommends education, diligence and hard work as one solution to individual poverty. Yet the Jewish people have had a wider vision in the past. There have been other virtues besides self-reliance, such as justice, compassion, charity and sympathy. The recommendations

of the Chief Rabbi are not merely an unrealistic solution to the
problems of our inner cities; they do not lay sufficient stress on the
richness and fullness of the Jewish heritage. The Jewish teachings we
have surveyed focus on the traditional commitment to those who are
downtrodden. In the past such prescriptions were directed primarily
to Jewry itself, since Jews lived in closed communities with relatively
little contact with the non-Jewish world. Today all this has changed.
In the modern world Jews have become full citizens of the countries
in which they dwell and are assimilated into contemporary society.
Such altered circumstances should provide the basis for a Jewish
commitment to all those who are downtrodden and marginalized,
whatever their race or religion.

As God's suffering servant through the ages, the Jewish people
should find solidarity with today's poor of paramount significance.
The prophets condemned every kind of abuse. Scripture speaks
of positive action to prevent poverty from becoming widespread.
Leviticus and Deuteronomy contain detailed legislation designed to
prevent the accumulation of wealth and consequent exploitation of
the unfortunate. Now that the ghettos have disappeared, modern
Jews should feel an obligation to take steps to eradicate poverty
and suffering wherever it exists. In particular, they should address
themselves to the economic deprivation that affects certain groups:
the young, who are frustrated by the lack of opportunity to obtain
training and work; manual labourers, who are frequently ill-paid and
find difficulty in defending their rights; the unemployed, who are
discarded because of the harsh exigencies of economic life; and the
old, who are often marginalized and disregarded. In all such cases,
the Jewish people – who have consistently endured hardship – should
feel drawn to the downtrodden of modern society, sharing in their
distress.

In attempting to accomplish this task, the plight of those living in
the inner cities is of central importance. Here the distinction between
the powerful and powerless is most clearly evident. In the cities – as
opposed to the suburbs – are to be found the unemployed, families
unable to cope, single parents, people with only part-time jobs,
individuals on welfare, drop-outs, and recent immigrants. In such
areas inhabitants are divorced from the powerful forces that shape
their lives: the inner city is the place of failure and hopelessness. The
graphic social divide between the rich and the poor is an everyday
reality for those who live in large metropolitan centres. All too often
the poverty of the inner city is the converse of middle-class suburban

life. The situation of the poor is an integral part of the elaborate hierarchy of wealth and esteem. The existence of rich suburbs is linked to the existence of ghettos and marginal sectors. A new consciousness is needed to remedy this situation, an awareness of the calamities of inner-city deprivation. By ministering to those at the bottom of society, Jews can affirm through their efforts that God is concerned with the plight of those facing adversity. In the inner-city Jews can embark on a task of reconstruction and restoration.

In this connection, special attention should be paid to the situation of the unemployed, who are generally found in the destitute parts of the inner city. Such individuals face particular difficulties in coping with their misfortunes. The unemployed do not know what to do with their time, and as a consequence, they are unfulfilled in essential areas: basic needs for human relationships, for financial income, for social status and identity, and for satisfaction and fulfillment. Helping those faced with such difficulties should be a high priority. The Jewish community can take the lead in assisting those out of work. Recently a number of writers have made a variety of suggestions about the kinds of activities that could be undertaken: ways must be sought for creating new work opportunities; labour not traditionally regarded as paid work (such as housework) must be accepted as valid and necessary; new manufacturing enterprises that stimulate the job market should be encouraged; apprenticeships for the young should be reintroduced; jobs need to be spread out through job sharing and part-time work; education must be seen as a preparation for life; voluntary activity should be stimulated and seen as a legitimate means of helping those in need.

In the quest to alleviate distress and disillusionment, Jews can make substantial contributions to those at the bottom of the social scale. Liberation from frustration and disappointment involves a reappraisal of life and labour: it is a task that can bind together the Jewish community in the quest for a meaningful life for all.

7
Judaism and Christian Anti-Semitism

In a recent issue of *Christian Jewish Relations*,[1] Johannes Cardinal Willebrands argues that Christianity is not anti-Semitic. The New Testament, he explains, contains numerous direct as well as indirect pro-Semitic statements, and at a deeper level the writers of the New Testament continually place Jesus and his mission within the Jewish tradition. Jesus' (Yeshu) Jewish origins are highlighted; Jesus' ministry was directed in the first place to Israel; New Testament apocalyptic images have a Jewish origin. Thus Willebrands contends: 'It is not at all easy to find a book more Semitic, or more Jewish, than the New Testament. To try to tear off from the New Testament its Semitic substance, would simply mean to destroy it, lock, stock and barrel'.[2]

THE NEW TESTAMENT WRITERS

Regarding statements in the New Testament which are critical of Jews, Willebrands asserts that they should not be interpreted as a condemnation of Judaism. Even Paul's criticism of the Law presupposes that the Law is good in itself. Further, the New Testament does *not* accuse the Jews of deicide even though the leaders of the Jewish people seem to have played some role in Jesus' death. Thus it is a mistake to think that all Jews are damned and rejected of God. Concerning the Pharisees, Willebrands quotes several references in the New Testament to counterbalance other negative descriptions. On this basis he writes, that 'the Pharisees . . . were certainly not the hypocritical repulsive bigots that a certain Christian tradition has made them out to be'.[3]

Finally Willebrands maintains that the Christian profession of faith in Jesus does not imply that the Jewish people is unworthy of respect. Indeed, he argues that if Christian commitment suggests a reference to Judaism, it is a positive one because it is from the Jewish faith that the notion of Messiahship is derived. Thus he writes: 'the Christ-Messiah links us to Judaism, because he was and remains a Jew, and with him Judaism enters into Christianity through the main door'.[4] For Willebrands, New Testament Christianity is not inherently anti-Semitic, yet he does admit that through the centuries Christians have unjustly been prejudiced against Jews. Nevertheless, he believes a distinction should be drawn between Christian belief and practice and historical and cultural realizations of the faith. 'It must be admitted . . .', he writes, 'the most, if not all, historical embodiments of Christianity this side of history, do not easily live up socially and culturally, to the requirements of our own religious profession'.[5]

These observations will no doubt be warmly welcomed by the Jewish community. After the Holocaust, it is reassuring to read such a positive pronouncement about Christianity and anti-Judaism by a prominent figure in the Catholic Church. Yet the question remains whether Willebrands views are valid; is he right in thinking that Christianity and anti-Semitism are intrinsically incompatible? No doubt there are good reasons to accept his picture of Jesus' teaching – Jesus' denunciation of the religious establishment does appear to be a criticism of the leaders of the nation rather than Judaism itself. But it would be a mistake to identify New Testament Christianity with the Christian tradition. Christianity has been an ongoing faith for nearly two millenia, and it is to this religious heritage that one must look to find an answer to the question whether Christianity is intrinsically anti-Jewish.

THE EVOLUTION OF CHRISTIAN ANTI-SEMITISM

In his discussion, Willebrands ignores the fact that from the very earliest period Christians affirmed Jesus as Christ and Lord. According to Christian exegetes of Scripture, the Messianic hope was fulfilled by Jesus; Christian teachers sought to justify this belief by reinterpreting the concept of Messiaship as an inward and spiritual transformation rather than one involving a public, historical event. According to traditional Christian theology, it is the Church rather than the Jewish community which is the true heir to the promises made to Abraham. By rejecting Jesus as Saviour, Jews no longer constitute God's elect and as a punishment for their hardheartedness, the Ancient Temple was destroyed and the Jewish people have been driven into exile. In the light of this Christological conception of history, the Church taught that the Jewish community must continue as a despised nation as proof of Divine retribution – such a theological position was enshrined in official policy, combining social denigration with pressure for conversion.

Thus, throughout the history of Christianity, anti-Judaic attitudes and practices were grounded in a theology of fulfilled Messianism. As Christ and Lord, Jesus superseded the tradition into which he was born and opened the way of salvation to all humanity. Christian anti-Semitism is not, as Willebrands contends, an historical and cultural aberration; it is at the heart of traditional Christology and within this context it is possible to understand the horrific denunciation of Jews and Judaism through the ages. As early as the 3rd Century, for example, Origen proclaimed that the Jewish people deserve to suffer because they have rejected Jesus as Christ. 'We may thus assert in utter confidence', he writes, 'that the Jews will not return to their earlier situation, for they have committed the most abominable of crimes, informing this conspiracy against the Saviour of the human race'.[6] In a similar vein, Gregory of Nyssa castigated the Jews for their involvement in Jesus' death as well as their abundant sinfulness: 'Murderers of the Lord, assassins of the prophets, rebels, and detesters of God, they outrage the Law, resist grace, repudiate the faith of their fathers. Companions of the devil, race of vipers, informers, calumnators, darkeners of the mind, pharisaic leaven, Sanhedrin of demons, accursed, detested, lapidators, enemies of all that is beautiful . . .'[7]

THE PASSION PLAYS AND WRITERS' VIEW OF THE JEWS

These patristic views became the dominant attitude of the Church toward the Jewish people and were most graphically expressed in the medieval passion plays. In scenes of the Crucifixion especially, Jews were portrayed as brutal tormentors. Thus, for example, we read in a French play of the period that Jews tormented Jesus before he was put to death. In this passage several Jews comment on Jesus' suffering and torture him.

ROULLART
See the blood streaming
and how his whole face is covered.

MALCHUS
Here, false and bloody man,

> I pity not your pain
> More than that of a vile trickster
> That nothing avails, he is so
> low.

BRUYANT

> Let us play at pulling out his
> beard
> That is too long anyway.

GRIFFON

> I have torn at him so hard
> That the flesh has come away
> too.

DILLART

> I would take my turn at tearing
> So as to have my share as well.

DRAGON

> See what a clump this is
> That I pull away as if it were
> lard.

BRUYANT

> But see how I go about it now.
> Behold he has not one left.[8]

It is not surprising that Jews were persecuted as a result of such depictions; by identifying with Jesus' agony, Christians transferred their projected personal resentments onto the Jewish people. Such hatred of Jews continued through the centuries, giving rise to various kinds of accusations against them such as ritual murder, defamation of the host, and so on. In addition, Church leaders frequently issued proclamations and pamphlets in which anti-Semitism was legitimized on theological grounds. In a notorious critique, for example, Martin Luther attacked numerous crimes. In *Against the Jews and their Lies*, he wrote: 'Know O adored Christ, and make no mistake, that aside from the Devil, you have no enemy more venomous, more desperate, more bitter than a true Jew who truly seeks to be a Jew'. The Jews, he believed, are venomous serpents; they rob, pilage and corrupt. On a practical level, Luther propounded a series of revenges against them: 'that their synagogues be burned, their books confiscated, that they be forbidden to pray to God in their own way and that they be expelled from the lands in which they live'.[9] In a later pamphlet he declared: 'The Jews are worse than the devils. O God, my beloved father and Creator, have pity on me who in self-defence must speak so scandalously of Thy Divine and eternal Mystery against Thy wicked enemies, the devils and the Jews'.[10]

Here in Luther's expression of enmity is enshrined the fundamental Christian hostility to the Jewish people. For the Church, Jews are Christ-killers, devils, pollutors of Christian culture and civilization. These attitudes have for centuries been at the heart of Christian theology – to deny their existence (for even the most lofty motives) is to falsify the tradition. What then can be done? Cardinal Willebrands is surely right that Christian anti-Semitism poses serious difficulties for the post-Holocaust Christian community. But arguably, a more radical remedy than this reassessment of New Testament teaching is needed if anti-Judaism in the Church is to be overcome.

REINTERPRETING CHRISTOLOGY

Recently the Christian theologian Rosemary Radford Reuther made just this point. It is not possible to rethink anti-Judaic patterns, she writes, without questioning their Christological basis. Christians must formulate their faith in Jesus as anticipatory rather than final. Jesus, she believes, did not fulfil all Jewish hopes for the Messiah; rather he announced this Messianic hope but died on the cross of unredeemed history.[11] Reuther's reorientation of Christology, in which Jesus is not seen as absolute, allows room for the Jewish people as true and faithful witnesses to God. Given this understanding it no longer makes sense to abuse Jews for failing to recognize Jesus as Messiah and Lord.

Such a reinterpretation of Christian theology has gained increasing acceptance among a growing number of Christian scholars. Professor John Hick, for example, speaks of a Copernican revolution in theology which involves a radical transformation of the Christian view of religious pluralism. It demands, he writes, 'a paradigm shift from a Christianity-centred or Jesus-centred to a God-centred model of the universe of faiths. One then sees the great world religions as different human responses to the one Divine reality, embodying different perceptions which have been formed in different historical and cultural circumstances'.[12] Similarly, the Roman Catholic priest Raimundo Panikaar endorses a new map of world religions. For Panikaar, the mystery within all religions is both more than and yet has its being within the diverse experiences and beliefs of the world's religions: 'It is not simply that there are different ways of leading to the peak, but that the summit itself would collapse if all the paths disappeared.[13] Such a vision of the universe of faiths implies that no religion can claim final or absolute authority.

A similar position is advanced by Dr Stanley Samartha. God, he believes, is the Mysterious Other: 'The Other relativizes everything else. In fact, the willingness to accept such relativization is probably the only real guarantee that one has encountered the Other as ultimately real'.[14] By relativizing all religious figures and revelation, Samartha does not intend to deny their necessity or reduce them to a common denominator. The Mysterious Other must confront humanity through particular mediations, yet no particular manifestation is universally valid. A particular religion such as Christianity can claim to be decisive for some people, but no religion is justified in claiming that it is decisive for all.

Again, Professor Paul Knitter argues that the theocentric model is a valid reinterpretation of Christian tradition and experience. Jesus should not be understood as God's complete revelation – exclusivist language in the New Testament should be seen as essentially confessional in nature. Such Christological language, he asserts, is much like the language a husband would use of his wife: 'You are the most wonderful woman in the world', and so on. In the context of a marital relationship these claims are true, but only as an expression of love. Similarly it is possible for Christians to express their dedication to Jesus without adopting an absolutist position. Utilizing the analogy of marriage, Knitter writes: 'The deeper the commitment to one's spouse and the more secure the marriage relationship, the more one will be able to appreciate the truth and beauty of others. Therefore, not only does commitment to Jesus include openness to others, but the greater the commitment to him, the greater will be one's openness to others'.[15]

CONCLUSION

Such redefinitions of Christology provide a new basis for viewing other faiths. Traditional Christianity – with its insistence on finality – simply does not fit what is being experienced in the arena of religious pluralism. In place of a Christocentric conception of God's activity, these theologians are proposing Theocentrism; it is not Jesus, but God who is at the centre of the universe of faiths. Within such a context, Judaism can be seen as an authentic and true religious expression, and such a paradigm-shift calls for a critical reassessment of the Church's attitude to the Jews. Here then is a framework for positive Jewish-Christian encounter and religious harmony. Such a new vision truly paves the way (in Willebrand's words) 'to bring Jews and Christians together as sons and daughters of Abraham, distinct yet related, asking and receiving forgiveness, reconciled at last'.[16]

8

Obstacles
to Jewish-Christian
Encounter

In a discussion of Jewish-Christian relations in *Immanuel*, a semi-annual bulletin of religious thought in Israel, the Rev. C. Schoeneveld argues that the clash between conflicting theological presuppositions in Judaism and Christianity has made it impossible for Jews and Christians to find room for one another in religious dialogue. 'It seems', he writes, 'that Jews and Christians start from two contradictory and mutually exclusive positions, both of which are claimed to be the true understanding of God. The crucial issue between Judaism and Christianity is here the Christian claim that God became Man. For Israel God cannot be man or become man. For the Church, God can be man and does become flesh. Here is the deep gulf: for Judaism God's holiness and power, so to speak, forbid him to be man: for Christianity God's holiness and power, so to speak, enable him to be man. Two different understandings of God are here at stake; which understanding of God is the true one? If the Jewish understanding of God is the true one, then Christians are idolaters; if the Christian understanding is the true one, then the Jews were blind and unfaithful and did not pay attention to God's gracious visitation to them'.[1]

CONFLICT BETWEEN CHRISTIAN AND JEW

This conflict noted by Schoeneveld has led to bitter strife from New Testament times until the modern period. In the *Acts of the Apostles*, Chapter 7, Stephen became the first Christian martyr when he was stoned by the Jews for his faith in the heavenly Son of Man. Similar hostility is reflected in rabbinic sources. In the *Jerusalem Talmud*, for example, we read: 'When Nebuchadnezzar used the expression "He is like a Son of the gods", [Daniel 3:25] an angel came down from heaven, smote him on the mouth and said, "Blasphemer! Does God have a son?"[2] Similar antipathy can be found in the writings of the early Church. Origen, for example, in *Contra Celsum* argues, 'We may thus assert that the Jews will not return to their earlier situation, for they have committed the most abominable of crimes in forming this conspiracy against the saviour of the human race . . .'[3] In other words, he is maintaining that God has punished the Jews because of their rejection of Jesus.

This enmity continued all through the Middle Ages and it eventually gave rise to a number of religious debates. In Barcelona there was a disputation in 1263, during the course of which the King of Aragon posed the following questions to Rabbi Moses Nahmanides: 'Has the Messiah already appeared? Is the Messiah promised by the Prophets a human or Divine figure? Who holds the correct faith, the Christians or the Jews?' In reply to the first question Nahmanides argued that the promises in the Old Testament for the Messianic Age had not yet been fulfilled; war, bloodshed, injustice and outrage still hold sway on the Earth. He also argued that Jesus has not freed men from the guilt of original sin since the punishments decreed by God for the sin of the first man (according to Christian doctrine) continue to remain in force. In answer to the second question, Nahmanides replied that in the Jewish tradition the Messiah is to be human rather than Divine and finally, in answer to the third question, he declared that Christian doctrine is fundamentally irrational and therefore could not be true.[4]

Other Jewish responses to such questions can be found in mediaeval rabbinic writings. Saadya Gaon, in *Emunot ve-Deot* argued that Christianity is a human creation which falsely maintains that it is Divinely revealed.[5] In the *Kuzari*, Judah ha-Levi maintained that Christianity professes false doctrines which distort Divine truth.[6] Again Isaac Troki, in *Hizzuk Emunah* attempted to show that Christological interpretations of the Old Testament have no solid foundation.[7]

It was not until the 17th century, in a debate between the Christian, Phillip van Limborch, and the Jew, Isaac Orbio de Castro, that Jews and Christians were able to achieve some measure of tolerance; even then neither protagonist had a sympathetic understanding of the other's faith. Orbio, on the one hand, stated that it is a mistake to read Christological doctrines into the Old Testament: Limborch, on the other hand, argued that Jesus was greater than Moses and that it is necessary to have faith in Jesus Christ in order to achieve salvation.[8]

In the 18th century, in the dialogue between Moses Mendelssohn and Johann Caspar Lavater, a similar lack of understanding was found despite Mendelssohn's belief that Christianity was, in some respects, true. On the basis of a rejection of the Christological interpretation of passages in the Old Testament, he attempted to demonstrate the irrationality of the doctrines of the Trinity, the Incarnation, the Resurrection, the Ascension and the Redemption claimed to have been wrought through Jesus.[9]

In the following century there were other Jewish thinkers who discussed the relationship between Judaism and Christianity. Salomon Formstecher, for example, in *Religion des Geistes*, declared that Judaism was the true world religion whereas Christianity was disguised Paganism.[10] Similarly, in the *Revelation According to the Doctrine of the Synagogue*, Salomon Ludwig Steinham argued that Christianity was a mixture of Jewish and Pagan ideas and alleged that the doctrine of the Incarnation is self-contradictory.[11]

There have been similar conflicts this century. In the discussion between Martin Buber and Karl Ludwig Schmidt, theological differences between Judaism and Christianity were highlighted. At the beginning of the debate, Schmidt asked: 'The only important question is whether nearly two thousand years ago the Jewish nation, the Jewish Church of the time, did not harden their hearts against the Messiah sent by God, thereupon, through the destruction of Jerusalem, losing the focus of their ramified diaspora, and thenceforth living in the diaspora, in dispersion, without a spiritual centre'. In response Buber stated, 'We cannot ascribe finality to any one of His [God's] revelations, nor to any one [revelation] the character of the Incarnation. Unconditionally, that futuristic Word of the Lord points to the Beyond at every moment of passing time; God transcends absolutely all of his manifestations'.[12]

Recently some Jewish writers have discussed Jewish-Christian relations in the light of the Holocaust. Richard Rubenstein, for example, in *After Auschwitz* maintains that Jews and Christians can develop personal relationships only when there exists theological ambiguity and uncertainty. He writes: 'When the Jew holds firmly to the doctrine of the election of Israel and the Torah as the sole content of God's revelation to mankind, the Christian insistence upon the decisive character of the Christ event in human history must be, at best, error and, at worst, blasphemy'.[13] Similarly, he continues, when the Christian 'is convinced that the Divine-human encounters recorded in Scripture find their true meaning and fulfillment in the Cross, Jews are at best the blind who cannot see; at worst, they are the demonic perverters, destroyers and betrayers of mankind's true hope for salvation'.[14]

Historically then, it an be seen that the central obstacle to real Jewish-Christian dialogue has been the clash between religious claims. In the *Jewish-Christian Argument*, the eminent Jewish New Testament scholar H.J. Schoeps writes 'For nineteen centuries, Jews and Christians have passed through the world beside each other. There has been no lack of side glances, but true dialogue never developed – nor in fact could it develop. During the first centuries, the Jewish side had no other interest besides refuting Christian re-interpretations of Jewish doctrines, holding themselves aloof from true encounter through "refutations" of their opponents. When Christianity acceded to power, Christians no longer had any serious desire to engage in discussion with the Jews for the latter's very impotence was seen as an overwhelming instance of God's punishment. Within the intellectual arena of mediaeval scholasticism, Jews and Christians could properly have only the concern of justifying their own religion while, at the same time, flatly refusing to acknowledge the other's claim to truth.'[15] There has been more scope for understanding and dialogue in the modern period, but, in fact, Jews and Christians have continued to emphasise the theological gulf that separates their faiths.

POSITIVE SIGNS IN DIALOGUE

Today, however, this theological gulf has narrowed since within Christianity itself there is serious disagreement about the doctrine of the Incarnation. Indeed, the present-day debate between conservative and liberal Christian theologians has a very definite resemblance to previous Jewish-Christian debate. The similarity is brought out clearly in the Preface of the *Truth of God Incarnate*: 'Our main concern is not with the book (*The Myth of God Incarnate*)[16] and its publication; rather with the issues it brings up. Were the early Christians mistaken in ascribing deity to Jesus? Has the Church been guilty of idolatry ever since? What actually is the New Testament evidence? Is it reliable? Can the contentions of historic Christianity confidently be jettisoned after two thousand years? These are the questions that the man in the street will be asking himself . . .'[17] This could be a verbatim report from a Jewish-Christian confrontation; in fact, it is directed against a volume of essays produced by seven of today's eminent Christian thinkers and published under the title *The Myth of God Incarnate*.

As is made clear in the Preface of *The Myth of God Incarnate*, the authors are not original in their refusal to understand the traditional doctrine of the Incarnation literally. In their own words, 'There is nothing new in the main theme of the book . . . A growing number of Christians, both professional theologians and lay people, have been thinking along these lines'.[18] What the publication of the volume does indicate, however, is that non-traditional interpretations of Christian doctrines are widely held even among those who hold influential positions within the Church itself. In view of this it seems possible that Jewish-Christian dialogue might be pursued with more profitable results than the theological impasse it has achieved in the past.

John Hick, in his book *God and the Universe of Faiths*, describes the traditional doctrine of the Incarnation as a 'Mythological idea. As such it cannot *literally* [his italics] apply to Jesus. But as a poetic image – which is powerfully evocative even though it conveys no literal meaning – it expresses the religious significance of Jesus in a way that has proved effective for nearly two millennia'.[19] He goes on to conclude the chapter 'Incarnation and Mythology' with these words: 'If we make the mistake (which lay at the root of all the Christological heresies) of trying to turn the myth into a hypothesis, we not only falsify its character but also generate implication which would make impossible any viable theology of religions'.[20]

These theological developments are not confined to Europe: the American thinker, Charles B. Ketcham, in his book *A Theology of Encounter*, re-interprets the doctrine of the Incarnation in the light of the thought of the Jewish philosopher Martin Buber. He writes, 'What Jesus represents is the fullness of the ontological reality of *Being*. His identity, his authenticity is effected by and ratified by his I-Thou relation with God . . . The a priori *Thou* for Jesus was fully responsive to God'.[21] He goes on to say that this understanding of the nature of Jesus avoids all the obvious intellectual problems of the Incarnation by not creating them.

These liberal interpretations of the doctrine of the Incarnation clearly remove the traditional impediment to authentic Jewish-Christian dialogue; the liberal Christian can no longer condemn the Jew for refusing to accept that Jesus of Nazareth was literally

'God of God, Light of Light, Very God of Very God, Begotten not made, being of One Substance with the Father' since that is exactly what he is doing himself. We must now ask whether such dialogue is possible from the Jewish side today.

CONTEMPORARY JEWISH-CHRISTIAN ENCOUNTER

As a result of centuries of religious conflict and hostility, Jews have felt and continue to feel suspicion and distaste for both Christians and Christianity. Even in this enlightened century, wounds have been inflicted by the Christian community. The destruction of the Holocaust is not to be forgotten; the Churches did not rise in a body to denounce Hitler's activities; the railway lines to Auschwitz were not bombed by the allies; there is not much Christian interest in the plight of Jews in the Soviet Union and even the much vaunted Vatican statement on Jewish innocence for the Crucifixion is mild and was only achieved after much argument. Against this background the position of many Jewish scholars is understandable. Real dialogue is obviously impossible in conditions of mutual distrust. Nearly two thousand years of being despised and persecuted has left its mark on the Jewish community. In spite of all this, there are positive signs which indicate a Jewish readiness to participate in dialogue and to study with and to learn from the dominant daughter religion.

As W. Jacobs notes in *Christianity Through Jewish Eyes*, perhaps the best basis for dialogue lies in scholarly exploration into the background of the New Testament.[22] Jesus and Paul were Jewish figures with Hebrew names. They kept the Jewish law, they worshipped in the Jewish synagogue, they participated at Jewish feasts. The pioneering work in this area done by such scholars as Samuel Sandmel,[23] H.J. Schoeps[24] and Geza Vermes[25] has aroused much critical interest from both Christians and Jews. Quite apart from broadening the Christian understanding of their own religious background, these works counterbalance many of the anti-Semitic elements of the New Testament.

Of course, much of the most fruitful Jewish-Christian dialogue is conducted on a personal level. The Jewish scholar Franz Rosenzweig conducted a long correspondence with his friend Ehrenberg who was a Jewish convert to Christianity. Both men were intensely religious, but beside their faith, they brought real friendship into their discussions. Rosenzweig wrote, 'The truth, the entire truth, belongs neither to them nor to us. We [the Jews] bear it within ourselves; precisely, therefore, we must first gaze within ourselves if we wish to see it. So we will see the star, but not its rays. To encompass the whole truth one must not only see the light, but also what it illuminates. They [the Christians], on the other hand, have been eternally destined to see the illuminated object, but not the light'.[26] Thus though Christians and Jews see the truth in different ways, before God there is only one truth. This attempt to show the fundamental unity between the two religions was the first real Jewish recognition of the truth claims of Christianity. Rosenzweig had a real understanding of Christianity and he realised his limitations as an outsider. His work could have been the beginning of a profitable dialogue, but it was generally neglected. Neither Jew nor Christian was ready for exchange at this level.

Rosenzweig was writing before the Second World War. As we have seen, the Christian theological climate has largely changed. No longer is a literal understanding of the doctrine of the Incarnation common to all Christians. Since the Second Vatican Council, Jews have been officially exonerated from blame for the death of Jesus. As a result of the work of New Testament scholars, both Christian and Jew, the anti-Semitic perspective of the New Testament has been explained and is more readily understood so it can be read and accepted as part of the Jewish heritage as much as the Christian. It is clear then, that the words of Shoeneveld, with which this essay opened, are no longer true. Jews and Christians no longer start from 'two contradictory and mutually exclusive positions'.

CONCLUSION

However, it is too soon to be optimistic. Two thousand years of distrust and persecution are not easily forgotten. Nonetheless, today while both Christianity and Judaism are seeking ways to adjust themselves and adapt to the increasing challenge of indifference and secularism, there is a real possibility for dialogue. Already Jews and Christians work together on common projects of fellowship and charity, but it should go further than this. Christian-Jewish dialogue has ceased to be the impossibility it once was. Admittedly a bridge has not yet been built between the two faiths, but at least a rope has been thrown over.

9

A New Vision
of Jewish-Christian Dialogue

In the previous essay, which was first published in the English journal *Theology*[1], I discussed whether it is now possible for Christians and Jews to engage in real dialogue given that a significant number of Christians have come to see the Incarnation as a myth. It seemed that this new, liberal interpretation of the doctrine of the Incarnation removes the traditional impediment to authentic Jewish-Christian dialogue since the liberal Church can no longer condemn the Jew for refusing to accept that Jesus was literally 'God of God'.

CRITIQUE OF A LIBERAL APPROACH TO DIALOGUE

In subsequent issues of *Theology* the position I put forward was criticized for several reasons. In a letter to the editor, E.L. Mascall stated that he could see no grounds for hope in my suggestion. What is needed instead, he believes, is for Christians who accept the traditional doctrine of the Incarnation and Jews committed to their heritage to 'set out on a sympathetic project of mutual exploration and understanding; they would no doubt be in for some very hard work, but might be very fruitful'.[2]

In another letter to the editor in the same issue, David Cockerell pointed out that his experience of Jewish-Christian encounter was a positive one: 'Our warm and generous Jewish neighbours showed a willingness to share and discuss religious ideas'. Possibly, he suggests, real exchange should take place on such a spontaneous, neighbourly level for it is only when the theological 'experts' get to work that 'the air turns blue and the knives are drawn'.[3] Further, like Mascall, Cockerell believes that in dialogue Jews and Christians should confront the differences between the two faiths. Christians should not have to be saddled with what seems to many to be reductionist interpretations of their faith as a precondition for entering into conversation with people of other faiths. 'We begin to learn from each other, and so grow closer together, when we come together genuinely to listen to and to learn from the insights of others – but their integrity and ours, is not respected where they – or we – are expected to whittle away the areas of substantial difference which exist between us.'[4] In this light the aim of interfaith dialogue is to create an environment in which differences can become a point of growth.

This same point was taken up by Valerie Hamer in 'A Hair's Breadth' in the next issue of *Theology*. Like Mascall and Cockerell, Hamer contends that dialogue does not commit us to drawing closer in belief but rather in mutual understanding. Thus, she states that dialogue may well illustrate how far apart Jews and Christians are, and this should not be an obstacle to friendship and tolerance between Jews and Christians. 'The fact that Christians are re-examining the traditional doctrine of the Incarnation', she writes, 'should have no bearing upon the progress of dialogue. The question of the Incarnation is an internal Christian issue . . . however, it is not part of dialogue for one party to make any comment upon or show partisanship in the internal affairs of the other'.[5]

The view of dialogue that Mascall, Cockerell and Hamer adopt is one shared by a number of modern theologians. Leslie Newbigin, for example, in 'The Basis, Purpose, and Manner of Inter-Faith Dialogue' argues that the Christian who participates in dialogue with other faiths must subscribe to the tenets of the Gospel tradition. 'He cannot agree that the position of final authority can be taken by anything other than the Gospel . . . Confessing Christ-Incarnate, crucified, and risen – as the light and the true life, he cannot accept any other alleged authority as having the right of way over this . . .'[6]

This understanding of dialogue, however, is not far removed from the old attitude of Christian superiority and a rejection of non-Christian traditions. If Jesus is regarded as 'true light and true life' it is hard to see how interfaith discussion can take place on a sympathetic level. Here the Church speaks out of the belief that God has entered human history in the person of Jesus Christ. For those who adopt this position, the Christian revelation is uniquely true. And if, as Newbigin and others suggest, the partner in dialogue adopts an equally confessional stance, all that can be gained is an insight into one another's convictions, Furthermore, insofar as they hold to the absolute truth of their respective faiths, they may well try to convert one another.

THE CONFESSIONAL STANCE IN DIALOGUE

At best such a confrontation between believers would be an educational exercise in which those engaged in conversation could learn about one another's theology. In the 'Goals of Inter-Religious Dialogue', Eric Sharpe defines this type of encounter as 'discursive dialogue' in which there is 'meeting, listening and discussion on the level of mutual competent intellectual inquiry'.[7] This kind of interchange is important, but it is far removed from dialogue at the deepest level in which Christians and non-Christians are engaged in a mutual quest for religious insight and understanding. Interfaith discussion must move beyond the stage of confessional or discursive encounter to a position of openness and receptivity. Such an approach is well formulated in the 'Guidelines for Inter-Religious Dialogue' proposed in 1972 by Stanley Samartha of the World Council of Churches in which he recommends that dialogue should be truth-seeking: 'Inter-religious dialogue should also stress the need to study fundamental questions in the religious dimensions of life . . . World religious organizations should support the long-range study of the deeper questions which today ought to be taken up not just separately by individuals of each religion, but also together in the larger interests of mankind'.[8]

The difficulty is that when interfaith dialogues are organized they frequently lose sight of this goal, and instead of engaging in a mutual quest, participants adopt a confessional attitude or decide to teach members of other faiths about their practices and beliefs. This was particularly evident in the consultation between Anglicans and Jews held at Amport House at Andover, England in November 1980. Despite the primary objective to discuss an issue of mutual concern – law and religion in contemporary society – it became clear that religious convictions about the nature of Jesus and the Christian revelation stood in the way of a constructive exploration of shared problems. This confrontation is thus a concrete illustration that the kind of dialogue envisaged by Mascall, Cockerell, Hamer and Newbigin inevitably is constrained by conflicting theological presuppositions.

The subject of this encounter between Anglican and Jewish leaders focussed on three basic questions: (1) What is the legitimacy or need of an objective law of God beyond situational ethics? (2) Is the religious objection to 'permissiveness' more than a mere return to religious triumphalism? (3) Have Jews and Christians any insights about the line to be drawn between individual personal freedom and the authority of the State? The Conference lasted three days, and according to the Archbishop of York and the Chief Rabbi, the participants 'did begin to see the value and relevance of exploring our different religious heritage to come up with clues that have at least a sporting chance to be taken seriously'.

Despite this claim, it is clear from the papers published in *Christian Jewish Relations*[9] that prior religious commitments made such a joint quest extremely difficult. From the Christian side, the centrality of Jesus continually came to the fore. Thus, in 'Law and Religion in Contemporary Society', G.R. Dunstan draws attention to the fact that St Paul argued that ritual ordinances – what he called 'the works of the law' had been fulfilled by the self-offering of Jesus and need not be demanded of those who partook of the benefit of his sacrifice. Yet he affirmed the demands of the moral law in its full rigor – fulfilled to a new depth what he perceived it to be in the life and teaching of Jesus. 'Obedience was due in grateful and loving response to God's love, or grace, as seen in Jesus.' For Paul, baptism 'into Christ implied baptism into his obedience, a partaking of his sacrifice' (Rom. 12). St Paul is thus the authoritative teacher of New Testament ethics: 'he had to give his Gentile Churches, made up of men and women with no common religious culture or bond, a common morality, a 'way' to walk in, a Christian "*halakah*"'.[10]

This understanding of morality as obedience to God's love in Jesus has no connection with Jewish ethics. Dunstan thus offers no suggestions how Jews and Christians could reach some sort of agreement in the area of ethics. Rather he points to the fact that in the area of medical ethics (which he had discussed with the Chief Rabbi for several years), there were deep divisions between the two traditions. Clearly then, in Dunstan's discussion of law in society, the obstacle to fruitful dialogue is the Christian conviction that the moral law is ultimately grounded in Jesus Christ. Similarly, in 'The Place of Law in contemporary Society' A. Phillips emphasizes that 'Christianity rests entirely on the authority of Jesus alone, what he was and did. The Christian is called to identify with Christ by taking up his cross and following (Matt. 16.42). It is in this self-denying cross that his ethics are located'. Membership of the Israel of the New Covenant was not determined by obedience to any Christian law, but it was subjected to the new situation created by the Christ event. Further, Phillips contends that for Christians, 'the spirit, under whose direction all ethical rulings must be made' continues to guide into all truth (Jn. 16.13).[11]

In 'A Christian Understanding of Law and Grace' C.F.D. Moule also locates the moral law in the personhood of Christ. The thesis of his paper is the conviction that the Christian Church is the Israel of the New Covenant and that a right relation with God depends solely on trusting him for his forgiveness which has taken shape in history and continues to take shape in the death and aliveness of Jesus. 'There is no way', he writes, 'of being within the Covenant except trust in God – the God whom Christians find supremely and decisively in Jesus'.[12] If Jesus is one with God and one with humanity, his death and resurrection are at one and the same time the affirmation of law and grace. The main thrust of the Mosaic revelation thus extends beyond itself – into the Christian revelation.

The understanding of Jesus as God Incarnate is therefore central to a Christian conception of ethics, but as Moule himself remarks, this standpoint 'cannot be without offence to the Jew'. And, though these papers are illuminating in various ways, they do not facili-tate Jewish-Christian dialogue. Fundamentally they are confessional and educative. Jesus is seen as the climax of human history, and Christianity is understood implicitly and at times described explicitly as the fulfillment of God's revelation.

From the Jewish side, there is likewise an appeal to revelation as the basis of morality. In 'Law as a Basis of a Moral Society', W.S. Wurzburger draws a distinction between philosophical doc-trines which base law upon morality and the Jewish tradition in which 'morality ultimately derives its normative significance from the transcendent authority of the law. Jewish ethics attributes the "imperativeness" of the moral law to the property of being com-manded by God on Mt. Sinai, a view in direct opposition to the Christian view that ethics must be grounded in Jesus Christ – the word made flesh'.[13]

The contrast in approach is explained in some detail by U. Tal in 'Law, the Authority of the State, and the Freedom of the Individual Person'. It is not unity, he argues, but rather plurality which Judaism should seek in dialogue: 'In the realm of pure theology the fundamental principle of Christianity, that Jesus is the Christ, the Messiah in whom in the dispensation of time . . . all things . . . both which are in heaven and which are on earth (Eph. 1.10) will have been re-established and reconciled (2 Cor. 5.18), is unacceptable to

Judaism. As long as Judaism remains faithful to the tradition of the ontological all-inclusiveness of the Torah it cannot accept . . . that God hath made the same Jesus, whom ye have crucified, both Lord and Christ (Acts. 2.36; Heb 5.5.; Ps. 2.7)'.[14]

In the concluding paper 'Review of Christian-Jewish Relations', C.M. Reigner points to the fact that Christian-Jewish dialogue must be based on a recognition of 'the fundamental differences' between the two faiths, yet it is difficult to see how dialogue understood in this sense can go beyond the confessional or the educative stage.[15] No doubt the participants in this conference learned a great deal from one another, but because of the Christians' commitment to the traditional understanding of the Incarnation and the Jews' refusal to look beyond the Jewish conception of revelation as the basis for the moral law, no progress was made in formulating a common approach to the problems outlined. This encounter is an example of the type of interfaith dialogue recommended by Mascall, Cockerell, Hamer, Newbigin and others; yet by bearing witness to their respective faiths, it consisted simply in the display and comparison of irreconcilable beliefs. What is needed, however, is for participants in such discussions to adopt an *open*-minded and inquiring disposition in exploring fundamental questions. As can be seen from this consultation, this can happen only if the doctrine of the Incarnation is understood in such a way that Christians will recognize the separate validity of non-Christian religious traditions.

For Jewish participants in dialogue, there must also be the same level of tolerance. In the past Jews have maintained that their religion is at the centre of the Universe of faiths; Sinaitic revelation is thus understood as a unique divine act which provided a secure foundation for the religious traditions of Israel. From the Pentateuchal revelation Jews believe they can learn God's true nature, His dealings with His chosen people, and the promise of the world to come. In this fashion the Written Torah as well as the rabbinic interpretation of Scripture is perceived as the yardstick for evaluating the truth claims of Christianity, and the significant feature of this view is that Christianity is regarded as true only in so far as its precepts conform to the Jewish faith.

If Jewish-Christian dialogue is to take place on the most profound level, such a Judeo-centric picture of revelation must be replaced by a more tolerant view in which God is understood as disclosing Himself to each and every generation and to all mankind. Thus, neither in Judaism nor in Christianity nor for that matter in any other religion is revelation complete and absolute. In such a model of God's activity, it is God Himself who is at the centre of the Universe of faiths with both Judaism and Christianity encircling Him and intersecting only at those points where the nature of Divine reality is truly reflected.

AREAS OF ENCOUNTER

Given that Christians and Jews are prepared to begin from this starting point, there are a number of central issues, of which the following are a few representative examples, which Jews and Christians could fruitfully explore together:

(1) *Symbols* – The two faiths could profitably discuss the nature of religious symbols as long as neither Jew nor Christian adopts the standpoint that the symbols in his respective faith are intrinsically superior. Not very much is known about the logic of symbols. We do not understand why, for example, people chose to use certain symbols, why they give up some symbols, why they remain unmoved by symbols that others find meaningful, and why they are moved by a symbol that others find offensive. If discussion took place across religious lines, it might be possible to gain greater insight into what is involved in religious symbolism.

(2) *Worship* – In Judaism and Christianity worship is a response to God, an acknowledgement of a reality independent of the worshipper. Assuming that neither the Jewish nor the Christian participants maintain that their conception of God is uniquely true, it would be useful to discuss the ways in which various forms of worship give some glimpse into the nature of the Godhead. Furthermore, it might be possible to explore ways in which the liturgical features of one tradition could be incorporated into the other. The Passover Seder, for example, is regarded by most scholars as the ceremony celebrated at the Last Supper. In this respect it is as much a part of the Christian as the Jewish tradition and could become an element of the Christian liturgy. Similarly, the Psalms are shared by both Christians and Jews, and their recitation in the Christian musical tradition could enter into the Jewish liturgy. These are simply two examples of the ways in which Jews and Christians could enrich the liturgical dimensions of one another's faith.

(3) *Ritual* – Like worship, ritual plays a fundamental role in Judaism and Christianity and there are areas worthy of joint investigation as long as neither party adopts an attitude of religious superiority. First, an examination of formal and elaborate practices

as well as simple actions could reveal the various ways in which the believer interprets his action as making contact or participating in God's presence. Second, a comparative study of ritualistic practices could illustrate the ways in which an outer activity mirrors an inner process – a relationship fundamental to the concept of ritualistic behaviour. Third, it might be beneficial to look at various contemplative and mystical activities in these faiths which allegedly disclose various aspects of God and enable the practitioner to reach a high state of consciousness.

(4) *Ethics* – Orthodox Jews believe that God chose them to be His special people and gave them His law through the revelation on Mt Sinai. The moral law is thus embodied in immutable, God-given commandments. For the traditional Christian, Christ is the end of the law, thereby superseding the Torah as the mediator between God and man. Allowing that both sides adopt a more flexible stance to moral attitudes within their respective traditions, it would be worthwhile to embark on a exploration of Jesus' critique of Pharisaic Judaism. Such an investigation would help to illuminate the tension between specific rules and general principles as well as the relationship between action and intention.

(5) *Society* – Religions are not simply systems of belief and practice; they are also organisations which have a communal and social dimension. Given that neither the Jewish nor the Christian partner in dialogue assumes at the outset that his faith possesses a better organisational structure and a more positive attitude toward modern society, it would be helpful to examine the way in which each religion understands itself in relation to the world. In addition, since Judaism and Christianity have religious hierarchies, an analysis of the nature of institutional structures, the training of leaders, and the exercise of authority could clarify the ways in which religious traditions reflect the non-religious characteristics of the societies in which they exist. In the face of modern secularism, such an examination is of particular consequence since, more than ever before, religions find themselves forced to adapt to a rapidly changing world.

CONCLUSION

These subject areas by no means exhaust the possibilities for dialogue, but they do indicate the type of discussions that could take place. Of course, such issues could be discussed by traditionally-minded Christians and Jews, but, as was illustrated in the case

of the encounter at Amport House, such debate is inevitably constrained by conflicting religious presuppositions: as in the past, the
Christian belief that Jesus was literally God Incarnate and the
Jewish conviction that Judaism is the supremely true faith are
central stumbling-blocks to a mutual quest for religious insight and
understanding. However, today there is the possibility, as never
before, for authentic interfaith dialogue of the deepest kind. If Jews
and Christians can free themselves from an absolutist standpoint in
which claims are made to possess ultimate and exclusive truth, the
way is open for a radically new vision of Jewish-Christian relations.

10
Judaism
and the Theology of
Liberation

For nineteen centuries Jews and Christians lived alongside one another; nevertheless, positive dialogue between these two faiths has only recently taken place, for several reasons. First, there is increasing scholarly exploration into the background of the New Testament. Jesus and Paul were Jewish figures; they kept the Jewish law; they participated at Jewish feasts. The pioneering work in this area done by such scholars as Samuel Sandmel (in *We Jews and Jesus*),[1] H.J. Schoeps (in *Paul: The Theology of the Apostle in the Light of Jewish Religious History*),[2] and Geza Vermes (in *Jesus the Jew*)[3] has aroused much critical interest from both Christians and Jews. Quite apart from broadening the Christian understanding of their own religious background, these works, as we have said, counterbalance the anti-Semitic elements of the New Testament. Secondly, fruitful Jewish-Christian encounter seems to be more of a possibility today because it is conducted on a personal level. Over the past few years encounters between Jews and Christians have been undertaken in friendship and understanding in Israel, Europe and the United States; such amicable dialogue has resulted in the formation of numerous associations of Jews and Christians throughout the world.

A third factor contributing to interfaith encounter concerns a significant theological development within the Church. In South America, as well as in other countries in the Third World, a new Christian theological development has been taking place in the last few decades. 'Liberation theology', as it is frequently called, has captured the imagination of both Roman Catholics and Protestants. Combining theory with practice, this movement attempts to utilize the insights of Marxist social criticism in forging a new vision of the

107

Christian message. Most importantly for Jewish-Christian encounter, liberation theologians have gone back to their Jewish roots in the Hebrew Bible. Suddenly Jewish and Christian writers find themselves using the same vocabulary and motifs, and this bond paves the way for a mutual examination of commonly shared religious ideals.

A NEW UNDERSTANDING OF JESUS

In the past Christians have understood Jesus as the risen Christ who sits at the right hand of the Father. In line with traditional Christology, liberation theologians also see Jesus in similar terms: He is the Messiah; He is the Word made flesh; He is the Incarnate God. Nevertheless, liberation theologians repeatedly emphasize that their concern is not to theorize abstractly about Christological doctrines. Such traditional theological reflection, they believe, has been misguided since it has tended to obscure the human figure of Jesus. Frequently Christ has been reduced to sublime abstraction, which has led to a spiritual conception of the Son of God divorced from Jesus' concrete historicity. Such a theoretically abstract presentation of Christ has also given rise to the view that Jesus was a pacifist who loved all human beings and died on behalf of all people in order to free them from sin. According to liberation theologians such an emphasis distorts the real nature of Jesus in that it exempts him from history and uses Christianity as a support for ideologies espousing peace and order.[4] Further, liberation theologians point out that if Christ is seen as the absolute in abstract terms, there is a tendency to neglect earthly matters; in particular, the emphasis on the absoluteness of Christ can bring about an unquestioning acceptance of the social and political status quo.[5]

In the light of these objections to traditional Christian speculation, liberation theologians have insisted that the historical Jesus should be the starting point for Christological reflection. In this endeavour Biblical hermeneutics cannot be taken to mean simply the art of understanding ancient texts; rather it also involves an identification with Jesus' life and message. This is so, liberationists maintain, since the tradition of the primitive Church preserved of Jesus only that which represented his function in the life of the faith of the community. Thus, understanding Jesus cannot be reduced to a scientific 'investigation'; instead, as Leonardo Boff explains, 'to really comprehend who Jesus is, one must approach him as one touched by and attached to him. Defining Jesus we are defining ourselves.

The more we know ourselves, the more we know Jesus'.[6]

Following this impetus, liberation theologians see a structural similarity between the situation in Jesus' time and in the modern world. Oppression and persecution in contemporary society as in 1st Century Palestine, they believe, are contrary to the Divine plan for mankind. In the Gospels Jesus initiated a programme of liberation; yet his struggle against the Jewish authorities illustrates the conflict that any project of liberation will provoke. The historical Jesus thus clarifies the chief elements of Christological faith: by following his life and cause in one's cwn life, the truth of Jesus emerges. As Leonardo Boff explains, 'Jesus does not present himself as the explanation of reality; he presents himself as an urgent demand for the transformation of that reality'.[7] By offering a critique of humanity and society, Jesus points the way to the fulfillment of the Kingdom of God.[8]

For Jews, liberation theology thus offers a new orientation to Jesus. Previously Jews and Christians have been unable to find common theological ground – instead of attempting to forge a bridge between the two faiths, Jews have repudiated Christian claims about Jesus' divinity while Christians have denounced Jews for their unwillingness to accept Christ as their Saviour. The doctrines of the Trinity, the Incarnation and the understanding of Jesus as the Messiah have separated the two traditions and have served as stumbling blocks to fruitful interfaith encounter. Today, however, liberation theology offers a profoundly different direction to Christian thought. Unlike theologians of the past, these writers are not concerned to analyze Jesus' dual nature as God and man; abstract speculation about the central issues of traditional Christology (divine personhood, hypostatic union, and so on) has been set aside. Instead, liberation theology focusses on the historical Jesus as the starting point for Christian reflection. As Jon Sobrino, the Spanish theologian, writes: 'Our Christology will . . . avoid abstractionism and the attendant danger of manipulating the Christ event. The history of the Church shows, from its very beginning . . . that any focusing on the Christ of faith will jeopardize the very essence of the Christian faith if it neglects the historical Jesus'.[9]

What is of crucial significance for Jewish-Christian dialogue is the primary emphasis here on understanding Jesus as a 1st-century Palestinian Jew. It is the flesh-and-blood Jesus of history who is of fundamental importance for liberation theologians; the concrete preaching and actions of Jesus himself provides the basis for the formulation of Christian theology. The historical context of the Gospels is in this way reclaimed for Christians, and Jesus' teaching in the New Testament is related directly to God's design as recorded in the Old Testament. In particular, Jesus is viewed as following in the footsteps of the great prophets of Ancient Israel. As I. Ellacuria insists, prophecy in the Old Testament and Jesus' mission in the New Testament must be related. 'The prophecy of the Old Testament', he writes, 'takes on its full ascendant import only in terms of what Jesus himself represents. By the same token the meaning of Jesus himself would escape us if we disregarded the history of prophecy'.[10]

From an historical standpoint then the picture of Jesus that emerges from the Gospel narratives is inextricably connected to his Jewish background. The consequence of this for Jews is profound for it opens the way to a fresh vision of Jesus' mission. His criticism of the religious establishment, like that of the pre-exilic prophets, should not be understood as a rejection of Judaism itself, as it certainly was not, but as a call to the nation to return to the God of their fathers. Seen in its true light, Jesus' teaching stands in the tradition of the ethical prophets of Ancient Israel, and it is to the prophetic books of the Bible that we must turn to find the crucial links that relate Jesus to his Jewish past. In this context the Jew can recognize Jesus as following the prophetic tradition even though he cannot say with the Christian liberation theologian that Jesus is 'God of God, light of light, very God of very God, begotten not made, being of one substance with the Father'.

THE KINGDOM OF GOD

Liberation theologians insist that the Kingdom of God as understood by Jesus is not the denial of history, but the elimination of its corruptibility. In the words of the Argentinian theologian José Miguez Bonino: 'God builds his Kingdom from within human history and its entirety; His action is a constant call and challenge to man. Man's response is realized in the concrete area of history with its economic, political and ideological options'.[11] The growth and ultimate fulfillment of the Kingdom rests on a struggle against exploitation, alienation, oppression and persecution; it embraces all: the world, society, and the individual. It is this totality which is to be transformed through the activity that God has initiated but not yet fully completed.

Within this unfolding of God's eschatological scheme, liberation theologians maintain that Christians have a crucial role. It is the responsibility of each person to engage in the quest for the liberation of the oppressed – this is a task which obliges all Christians to offer assistance not only in the religious and spiritual domain, but in the sphere of politics, economics and culture. According to P. Bigo, 'It is not enough to say that doing so is a condition for salvation; it is the very coming of the Kingdom in its temporal form'.[12] The way of the Kingdom implies the building of a just society. As Gutierrez notes, a situation of injustice is incompatible with the Kingdom: 'the building of a just society has worth in terms of the Kingdom, or in more current phraseology, to participate in the process of liberation is already in a certain sense, a salvific work'.[13] Entrance into the Kingdom is open only to those who practice justice and distribute to the poor whatever they have over and above their real needs.

The heart of the Gospel message is subversive; it embodies the Israelite hope for an end of the domination of man over man. The struggle for the establishment of God's Kingdom involves the overthrow of established powers – political involvement is imperative. To know God is to be concerned for the creation of a new order regulated by the principle of love. In the words of M. Echegoyen: 'Our hope may refer to the Kingdom, to the second coming of Christ, but it begins here and now, in this society in which I happen to live and for whose transformation – humanization – I am inescapably responsible . . . loving one's neighbour, which is the first commandment by definition, today means working to change the structures that can destroy my neighbour, the people, the poor'.[14] For liberation theologians such change involves the eradication of poverty which is incompatible with a Kingdom of love and justice. Some theologians even go so far as to advocate the necessity of violent revolution as a means of altering the economic structures of society.[15]

In the writings of these theologians then there is a common conviction that the rights of the poor must be upheld in a quest for the liberation of the oppressed. Peace, justice, love and freedom are dominating motifs in their understanding of the coming of God's Kingdom. Breaking with traditional Christian theology, liberation theologians emphasize that these are not internal attitudes – they are social realities which need to be implemented in human history. Gutierrez eloquently formulates this shift away from the values of the past: 'a poorly understood spiritualization', he writes, 'has often made us forget the human consequences of the eschatological promises and the power to transform unjust social structures which

they imply. The elimination of misery and exploitation is a sign of
the coming of the Kingdom'.[16] Thus the Kingdom of God, contrary
to what many Christians believe, does not signify something that is
outside this world. It involves the effort of each individual to bring
about a new order, a mission based on Jesus' actions and teachings
as recorded in the gospels.

What is of central importance for Christian-Jewish encounter is the
liberationist's insistence that the coming of the Kingdom involves
individual participation in the creation of a new world. Though
Judaism rejects the Christian claim that Jesus has ushered in the
period of Messianic redemption, Jews have steadfastly adhered
to the belief that God is a supreme ruler who calls all men to
join him in bringing about the Kingdom of God on earth. This
understanding is an essential element of Psalmist theology, and it
is a central theological motif of the Hebrew Bible. In later rabbinic
literature, this vision of man's role in bringing about God's Kingdom
is elaborated further.

According to the rabbis, the Kingdom of God takes place in this
world; it is established by man's obedience to the Divine will. The
Kingdom of God consists in a complete moral order on earth –
the reign of trust, righteousness and holiness among all men and
nations. The fulfillment of this conception ultimately rests with the
coming of the Messiah; nevertheless, it is man's duty to participate
in the creation of a better world in anticipation of the Messianic
redemption. In the words of the rabbis: 'Man is a co-worker with
God in the work of creation'.[17]

According to rabbinic theology, man is the centre of creation, for
it is only he among all created beings who can through righteousness
make the Kingdom glorious.[18] In rabbinic midrash, the view is
expressed that God's Kingship did not come into operation until
man was created: 'when the Holy One, blessed be He, consulted
the Torah as to the creation of the world, he answered, "Master
of the world, if there be no host, over whom will the King reign,
and if there be no peoples praising him, where is the glory of the
King?"'.[19] It is only man then who can make the Kingdom glorious;
God wants to reign over free agents who can act as His co-partners in
perfecting the world. What God requires is obedience to His ways of
righteousness and justice: 'You are my lovers and friends'. 'You walk
in my ways', God declares to Israel. 'As the Omnipotent is merciful
and gracious, long-suffering and abundant in goodness so be ye . . .
feeding the hungry, giving drink to the thirsty, clothing the naked,

ransoming the captives, and marrying the orphans'.[20] Throughout
Biblical and rabbinic literature, Jews were encouraged to strive for
the highest conception of life in which the rule of truth, righteousness
and holiness would be established among mankind. Such a desire is
the eternal hope of God's people – a longing for God's Kingdom as
expressed in the daily liturgy of the synagogue.

Here we can see the point of intersection between the Jewish
faith and Christian liberation theology. For both Jews and liberation
theologians the coming of the Kingdom in which God's heavenly rule
will be made manifest is a process in which all human beings have a
role. It involves the struggle for the reign of justice and righteousness
on earth. The Kingdom is not – as has been the case in traditional
Christianity – an internalized, spiritualized, other-wordly conception.
Rather it involves human *activity* in a historical context. Drawing on
the Old and New Testaments, liberation theologians have attempted
to demonstrate the tasks Christians must undertake in the building
of the Kingdom. Similarly, the rabbis elaborated the teaching of the
Torah about man's partnership with God in bringing God's rule. For
both faiths, the moral life is at the centre of the unfolding of God's
plan for humanity. Such a shared vision should serve to unite Jews
and Christians in a joint undertaking to transform our imperfect
world in anticipation of the Divine promise of the eschatological
fulfillment at the end of time.

THE EXODUS

For liberation theologians Jesus is the liberator who paves the way
for the realization of the Kingdom of God on earth. In presenting
this message of hope liberation theologians repeatedly emphasize
the centrality of the exodus from Egypt. 'The Exodus experience',
Gutierrez writes, 'is paradigmatic. It remains vital and contemporary due to similar historical experiences which the People of
God undergo . . . it structures our faith in the gift of the Father's
love. In Christ and through the Spirit, men are becoming one in the
very heart of history'.[21] Thus these Christian theologians look to the
history of the Jewish people for inspiration in their struggle against
exploitation and oppression in contemporary society, and this Divine
act of redemption of the Israelite nation provides a basis for a critique
of traditional Christian thought and modern society.

Liberation theologians stress that the Exodus was not simply
an event in the history of the Jewish people; instead it evoked

a deep response on the part of the ancestors of those who had been liberated. As J.S. Croatto writes: 'The word [Exodus] was "recharged" with fresh meanings by successive hermeneutical re-readings up to the time that it was fixed permanently as expressing a whole world-view in the Exodus account in its present form'.[23] The profundity of the Exodus therefore consists in its significance for later generations; the past holds a promise for those who understand its relevance. The Exodus is fraught with meaning. For Third-World theologians it is an account of liberation of oppressed peoples, and using this framework, they believe it is possible to understand the plight of those who are presently afflicted from the perspective of the Biblical Exodus – the situation of peoples in economic, political, social or cultural 'bondage'.[24]

In this context liberation theologians stress Moses' crucial role in the process of liberation. The Argentinian theologian Enrique Dussel, for example, begins his study of the history and theology of liberation by focussing on Moses' call to lead his people out of captivity.[25] Moses had fled to the desert because he had killed an Egyptian. He lived comfortably as a herdsman with his wife, his father-in-law and his flocks. But one day he heard God speak to him out of a bush. 'Moses, Moses', God cried, 'I have seen the affliction of my people who are in Egypt, and have heard their cry because of their taskmasters; I know their sufferings, and I have come down to deliver them out of the hand of the Egyptians . . . Come I will send you to Pharoah that you may bring forth my people, the sons of Israel, out of Egypt'.[26] this Divine encounter is represented by Dussel as follows:[27]

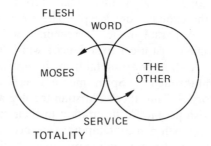

Here God – the Other – reveals Himself to Moses: Moses heard God's command: 'Liberate my people out of Egypt'. Established in the totality of fleshly, daily life, Moses responded by becoming the liberator of his people. We, too, are being called continually, Dussel contends, but we do not hear anything. Yet, like Moses, we must awaken ourselves to the Divine command. As Dussel writes: 'God . . . keeps on revealing himself to us as the Other who summons us. He is the first Other. If I do not listen to my fellowmen in bondage, then I am not listening to God either'.[28]

Liberation theologians also utilize the Exodus narrative to explain that God guides the destiny of the persecuted. In the flight from Egypt the Bible stresses that God leads the people: He did not take them out by way of the land of the Philistines although that was near for God said, 'Lest the people repent when the see war and return to Egypt. But God led the people round by way of the wilderness towards the Red Sea'.[29] When the Egyptian army attempted to capture the Israelites, God intervened so that they were saved. Once Israel had crossed the Red Sea, God sustained them in their wanderings: God gave them sweet water at Marah; He sent them manna and quail in the desert; He gave them safe passage through the Transjordan; He delivered the Amorite Kings into the hands of the Israelites. Not only did God deliver and protect His people, He also led them to their own land where they were no longer oppressed. Before Moses' death, God proclaimed to Joshua: 'I myself will be with you'. And he stated that he would be with Joshua as He was with Moses. The conquest is thus the second stage of God's deliverance, and even the prostitute of Jericho knew that God would take the side of His people as he had in the past: 'I know that the Lord has given you the land . . . we have heard how the Lord dried up the water of the Red Sea before you when you came out of Egypt . . .'[30]

Thus it is clear that the experience of the Exodus is typologically significant for liberation theologians; it is a paradigm of Divine liberation of the oppressed and persecuted. And just as the Exodus is a key element in liberation theology, so it has been in the self-understanding of the Jewish people through the centuries. In the Biblical period, details of the Exodus were recorded in cultic sayings, in Wisdom literature, and by the prophets and after the Exile the Exodus continued to play a dominant role in the Jewish faith. In particular, the Festival of Passover was regarded as crucially important in the religious life of the people. A.L. Finkelstein remarks: 'The Passover celebration commemorates an event which will probably symbolize for all time the essential meaning of freedom, namely freedom devoted to a purpose. When Israel came forth from bondage, it was not simply to enjoy liberty, but to make of liberty an instrument of service . . . the Israelites alone made the moment of their origin as a people one of permanent self-dedication to the principle of universal freedom as the essential prerequisite for spiritual growth. Hence the event has meaning for all living peoples'.[31]

In post-Englightenment Judaism, modern writers have emphasized the significance of the themes of liberty, redemption and freedom as found in the Passover festival. Franz Rosenzweig, for example, argues that there is an intrinsic connection between the Passover and the Sabbath. The Sabbath, he maintained, is a reminder of the Exodus from Egypt: 'The freedom of the man-servant and the maid-servant which it proclaims is conditioned by the deliverance of the people as a people from the servitude of Egypt. And in every command to respect the freedom of even the man-servant, or even the alien among the people, the law of God renews the awareness of the connection holding between the freedom within the people, a freedom decreed by God, and the freeing of the people from Egyptian servitude, a liberation enacted by God'.[32] Furthermore, the Passover meal is a symbol of Israel's vocation as a people; the deliverance of the nation affords a glimpse of its destiny. It is not only today that enemies rise up against the Jews; they have arisen in every generation, and God has always taken the side of his chosen people, for they have survived their enemies. All this points to the ultimate redemption as prophesied by Isaiah – of the day when the wolf shall dwell with the lamb and the world shall be as full of the knowledge of the Lord as the sea is of water.[33]

The moral implications of the redemption from Egypt are emphasized in *The Ethics of Judaism* by Moritz Lazarus. The Exodus, he writes, has a predominant place in the Biblical and rabbinic cycle of religious ideas. The most exulted moral statutes in the Torah concerning the treatment of strangers are connected with the Exodus, and are, from a psychological point of view, impressively inculcated by means of the injunction: 'Ye know the heart of the stranger'. The prophets and the psalmists employ this event to illustrate God's providence and grace, and the rabbis deduce from it the two fundamental aspects of Jewish ethics: the notion of liberty and man's ethical task. Throughout the history of Judaism, Lazarus maintains that 'the notion of liberty, inner moral and spiritual liberty, cherished as a pure, exalted ideal, possible only under and through the Law, was associated with the memory of the redemption from Egyptian slavery, and this memory in turn was connected with symbolic practices accompanying every act, pleasure, and celebration'.[34]

Kaufmann Kohler saw in the Passover a symbol of thanksgiving and hope which sustained the Jewish nation in their tribulations: 'The Passover festival with its "night of Divine watching" endowed the Jew ever anew with endurance during the dark night of medieval tyranny and with faith in "the Keeper of Israel who slumbereth not nor sleepeth"'. Moreover, he believed that the feast of redemption promises a day of liberty to those who continue to struggle under oppression and exploitation: 'The modern Jew begins to see in the reawakening of his religious and social life in Western lands the token of the future liberation of all mankind. The Passover feast brings him the clear and hopeful message of freedom for humanity from all bondage of today and of spirit'.[35]

In *Creed and Life* Morris Joseph also focusses on the contemporary significance of Passover. It is, he believes, the greatest of all the historical festivals in that it brings the Jew into close contact with the past. No other festival, he contends, so powerfully appeals to historical sympathies. At the Passover ceremony the Jew is at one with his redeemed ancestors; he shares with them the consciousness of their freedom, their sense of nationality that is beginning to stir in their hearts. 'He shares', he writes, 'their glowing hopes, the sweet joy of newly recovered manhood'. Through God's redemption the Israelites were able to free themselves from despair, and they share in this deliverance. 'We march forth', he states, 'with them from the scenes of oppression in gladness and gratitude. The ideal of the rabbis fulfills itself. "In every generation it is for the Jew to think that he himself went forth from Egypt"' (Pesahim 10:5).[36]

Ahad Ha-Am concentrates on Moses the Liberator as an ideal type of hero. Moses, he points out, was neither a warrior, nor statesman. Instead he was a prophet who put justice into action. Confronted by acts of iniquity, he took the side of the victim – the early events of his life in which he struggled against injustice served as a prelude to his revolt against Egyptian oppression: 'That great moment dawned in the wilderness, far from the turmoil of life. The prophet's soul is weary of the endless struggle, and longs for peace and rest. He seeks the solitude of the shepherd's life, goes into the wilderness with his sheep, and reaches Horeb, the mountain of the Lord. But even here he finds no rest. He feels in his innermost being that he has not yet fulfilled his mission . . . Suddenly the prophet hears the voice of the Lord – the voice he knows so well – calling to him from some forgotten corner of his innermost being: "I am the God of they father . . . I have surely seen the affliction of My people that are in Egypt . . . Come now, therefore, and I will send thee unto Pharaoh, that thou mayest bring forth My people the children of Israel out of Egypt"'.[37]

In the account of the Exodus from Egypt, therefore, the faith of Israel is portrayed as a response to God's will. What is required of Israel is obedient participation in the act of emancipation. For liberation theologians this Biblical anchorage leads to a practical orientation of the faith: praxis, rather than theological reflection, is understood as the key to Christian witness. Liberation theologians stress that theology must start from actions committed to the process of liberation; theology is conceived as a critical reflection on praxis. For Jews this emphasis on the concrete dimension of faith is vital. The Jewish hope lies in God's rule on earth – this is the goal of the history of the world in which the Jewish people have a central role. Throughout the Bible and in rabbinic literature ethical behaviour is the predominant theme – by doing God's will the Jew can help to complete His work of creation. As in the case of liberation theology, the Jewish religion focusses on orthopraxis rather than theological orthodoxy. Theological speculation is not seen as authoritative; instead moral praxis is at the core of the faith. Deeds of goodness rather than dogma take precedence; in this Jews and Christian liberation theologians are united in the quest for the total elimination of human wickedness.

AREAS OF SOCIAL CONCERN

This shared vision then can serve as a bridge between the two traditions. Liberation theology's return to traditional Jewish ideals should make it possible for both faiths to work together as never before in areas of social concern. In this liberation theologians have paved the way for such common endeavour by explaining how ethical values rooted in the Bible can be put into practice.

For liberation theologians the poor are the starting point of theological reflection rather than abstract metaphysical theories; the view 'from below' is essential. Liberation theology claims that it is in the situation of the poor that God is to be found; as in

Scripture, God is the saviour of the enslaved. What is required then is solidarity as a protest against the poverty in which the poor are forced to live. As Gutierrez explains, it is a 'way of identifying oneself with the interests of the oppressed classes and challenging the exploitation that victimized them'.[38] Poverty is something to be fought against and destroyed; God's salvation is achieved in the process of liberation. The problems and struggles of the poor are our own – the vocation of every person is to opt for human love and compassion. As Cussianovich explains 'Solidarity with the poor implies a commitment to turn human love into a collective experience from which there is no turning back'.[39]

As God's long-suffering servants, the Jewish people should find this message of solidarity with the poor of paramount significance. In the Bible the prophets condemned every kind of abuse. Scripture speaks of positive action to prevent poverty from spreading – in Leviticus and Deuteronomy there is detailed legislation designed to prevent the amassing of wealth and consequent exploitation of the unfortunate. Jews should thus feel an obligation to eliminate poverty and suffering from contemporary society. In particular, they should address themselves to the economic problems that affect various groups: the young who are frustrated by the lack of opportunity to obtain training and work, labourers who are frequently ill-paid and find difficulty in defending themselves, the unemployed who are discarded because of the harsh realities of economic life, and the old who are often marginalized and disregarded. In all such cases, the Jewish people – who have consistently endured hardship – should feel drawn to the oppressed of modern society, sharing in their misery.

In pleading the case of the poor, liberation theologians – who are predominantly South American – have focussed on the plight of the oppressed in the Third World. The underdevelopment of the poor countries, they point out, is the consequence of the development of other countries. In the words of Gutierrez, 'the dynamics of the capitalist economy led to the establishment of a centre and a periphery, simultaneously generating progress and growing wealth for the few and social imbalances, political tensions, and poverty for the many'.[40] The countries of Latin America were born in this context; they emerged as dependent societies in consequence of economic exploitation. Such unequal structures dominate and determine the character of the particular cultures of these countries, and they necessitate a defence of the status quo. Even modernization and the introduction of a greater rationality into the economies of these societies is required by the vested interests of the dominant groups. Imperialism and colonization are the hallmarks of the past and present economic and cultural climate. From a cultural point of view as well such imbalance between 'developed' and 'underdeveloped' countries is acute – the underdeveloped areas are always far away from the cultural level of the industrialized centres.

The perception of the fact of this dependence and its consequences has made it possible to formulate a policy of reform. According to liberation theology, human freedom cannot be brought about by a developmentalist approach that maintains élitism. Instead liberationists grapple with the existing relationships based on injustice in a global frame. By analyzing the mechanisms that are being used to keep the poor of the world under domination, liberation theologians assert that authentic development can only take place if the domination of the great capitalistic countries is eliminated. What is required is a transformation that will radically change the conditions in which the poor live. In this process, human beings are seen as assuming conscious responsibility for their own destiny. As Gutierrez explains: 'this understanding provides a dynamic context and broadens the horizons of the desired social changes. In this perspective the unfolding of all of man's dimensions is demanded – a man who makes himself throughout his life and throughout history. The gradual attainment of true freedom leads to the creation of a new man and a qualitatively different society'.[41]

These themes of liberation and emancipation should have important resonances for the Jewish community. As we have seen, the Biblical narrative portrays the Ancient Israelites as an oppressed nation redeemed by God. Throughout history the Jewish people have been God's suffering servant – despised and rejected of men, smitten and afflicted. Through such suffering Jews are able to gain a sympathetic awareness of the situation of others. The lesson of the Passover is at the heart of Jewish aspirations for all humanity, as we read in the Passover liturgy: 'May He who broke Pharoah's yoke for ever shatter all fetters of oppression and hasten the day when swords shall, at last, be broken and wars ended. Soon may He cause the glad tidings of redemption to be heard in all lands, so that mankind – freed from violence and from wrong, and united in an eternal covenant of brotherhood – may celebrate the universal Passover in the name of our God of Freedom'.[42] In this spirit, it is possible for Jews to heed the plea of those who are downtrodden in the Third World; linked with liberationists, they can press for a restructuring of the economic sphere. By combatting exploitation and indifference, it is possible for both Jews and Christians to participate in the struggle to bring about a better way of life.

This preoccupation with the Third World does not preclude concern for the oppressed in the First World countries. Liberation theologians stress that in the First World there are also grave inequalities between rich and poor. Despite the higher general standard of living in these countries, there nevertheless exist for many sub-standard living conditions, poor health, concern about jobs, and constant worry about money. Further, as L. Cormie points out, 'the epidemic rates of alcoholism and other forms of drug abuse, of rape, wife-beating, child abuse, and other forms of violence, of psychosomatic diseases like certain kinds of ulcers and heart disease, suggest the depths of anguish and alienation which many experience in our society'.[43] He goes on to argue that there are essentially two different segments in the labour market: primary sector jobs involving high wages, good working conditions, employment stability and job security, and secondary sector jobs involving low wages, poor working conditions, harsh and arbitrary discipline and little opportunity for advancement.[44]

Consumerism is a dominant ideology that contributes to such inequality – the most important questions are frequently concerned with how to save taxes and where to get the best prices for goods. As D. Solle explains: 'this attempt to focus our interests and life priorities on hairspray, cat food, and travelling to the Virign Islands represents an assault on the One in whose image I am created. It is an assault on human dignity. Consumerism means that my eyes are offended, my ears are obstructed, and my hands are robbed of their creativity'.[45] Exploitation in the First World is thus different from what is found in Third World countries. Inhabitants of the First World nations have become enmeshed in a cultural system that frequently perceives value in quantitative economic terms with an emphasis on having rather than being. Such hedonistic tendencies – generated by fiercely competitive economic interests – tends to divide the affluent from the poor. And nowhere is this more apparent than in the situation of the black community. In the United States, for example, as L. Cormie explains, slavery did not disappear with the disintegration of the plantation economy; in the period after the Civil War most blacks were relegated to work as sharecroppers. And even after the expansion of Northern industries, most blacks were channelled into the least desirable jobs and forced to live in the dilapidated city areas. Only a minority of blacks have been able to gain access to the privileges and status promised by the American dream.[46]

Having once laboured under the Egyptian yoke as slaves of Pharaoh, Jews today should be able to sympathize with the plight of such underprivileged sectors in the First World. In these countries, as in the Third World, the gap between the rich and the poor needs to be bridged, and facing such a challenge Jews should be able to unite with their liberationist brothers. The attempt to build a more just society should propel Jews into the vanguard of those who attempt to restructure institutions along more egalitarian lines. By putting themselves in the shoes of the disadvantaged, Jews can envisage what life must be for the underprivileged. In this way Jews – along with liberationists – can bring to the community policies of caring and sharing; this is theology 'from below', from the standpoint of those who are neglected and marginalized. By bringing their suffering to bear on these problems, the Jewish community can make a major contribution to the redemption of the poor.

In connection with this discussion of First World poverty, liberation theology has focussed on life in the inner-city. Here the distinction between the powerful and the powerless is most clearly evident. In the words of the English theologian John Vincent, these are 'the people' in the area of your town you don't go to, the place you pass through to get to city or suburb, the place you keep your children away from, the place you pray for, thanking God you do not belong there'.[47]

What is needed to remedy this situation is a new consciousness, an awareness of the calamities of inner-city deprivation. First-World theologians influenced by liberation theology contend that the proper Christian response is to engage in urban mission. By ministering to those at the bottom of society, Christians can affirm through their efforts that God is concerned with the plight of those facing adversity. Such activity constitutes an acted parable of the Kingdom, bringing into focus the meaning of the Gospel. Such a parable declares that the Christian cause is served best – not by places of power and influence – but by situations of vulnerability and powerlessness. According to liberationists, Christ is incarnate in the inner city. In his own time he belonged to the lower end of society; in today's world he is to be found also among the lowly. Urban mission thus aims to discover Jesus' message in the economic and cultural impoverishment of city life; from this vantage point, the Christian can strive to ameliorate the conditions of the downtrodden.

In pursuit of this goal, Jews too can enter into the life of the inner-city. Here they can embark on a task of reconstruction and restoration. Remembering their sojourn in the land of Egypt, they can identify with the impoverished; by going into the city, Jews can work alongside and for the betterment of the poor. The facts of the inner-city demand such commitment to change, and in this vocation liberationists can stand shoulder to shoulder with their Jewish brothers. Through urban mission Jews and Christians can affirm that hope for the modern world lies in a sympathetic response and dedication to the weak. Beginning at the bottom, it is possible to work for the creation of a community in which all people are able to regain their sense of pride and self-fulfillment. By labouring together in the neediest areas, the two faiths can join forces to bring about God's Kingdom on earth.

WOMEN'S EMANCIPATION

Liberation theology has also been concerned about the plight of women. Feminist theologians in particular have attempted to delineate the Biblical traditions encapsulating the liberating experiences and visions of the people of Israel so as to free women from oppressive sexist structures, institutions and internalized values. In the view of these writers, women have been and continue to be socialized into subservient roles – either they are forced into domestic labour or they hold badly-paid jobs. Only seldom do a few women manage to occupy jobs in male professions. According to the American theologian Rosemary Radford Reuther: 'Work segregation is still the fundamental pattern of society. Women's work universally is regarded as of low status and prestige, poorly paid, with little security, generally of a rote and menial character. The sexist structuring of society means the elimination of women from those activities that allow for and express enhancement and development of the self, its artistic, intellectual and leadership capacities'.[48] Throughout society, these theologians maintain, the full humanity of woman is distorted, diminished and denied.

To restore women's self-respect, liberationists focus on a number of Biblical themes – God's defence and vindication of the oppressed; the criticism of the dominant systems of power; the vision of a new age in which iniquity will be overcome; God's intended reign of peace. Feminist theology applies the message of the prophets to the situation of women; the critique of hierarchy thus becomes a critique of partriarchy. For these writers, images of God must include feminine roles and experiences, and language about God must be transformed from its masculine bias. For Christians, they believe, it is necessary to move beyond the typology of Christ and the Church as representing the dominant male and submissive female role. Within Church structures, women must be given full opportunities to participate at every level, including the ministry. In the civil sphere too women must be granted full equality before the law – a stance which calls for the repeal of all discriminatory legislation. There must be equal pay for equal work and full access to the professions. Many liberationists also insist on women's right to reproduction, self-defence, sex education, birth control and abortion as well as protection against sexual harrassment, wife-beating, rape and pornography.

In the Jewish community there has similarly been a growing aware-ness of discrimination against women. Over the last two decades a significant number of Jewish feminists have attempted to restructure the position given to women in traditional Judaism. In the past Jewish women were not directly involved with most Jewish religious activity. Today, however, Jewish women are trying to find ways to live as full Jews. In their attempt to reconcile Judaism and feminism these women are rediscovering various aspects of Jewish life: some study the place of women in Jewish history; others examine religious texts for clues to women's influence on Jewish life; while others redefine and feminize certain features of the Jewish tradition.

In seeking equal access with men, these feminists stress that women should be allowed to participate in the areas from which they have previously been excluded, namely, serving as witnesses in a religious court, initiating divorce proceedings, acting as part of a quorum for prayer, receiving rabbinic training and ordination as well as qualifying as cantors.

For these Jewish feminists, all formal distinctions in the religious as well as the secular sphere between men and women should be abolished. As Schneider explains: 'We have been trying to take charge of events in our own lives and in every area of what we call Jewish life: religion, the community, the family, and all our interpersonal relations'.[49] Given this impetus to liberate women from the restrictions of patriarchial structures, there is every reason for Jewish and Christian feminists to share their common concerns and objectives.

ECOLOGY

Not only do liberation theologians advocate a programme of liberation for all human beings; they also draw attention to human responsibility for the environment: ecological liberation is an important element in their policy of emancipation. Ever since the scientific revolution, nature has been secularized; no corner of the natural world has been immune from human control. Yet in this expansion of material productivity, the earth has been exploited to such a degree that pollution, famine and poverty threaten humanity's very existence. In this light, liberationists assert that human beings must accept responsibility for the environment. In the words of R. Reuther, 'the privilege of intelligence . . . is not a privilege to alienate and dominate the world without concern for the welfare of all other forms of life. On the contrary, it is the responsibility to become the caretaker and cultivator of the whole ecological community upon which our existence depends . . . We need to remake the earth in a way that converts our minds to nature's logic of ecological harmony. This will necessarily be a new synthesis, a new creation in which human nature and non-human nature become friends in the creating of a liveable and sustainable cosmos'.[50]

Such reform calls for changed attitudes to the natural world; liberationists argue that human beings must accept that balance in nature is an essential characteristics of the earth's ecosystem. Human intervention inevitably upsets such a natural balance; thus steps must continually be taken to restore equilibrium to the earth. In particular, environmentalists point out that care must be taken about the use of pesticides. Habitations previously available to many living creatures have been destroyed; for agricultural purposes, people should attempt to maintain diversity within nature and this requires a careful monitoring of the use of chemical substances. Pollution too has been regarded as a major problem in the modern world; industry, urban waste and motor transport have all adversely affected the environment, and conservationists maintain that adequate control must be exercised over the use of pollutants which infect air and water resources. Furthermore, environmentalists contend that human beings must take steps to preserve endangered species and avoid inflicting cruelty on wild and domestic animals. In all these endeavours there is a role for the Jewish community; the recognition that humanity is part of the ecological whole is fundamental to Jewish thought. According to the Jewish faith, man has been given authority over nature, and such responsibility should curb the crude exploitation of the earth for commercial purposes. Such a Divine fiat should foster a sympathetic understanding of the whole ecological situation engendering for Jews as for Christians an attitude of caring concern for all of God's creation.

These then are some of the areas in which Jews can unite with Christian liberation theologians to bring about God's Kingdom. In pursuit of a common goal of freedom from oppression, committed Jews and Christians can become a saving remnant in the modern world, embodying the liberating message of Scripture. Like Abraham they can hope against hope in labouring to build a more just and humane world. In the words of H. Camara, they can become an Abrahamic minority, attentive to the cry of oppression: 'We are told that Abraham and other patriarchs heard the voice of God. Can we also hear the Lord's call? We live in a world where millions of our fellow men live in inhuman conditions, practically in slavery. If we are not deaf we hear the cries of the oppressed. Their cries are the voice of God. We who live in rich countries where there are always pockets of under-development and wretchedness, hear if we want to hear, the unvoiced demands of those who have no voice and no hope. The pleas of those who have no voice and no hope are the voice of God'.[51]

CONCLUSION

Throughout history the Jewish people have been God's suffering servant, yet inspired by a vision of God's reign on earth they have been able to transcend their own misfortunes in attempting to ameliorate the lot of others. In the contemporary world, where Jews are often comfortable and affluent, this prophetic message of liberation can too easily be forgotten. Liberation theology, however – with its focus on the desperate situation of those at the bottom of society – can act as a clarion call to the Jewish community, awakening the people of Israel to their divinely-appointed task. The Jewish tradition points to God's Kingdom as the goal and hope of mankind – a world in which all men and nations shall turn away from iniquity and injustice. This is not the hope of bliss in a future life, but the building up of the Divine Kingdom of truth and peace among all peoples in the here and now. As Isaiah declared: 'I will also give thee for a light to the nations, that my salvation may be unto the end of the earth'.[52] In this mission the people of Israel and their Christian liberationist brethren can join ranks; championing the cause of the oppressed, afflicted and persecuted, both faiths can unite in common cause and fellowship proclaiming together the ancient message of the Jewish liturgy in their struggle to create a better world:

> O Lord our God, impose Thine awe upon all Thy works, and let Thy dread be upon all Thou hast created, that they may all form one single band to do Thy will with a perfect heart . . . Our God and God of our fathers, reveal Thyself in Thy splendor as King over all the inhabitants of the world, that every handiwork of Thine may know that Thou hast made it, and every creature may acknowledge that Thou hast created it, and whatsoever hath breath in its nostrils may say: the Lord God of Israel is King, and His dominion ruleth over all.[53]

Or, as Jesus put it rather more concisely:
'Thy Kingdom come, Thy will be done on Earth as it is in Heaven'.

11
Judaism
and the
Universe of Faiths

Recently there has been considerable discussion in Christian circles about the relationship between Christianity and the world religions. Traditionally Christians have insisted that anyone outside the Church cannot be saved. To quote a classic instance of this view, the Council of Florence in the fifteenth century declared that: 'no one remaining outside the Catholic Church, not just pagans but also Jews or heretics or schismatics, can become partakers of eternal life; but they will go to everlasting fire which was prepared for the devil and his angels. Unless before the end of life they are joined to the Church'.[1]

Increasingly, however, for many this view has seemed highly improbable in the light of contact with other faiths. An important document issued by the Catholic Church in 1965 (*Nostra Aetate*), for example, declared that the truth which enlightens every man is reflected also in non-Christian religions.[2] Nevertheless, while recognizing the value of other religions, this declaration maintains that the Christian is at the same time under the obligation to preach that Christ is the Way, the Truth, and the Life.[3]

Similar attitudes have also been adopted by various Christian theologians. Karl Rahner, for example, argues that salvation is open to adherents of other faiths since the devout Muslim, Hindu, Sikh or Jew can be regarded as an anonymous Christian – a status granted to people who have not expressed any desire for it.[4] Again, according to Hans Kung, the way is open to all men to attain eternal life in the world's religions. As Kung remarks, 'A man is to be saved within the religion that is made available to him in his historical situation'. In this manner the world's religions are 'the way of salvation, in universal salvation history; the general way of salvation, we can say, for the ordinary people of the world's religions, the more common, the "ordinary" way of salvation, as against which the way of salvation in the Church occurs as something very special and extraordinary'.[5]

Other Christian theologians have taken this view further by declaring that Christians must recognize the experience of God in Christ to be but one of many different Divine encounters with what has been given to different historical and cultural segments of mankind. In this light Christianity should lay no claim to superiority. In the words of Professor John Hick, the most important advocate of this view, 'in His infinite fullness and richness of being He exceeds all our human attempts to grasp Him in thought . . . the devout in the various great world religions are in fact worshipping the one God, but through different, overlapping concepts or mental icons of Him'.[6]

JUDAISM AND OTHER FAITHS

Recently in the modern Jewish world, however, scant attention has been paid to this issue of interfaith relations. Though there is an interest in the development of Jewish-Christian dialogue as well as isolated instances of Jewish-Christian-Muslim encounter, contemporary Jewish thinkers have not seriously considered the place of Judaism in the context of man's religious experience. This is regrettable since from the very earliest period Jews gave considerable thought to this crucial question.

In the Biblical period there was friction between Israel and other religions. Pagan deities were described in the Bible in the most negative way; they are 'elilim' – non-entities, loathsome and abominable. The worship of God is the way of faith; other religions are false. Yet despite such condemnation of pagan worship, the prophets did not plead for other nations to give up their gods. According to Deuteronomy, God permits the nations to serve their own deities: 'these the Lord your God allotted to other peoples everywhere under heaven'.[7] Indeed, it is even suggested that when non-Jews worship their gods, they are actually worshipping the God of Israel. According to Malachi, whose words can be interpreted in this way, 'from the rising of the sun even unto the going down of the same my name is great among the nations; and in every place offerings are presented unto my name, even pure oblations, for my name is great among the nations'.[8]

The rabbis continued the struggle against idolatry. The tractate Avodah Zarah in the Babylonian Talmud is devoted to the laws regarding the worship of other gods in the Greek and Roman religion as well as in Zoroastrianism, Christianity and Gnostic dualism. Nevertheless, rabbinic Judaism maintained that salvation is open to non-Jews as well as Jews as long as they observe the seven precepts of the sons of Noah. These are classified as follows: (1) Not worship idols; (2) Not to commit murder; (3) Not to commit adultery and incest; (4) Not to eat a limb torn from a living animal; (5) Not to blaspheme; (6) Not to steal; (7) To have an adequate system of law and justice.[9]

In the Medieval period in Europe the two rival faiths to Judaism were Christianity and Islam. The general view of Jewish thinkers in the Middle Ages was that Islam was not to be classified as idolatry, but there was considerable debate regarding Christianity.[10] But despite this uncertainty about the status of the Christian faith, it was not unusual to find some Jewish writers who regarded the teachings of Christians and Muslims as contributing to the spiritual life. Bahya Ibn Pakudah, for example, relied on Sufi teachers and defended his right to use them as teachers of religion.[11] Nevertheless, as religious faiths, Islam and Christianity were unanimously regarded as false, and there is simply no mention of Far Eastern religions in rabbinic sources.

By the time of the Enlightenment it was widely held among Jews that Christians and Muslims were in no way to be included in the harsh condemnation of heathens in classical sources. The general view was that these denunciations applied only to the ancient pagans and to contemporary idolators. Thus, Phineas Elijah Hurwitz writes that Jeremiah's injunction: 'Pour out Thy wrath upon the nations that know Thee not' (Jer. 10.25) refers to nations that do not know God, 'like the men of India and Japan who worship fire and water and who are called 'heathen'.[12] The legal authorities of this period all view Far Eastern religions in this way. This is the position, for example, of Rabbi Ezekkel Landau concerning a priest who married a Hindu woman according to Hindu rite, but later divorced her and repented of his actions. Jewish law rules that a priest who had once worshipped idols is not permitted to bless the people even after his repentance. But in this case Rabbi Landau permitted him to bless the people because his participation in a marriage service did not in and of itself constitute idolatrous worship. The clear assumption lying behind this decision is that the Hindu faith should be understood as idolatrous.[13]

THREE MODELS OF JUDAISM
AND THE WORLD'S RELIGIONS

From this brief survey we can see that from the earliest times
the Jewish community had a selectively tolerant attitude to other
religions. Jews did not attempt to convert non-Jews even though they
regarded their own faith as the touchstone of truth. Nonetheless, they
viewed all other religions as false except insofar as they agreed with
Judaism. No doubt this was the reason why rabbinic authorities did
not view Islam as idolatry whereas they maintained that polytheistic
religions such as Zoroastrianism, Gnosticism and Hinduism were
idolatrous. From this vantage point then Judaism is at the centre of
the universe of faiths, whereas all other belief systems encircle it
intersecting only at those points where there is common ground.
Such a view can be represented diagrammatically:

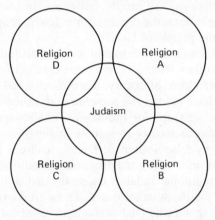

According to this traditional model, Judaism is at the centre
because it is absolutely true. Its source is God; at Mt Sinai God
revealed to Moses His holy Torah. It is this bedrock of certainty
which is the mainstay of the Jewish faith. Sinaitic revelation is seen
as a unique Divine act which provides a secure foundation for the
religious traditions of Israel. It is from the Pentateuchal account that
we learn of God's true nature, His dealings with the chosen people,
and the promise of the world to come. In this fashion the Written
Torah as well as the rabbinic interpretation of Scripture serves as
the yardstick for evaluating the truth claims of other religions.

The significant feature of this model is that it excludes the
possibility of God revealing Himself to others. It assumes that
throughout the history of the world, people have mistakenly believed
that they have had an encounter with the Divine, but in fact

God only made Himself known to the Jews. This accounts for the wide diversity and contradictory character of religious beliefs among the religions of the world. As to those religions which have ideas similar to what is found in Judaism, this concurrence is not due to God's intervention. Rather, the adherents of these religions would have arrived – possibly through the aid of human reason – at religious conceptions which simply happen to be true and therefore conform to what is found in the Jewish faith. Thus, for example the Muslim belief in one God who is eternal, omniscient, omnipotent and all-good is true, not because God revealed himself to Mohammed, but simply because it coincidentally corresponds with Judaism's understanding. Similarly, Christians would be viewed as coincidentally correct in their adherence to monotheism, but misguided in terms of their conception of the Trinity. On the other hand, polytheistic religions, such as the religious systems of the Ancient Near East and the Greek and Roman religions, are utterly fallacious. In all these cases the criterion of true belief is the content of the Jewish religion as revealed exclusively to the people of Israel.

Though such a model is consonant with the attitude of many Jews in the past, it suffers from a very serious theological defect. If God is the providential Lord of history, it is difficult indeed to understand why He would have hidden His presence and withheld His revelation from humanity – except for the Jews. To allow people from the beginning of human history to wallow in darkness and ignorance, weighed down by false notions of Divine reality is hardly what we would expect from a loving, compassionate and caring God. While it is true that traditional Judaism maintains that in the Hereafter all the nations of the earth will come to know God's true nature, this does not at all explain why God would have refrained from disclosing Himself to the mass of humanity in this life on earth.

Arguably what is much more likely is that in the past God revealed Himself not only to the Jews but to others as well. On this view, subscribed to by some modern Jewish thinkers,[14] Judaism would still be at the centre of the universe of faiths, encircled by other religions. But the significant difference between this second model and the previous one concerns the role of revelation. Here, non-Jewish religions would be regarded as true, not simply because adherents happened to have similar ideas to what is found in Judaism, but because of a real encounter with the Divine. Judaism would on this view be regarded as ultimately true; its doctrines would serve as a basis for testing the validity of all alleged revelations.

Thus it would be a mistake on this view to think that because a particular religion, such as Theravada Buddhism, has doctrines that directly contradict Jewish theology, God did not reveal Himself to the peoples of the Indian continent. On the contrary, it is likely He did but because of social, cultural and historical circumstances, this encounter was misunderstood or filtered though human interpretation in such a way that it became confused and distorted. On this account God would have manifested His general concern for mankind throughout history as well as his particular love for His chosen people.

The advantage of this second model is that it not only takes seriously God's love but it also comes to terms with the human spiritual quest. This is particularly important in the light of our increasing knowledge of religious cultures. Unlike the Biblical writers or the ancient rabbis, we know a great deal more about Christianity, Islam and the religions of the East; the comparative study of religions has made us more aware of the great riches of the religious faiths of the past. It is short-sighted in the extreme to dismiss these traditions as having no religious integrity. What is much more plausible is that in each stream of religious life, there have been great mystics, teachers and theologians who have in various ways experienced God's revelation and presence.

This second model preserves the centrality of the Jewish faith while giving credance to the claims of the followers other religions who have experienced the Divine. Nonetheless, it is questionable whether this picture of the universe of faiths goes far enough. Arguably even this modern approach to the religions of the world does not do full justice to God's nature as a loving father who truly cares for all his children. On this second model, it is the Jewish people who really matter. They are the ones who have received the full and ultimate disclosure of His revelation; other faiths have only a partial and incomplete view and are pale reflections by comparison. What is missing from even this more tolerant account is an adequate recognition of God's providential love and concern for all humanity.

What is far more likely, as John Hick has argued,[15] is that in each and every generation and to all peoples of the world, God has disclosed Himself in numerous ways. Thus, neither in Judaism, nor for that matter in any other religion, has God revealed Himself absolutely and completely. Instead, God's revelation was made manifest to different peoples in varied forms. In each case, the revelations and the traditions to which they gave rise were conditioned by such

factors as history, climate, language and culture. For these reasons
the form of the revelation has been characteristically different in
every case.

Such a conception of God's activity serves as the basis for an
arguably more accurate model of Judaism and the universe of
faiths. In this third model, God, rather than the Jewish tradition,
.is at the centre. Judaism, like other religions faiths, encircles Him
intersecting only at those points at which the nature of divine reality
is truly reflected:

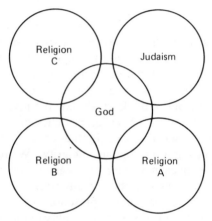

CONCLUSION

The advantage of this vision of Judaism in the context of the world
religions is that it is theologically more coherent with the Jewish
understanding of God, and it also paves the way for interfaith
encounter at the deepest levels. Already Jews work together with
members of other faiths on common projects of fellowship and
charity. Yet, if Jews could free themselves from an absolutist
Judeo-Centric position, the way would be open for interfaith dialogue of the most profound kind. With the Divine at the centre of
the Universe of faiths, Jewish dialogue with other religious traditions
would assume an altogether different and beneficial character. From
its Biblical origins Judaism adopted a generally tolerant attitude to
other religious traditions – what is possible today is for this spirit of
tolerance to deepen and serve as a foundation for a common quest
with like-minded adherents of other faiths for spiritual insight and
religious truth.

12
Ranking Judaism and Other Religions

Over the last few years there has been considerable debate about the relationship between the religions of the world; in particular Christians have been anxious to formulate a theology of other religions which transcends the traditional Christian belief that God's revelation and salvation are offered exclusively in Jesus Christ. In this context a number of theologians have questioned the finality of Christ and Christianity.

CHRISTIANITY AND RELIGIOUS PLURALISM

Professor John Hick, for example – the leading proponent of this view – speaks of a revolution in theology which involves a radical transformation of the concept of the universe of faiths. He claims that 'the great world religions [are] different human responses to the one Divine Reality, embodying different perceptions which have been formed in different historical and cultural circumstances'.[1] Similarly, the Roman Catholic priest, Raimundo Panikaar, argues for a revised form of ecumenism which strives for unity without harming religious diversity. Panikaar argues that the fundamental religious fact of the world's religions is the mystery known in every authentic religious experience. For Panikaar, this mystery within all religions is both more than and yet has its being within the diverse experiences and beliefs of the religions: 'It is not simply that there are different ways of leading to the peak, but that the summit itself would collapse if all the paths disappeared. The peak is in a certain sense the result of the slopes leading to it . . . It is not that this reality has many names as if there were a reality outside the name. This reality is the many names and each name is a new aspect'.[2] Thus he claims that no one religion can claim to be the ultimate truth.

Panikaar and Hick are not unique in their views. Similar positions are put forward by such theologians as Dr Stanley Samartha, formerly director of the World Council of Churches Programme on Dialogue[3] and Professor Paul Knitter of Xavier University.[4]

CRITERIA FOR GRADING RELIGIONS

The acceptance of such a theocentric model of the universe of faiths does not imply, however, that all religions are equally valid. Addressing himself to this point, Professor Hick in an extremely valuable discussion of this issue asserts that religious concepts and practices are not all on the same level of value or validity.[5] This is so among the different religions and even within individual religious systems. Indeed, he points out, throughout history the most significant religious figures have been critical of various ideas and attitudes: Gautama rejected the notion of the eternal atman; the Hebrew prophets criticized mere outward observances and practices; Jesus attacked the formalism and insincerity of the scribes and Pharisees; Muhammad rejected the polytheism of Arabian society; Guru Nanak and Martin Luther were critical of the traditions into which they were born.[6] Thus Hick maintains that assessing religious phenomena is a central feature of religious seriousness and openness to the Divine. It is legitimate to grade aspects of religions and place them in some order of merit. No-one, he believes, is going to think that all the features of the world's religions are on the same level of value or validity: different aspects 'have to be regarded as higher or lower, better or worse, Divine or demonic'.[7] Yet Hick is anxious to emphasize that while it is proper to assess religious phenomena, it is not realistic to grade the world's religions as totalities. 'Each of these long traditions', he writes, 'is so internally diverse, containing so many different kinds of both good and evil, that it is impossible for human judgement to weigh up and compare their merits as systems of salvation'.[8] Commenting on this view, Paul Griffiths and Delmas Lewis describe Hick as a non-judgemental inclusivist who is unwilling to make judgements about the claims of the world's religions,[9] but this is a mistake. Hick makes it clear throughout his discussion that it is the theologian's proper task to ascertain what aspects of a tradition are 'belief-worthy, revelatory, plausible, rightly-claiming allegiance'.[10]

The difficulty with Hick's position is not, as Griffiths and Lewis maintain, that he refuses to make judgements about the truth-claims of religions, but rather that the evaluative framework he outlines is open to serious criticism. The first criterion Hick proposes is theological coherence: 'We can try to assess such a system in respect of its internal consistency . . .'[11] Yet there is no self-evident reason why internal consistency should necessarily be regarded as a central virtue of a religion. It may well be that religious experience transcends ordinary categories of logical reasoning; furthermore, even if it were shown that a religious system is coherent in terms of belief and practice, this would not necessarily imply that it was in fact based on a true encounter with Divine reality. Allied with this notion of internal coherence is a second criterion of religious adequacy – 'its adequacy both to the particular form of experience on which it is based and to the data of human experience in general'.[12] Here, however, it is unclear how one is to determine whether a theology or philosophy within a religious tradition is adequate to the originating religious vision or successful in interpretating that vision to a new age. There is no doubt that the theologies of Thomas Aquinas, al-Ghazali, Maimonides, Shankara and Buddhaghosha are intellectually impressive, but are they true to the original vision on which they are based? Are they successful interpretations for subsequent believers? There is no obvious way to deal with these questions, and any answers will inevitably be based on subjective reactions and interpretations.

The third criterion Hick suggests is spiritual in nature. Here the test consists in ascertaining the extent to which religious ideas promote or hinder the aims of salvation and liberation. 'And by salvation or liberation', Hick writes, 'I suggest that we should mean the realization of that limitlessly better quality of human existence which comes about in the transition from self-centeredness to Reality-centeredness'.[13] In explaining this principle, Hick gives examples from several religions: Christians give themselves to God in Christ in a total renunciation of the self-centred ego and its concerns; Muslims give themselves in total submission to God; Hindus strive for union with the Ultimate through meditation and selfless action. While it is true that within the world's religions this theme of selflessness in different forms is an important feature, there are other central motifs as well. Whether this aspect should be the touchstone of religious validity is open to debate. Religious systems provide different and varied spiritual fruits – it is certainly plausible that other spiritual attitudes and concerns are of equal or even superior value than ego-renunciation and self-giving to the Real.

The final criterion Hick proposes is moral assessment.[14] In recommending this standard Hick extols the lives of various saints of the world's religions, yet he emphasizes that the actual histories of religious traditions frequently fall short of moral ideals. In this context he catalogues what he considers modern moral evils engendered by religious faith: the lethargy of Eastern countries in relation to social and economic problems; the West's exploitation of natural resources; Hindu and Buddhist otherworldliness in retarding social, economic and technological progress; the unjust caste system of India; the burning of widows in India; the cutting off of a thief's hands under Islamic law, and so forth.[15] In making these judgements Hick wishes to illustrate that in the history of all religious traditions there is both virtue and vice. Nevertheless, what is absent from this list is a systematic framework for ethical decision-making. Moral attitudes are notoriously difficult to assess. Does Hick recommend we adopt a teleological or deontological stance? When considering the viability of religious claims concerning the multifarious dimensions of human behaviour, what is to be the basis for making a correct judgement? These central questions are unfortunately left unanswered despite Hick's assurances that certain aspects of the world's faiths are morally inadequate, thereby rendering them religiously less viable.

A similar criticism applies to Hick's consideration of the moral character of religious leaders. What is important about such individuals, he writes, is the coherence between their teaching about God and the ways in which such teaching is reflected in their own lives. Taking the example of Jesus, Hick asserts that if Jesus had taught hatred, selfishness, greed, and the amassing of wealth by exploiting others he would never have been regarded as 'Son of God'. The same, Hick argues, applies to each of the great religious figures; on this basis, he believes it is possible to identify the operation of an ethical criterion in the recognition of a mediator of the Divine or the Real'.[16] Yet while it may empirically be the case that Jesus' followers would not have accepted him as Christ if his ministry had not conformed to his teaching, it does not necessarily follow that when such coherence is found in the life of a religious leader, that person has in fact had a true encounter with God. Nor for that matter should one necessarily conclude that a lack of coherence demonstrates the falseness of a religious leader's claims – when such a figure does not live out his message, this may well be the result of human weakness, temptation and sin.

Similar criticisms made of Hick's criteria can be levelled at the bases for grading religious faiths delineated by Paul Knitter in a recent study of Christian attitudes toward the world's religions.

According to Knitter, there are three guidelines for determining the truth-value of any religion or religious figure: (1) Personally, does the revelation of the religion or religious figure – the story, the myth, the message – move the human heart? Does it stir one's feelings, the depths of one's horizons?; (2) Intellectually, does the religion also satisfy and expand the mind? Is it intellectually coherent? Does it broaden one's horizons of understanding?; (3) Practically, does the message provide for psychological health of individuals, their sense of value, purpose and freedom? Does it promote the welfare, the liberation of all peoples?[17] As in the case of Hick's criteria, the answers to these questions will inevitably involve subjective interpretation and personal judgement. For example, the life and teachings of Jesus evoke a spiritual response on the part of Christians but have little meaning for Jews. Similarly, the Buddha is of profound significance for Buddhists but has little relevance for Muslims. Again, the legal system of Islam has no significance for Hindus. In all these cases, it is simply impossible to make an objective evaluation of the truth claims of the world's religions on the basis of an existential response. The same applies to the intellectual coherence of religious traditions: Jews, for example, find the Christian doctrines of the Trinity and Incarnation irrational and incoherent. For Christians the Theravada Buddhist's rejection of a supernatural deity undermines the spiritual life. Muslims regard Hindu polytheism as religiously abhorrent. Thus, Knitter's second criterion also fails to provide a firm foundation for evaluative judgement. The third criterion is equally problematic: how is one to assess whether particular religious beliefs promote psychological health and liberation? Orthodox adherents, for example (such as Orthodox Jews, Roman Catholics, traditional Muslims) regard liberal movements within their own faiths as misguided; liberals on the other hand argue that certain traditional elements of their faiths are psychologically constraining and hinder personal and communal growth. We can see therefore that Knitters suggestions, like Hick's, fall short of providing a satisfactory basis for ranking religions.

THE CRITERION OF VIABILITY

These proposals for evaluating religions and religious figures are ultimately unsatisfactory because they fail to provide clear-cut and generally accepted bases for evaluation. Yet this should not be a surprising conclusion. In the past adherents of a particular religion judged all other religions by the criteria of their own faith; the eclipse of such an exclusivist stance by a theocentric picture of the world's religions leads inevitably to a relativistic conception of the universe of faiths. Within such a framework, as we have seen, grading religions – whether on the basis of theological coherence, religious adequacy, spirituality, morality, existential response, psychological health, or liberating capacity – involves subjective, personal decisions grounded on fundamental presuppositions about the Divine reality and the human condition. Given such a situation, is it possible in any way to grade religions objectively? Hick is certainly correct that religious systems as totalities cannot be ranked since they are themselves composed of different streams of traditions. Nevertheless, it should be possible to evaluate separate movements within the world's religions on the basis of their viability, namely , their capacity to satisfy the spiritual demands and animate the lives of adherents. Within such a context there would be no need to appeal to any alleged universal standard of judgement; instead the criterion of viability could serve as the sole guideline for rating religions. If a movement within a particular religious system were seen to be effective in the lives of its followers, it would rank higher than another religious system which did not in fact satisfy the spiritual needs of adherents. Such a guideline would not yield judgements about the truth-claims of the various faiths yet it would furnish important information about the religious adequacy of the world's religions and enable one to place them in some hierarchical order on the basis of ascertainable evidence.

Modern Judaism furnishes an illuminating example of the possibilities of this means of grading religions. Through the centuries traditional Judaism has maintained that God revealed the Pentateuch to Moses on Mt Sinai. This belief implies that the whole Torah, including theology, history and law, is of Divine origin – everything contained in these books was revealed by the Almighty. This principle guarantees the validity of the legal system and serves as the foundation of the theological tenets of the faith. Yet, it has become increasingly difficult for most Jews to accept this fundamentalist belief in the origin of Scripture. The main challenges to the doctrine of Pentateuchal infallibility have united to produce a convincing picture of the Pentateuch as a work with a human history and coloured by human ideas, including human errors.[18] This shift in understanding has had far-reaching consequences for modern Orthodoxy. There is still a small segment of Orthodox Jews who hold fast to the traditional conception of the origin of the Torah. For them Orthodox Judaism is in every way a viable religious system, but in practice the majority of Jews who affiliate to Orthodox Judaism have set aside not only the central belief in Torah from Sinai but also its attendant notions. These lapsed Orthodox Jews no longer subscribe to the conviction that each and every word of the Pentateuch was dictated to Moses, nor do they accept that the ancient rabbis were infallible interpreters of the law whose decrees are perfectly in accord with God's will. Consequently they do not feel bound to observe the 613 scriptural commandments nor the thousands of rabbinic laws based on these precepts as recorded in the Code of Jewish Law. Instead lapsed Orthodox Jews observe only those segments of the legal tradition which they find of importance. It is not uncommon, for example, for such Orthodox Jews to insist on a strict observance of the food laws while neglecting the laws of ritual purity in other spheres (such as ritual immersion after menstruation).

Similarly, lapsed Orthodox Jews no longer feel bound to accept many of the theological beliefs inherent in the Torah, nor the principles of the Jewish faith as enshrined in Maimonides' formulation of the 13 cardinal beliefs of Judaism. Doctrines such as belief in the resurrection of the dead, final judgement, and reward and punishment in the Hereafter have been largely ignored or discarded. Thus, Orthodox Judaism as a system of belief and practice has ceased to be a viable religious system for the majority of those who describe themselves as adherents. Here then is an example of a religious system which has ceased to be effective for those who regard themselves (and are regarded by the Jewish community generally and the outside world) as Orthodox Jews. For these lapsed Orthodox Jews – as opposed to authentic Orthodox Jews who are firmly committed to the faith – traditional Judaism is no longer tenable as a religious system since its theological tenets preclude significant adaptation and change. Thus, in grading the world's religions on the basis of viability, it is clear that contemporary Orthodox Judaism in its lapsed phase would rank lower than any religious system which is fervently adhered to by a substantial majority of its followers.

In contrast to modern Orthodoxy (where there is a striking discrepancy between the demands of traditional Judaism and the life-style of lapsed Orthodox Jews) contemporary Reform Judaism is more consonant with the needs and expectations of its followers. Unlike Orthodox Judaism, the Reform movement is open to fundamental change since it has rejected the belief that the Pentateuch was given by God to Moses. This movement within world Jewry has broken ranks with Orthodoxy by declaring that the Pentateuch is a post-Mosaic, composite work – the product of a Divine encounter with Israel but with a strong human component. Laws as well as religious beliefs are thus seen to be the product of historical circumstances. On this basis Reform Jews have largely rejected the halachic aspects of traditional Judaism. Reform Judaism is conceived essentially as a prophetic faith, emphasizing moral conduct combined with prayer and worship. Within this context, Reform Jews feel free to dismiss the legal and theological features of traditional Judaism which they no longer regard as tenable. Without the theological constraints of Orthodoxy, Reformers maintain that it is legitimate to adapt the tradition to meet modern needs and concerns. At the centre of Reform belief is the conviction that the Torah – as understood in its widest sense – must be open and developing. God's revelation is seen not as a series of theoretical absolutes, but as progressive in character. Within this framework, the role of the Reform rabbi is to search the classic Jewish sources for guidance for everyday living as Jews in contemporary society.

Such openness inevitably leads to confusion about which aspects of the tradition should be retained and which discarded. Yet there is no doubt that the majority of those who identify as Reform Jews find Reform Judaism viable as a religious system. Its very flexibility and diversity enable its adherents to shape the tradition to meet their spiritual needs. One could argue that Reform Judaism as a polymorphous entity is not internally coherent and consistent, yet its pliable character does enable it to adapt easily to individual needs. In a ranking system then, Reform Judaism – whatever its intrinsic merits – would receive high marks as a viable system of belief and practice. Unlike Orthodoxy, which presents a theoretical framework of belief and practice which is largely neglected by so-called adherents, Reform Judaism offers a loosely-knit structure which is amenable to personal choice and individual taste. Its viability consists in its effectiveness as a religion to influence and shape the lives of its followers according to their existential needs.

THE APPLICATION OF THE VIABILITY CRITERION

These two examples from the Jewish world illustrate how the principle of viability can be used as a criterion for grading religious systems. Again, it must be emphasized that in evaluating a religion according to this standard, no judgement is being made about the validity of its truth-claims, nor is one attempting to ascertain whether the religion is in fact based on a true encounter with the Divine. All that is being judged is whether the religious system is practised and believed in by the majority of its co-called adherents. The process of grading religions is therefore essentially a sociological rather than a philosophical or theological exercise. The concern is not with inherent value, truth or validity, but with the capacity of a religious system to function effectively in the lives of its adherents: to do so there must be a correspondence between the tenets and practices of a religion and the way of life of those who allegedly subscribe to it. Ranking religions thus involves a comprehensive investigation into the present state of religious beliefs and practice in the world's religions.

One would need, for example, to examine the current state of affairs in the Muslim world. Do present day Muslims in fact accept the Qur'an as a perfect revelation from God? Is the Shar'ia an active force in shaping the lives of the Muslim community? Are both Sunnis and Shi'ites true followers of their separate traditions? How universal is the revival of Islamic fundamentalism in the Arab world? The answers to such questions should help to clarify the extent to which Islam as a religious system is a vibrant and active force in Muslim life. Similar questions could be posed regarding Christianity. Here one would need to examine the extent to which Christian beliefs and values are incorporated into the lives of members of the various branches of Christendom: Eastern Orthodox, Roman Catholic and Protestant. These groups obviously have different views of the essential features of the Christian life – what is at stake in a test of viability is the degree to which followers have incorporated the teachings of their respective traditions into their lives. A parallel case of religious diversity is found within Hinduism. With neither founder, creed, nor fixed pattern of observance, it is more difficult to measure the viability of the Hindu faith than in most traditions. Nevertheless, Hinduism embodies a certain ethos and a number of underlying conceptions (such as samsara, karma and moshka). Thus, as with other faiths, it should be possible to discover the degree to which Hinduism as a philosophy and way of life is meaningful for those who consider themselves Hindus.

Turning to other religions of the East, one could attempt to ascertain the extent to which the teachings of the Buddha serve as the focus of the lives of those who describe themselves as Buddhists.

Do they truly accept the Four Noble Truths as valid? Does the Noble Eightfold Path serve as the blueprint for living? Is the belief in Nirvana widely accepted? To take another example of an Eastern religion, is there for Jains a general acceptance of the doctrine of transmigration and rebirth? Is non-violence a characteristic of the lives of most Jains? Are they scrupulously vegetarian? Again, in this process of grading religious systems one would need to consider the effectiveness of new religions and quasi-religious cults to fulfil the spiritual needs of their followers. Are the adherents of such groups as Hare Krishna, Divine Light Mission, Unification Church, Transcendental Meditation and the like deeply dedicated? Do they actually accept the teachings of their various spiritual leaders? In all these cases the answers to these and similar questions would provide a basis for drawing up a hierarchical list of the world's religious systems based on the principle of viability.

CONCLUSION

It might be objected that grading religions in this way does not reveal what is of crucial importance – the relative inherent merits of the world's faiths. In one sense this is a fair criticism: the criterion of viability does not provide a touchstone for testing the truth-claims of a particular faith. But, as we have seen, ranking religions in terms of truth appears to be an impossible task since the criteria for judging religions in this manner are ultimately based on subjective judgement and personal predilection. Ranking religions on the basis of viability, however, would overcome this impasse by providing an objective procedure for evaluating religions on the basis of effectiveness. Drawing up such a viability map of the universe of faiths might well provide illuminating information in a number of important spheres: firstly, from a phenomenological standpoint, knowing about the realities of belief and practice in the world's religions could provide invaluable insights for the student of religion. All too often introductions to a religious heritage as well as more advanced studies offer only theoretical accounts of the elements of a tradition without indicating whether adherents actually accept the doctrines of their faith or attempt to infuse its teachings into their daily lives. Ranking the world's religions according to viability would help to fill this gap.

Secondly, such an investigation might well illustrate (as in the case of Orthodox Judaism) that some of the world's religions have today ceased to play a major role in the lives of so-called adherents. In the face of increasing secularism, this would not be a surprising situation, yet it is significant that the new cults seem to have attracted followers who are deeply committed. These modern movements appear to meet the spiritual needs of their disciples more successfully than mainstream traditions. In many cases converts to these cults have rejected the religions into which they were born because they find them spiritually bankrupt – in their place the cults offer them a discovery of the holy and experience of a transcendental reality. Such a development raises a number of serious questions about the effectiveness of the world's major religious traditions in contemporary society. Finally, in the same connection, ranking religions according to viability would help to illustrate whether Orthodox or liberal traditions have a greater hold on adherents. In the case of Orthodox Judaism, it is clear that the theological rigidity of Orthodoxy has undermined its vitality as a living faith, yet the opposite might be the case in other religions, such as Islam. This kind of information could contribute to an understanding of the dynamic of faith in a scientific age. These areas of concern are simply suggestive of the ways in which a test of viability could be of benefit. Though it would not determine the relative truth of the world's religions, such an approach is entirely consistent with a theocentric conception of the universe of faiths and could provide a sympathetic framework for appreciating and understanding the religious experience of humanity today.

Notes

Notes to Chapter 1: Jewish Faith and the Holocaust

1. E. Wiesel, *Night* (New York: Hill and Wang, 1960). As quoted by R. Rubenstein and J. Roth, *Approaches to Auschwitz* (London: SCM Press, 1987), p. 283.
2. Ibid., p. 285.
3. E. Wiesel, *The Trial of God* (New York: Random House, 1979), p. 129.
4. Ibid., p. 133.
5. R. Rubenstein and J. Roth, op.cit., p. 287.
6. E. Wiesel, *A Jew Today* (New York: Random House, 1978), p. 164.
7. R. Rubenstein, *After Auschwitz* (Indianapolis: Bobbs Merrill, 1966), p. 153.
8. R. Rubenstein and J. Roth,*Approaches to Auschwitz* (London: SCM Press, 1987).
9. R. Rubenstein, *After Auschwitz*, as quoted by R. Rubenstein and J. Roth op.cit., pp. 312–13.
10. Ibid., p. 315.
11. A. Cohen, *Tremendum* (New York: Crossroad, 1981) as quoted by R. Rubenstein and J. Roth, op.cit., p. 330.
12. Ibid., p. 331.
13. Ibid., p. 332.
14. Ibid., p. 333.
15. E. Berkovits, *Faith After the Holocaust* (New York: Ktav, 1973), pp. 5–6.
16. Ibid., p. 70.
17. I. Maybaum, *The Face of God After Auschwitz* (Amsterdam: Polak & Van Gennep, 1965), p. 36.
18. Ibid., p. 84.
19. E. Fackenheim, *Judaism* 16 (Summer 1967), pp. 272–3.
20. E. Fackenheim, *To Mend the World* (New York: Schoken, 1982).
21. Ibid., p. 250.

Notes to Chapter 2: The Afterlife in Contemporary Jewish Belief

1. K. Kohler, *Jewish Theology* (New York: Ktav, 1968), p. 279.
2. R.H. Charles, *A Critical History of the Doctrine of a Future Life in Israel, in Judaism, and in Christianity* (London: Adam & Charles Black, 1913), p. 157.
3. Kohler, op.cit., p. 282.
4. Ps. 28:1, 88:5; Nu. 16:33, Ps. 6:6; Is. 38:18.
5. Josh. 18.16; 2 Kings 23:10; Jer. 7:31–32, 19:6, 32:35.
6. Josh. 18:16.

7. Jer. 2.23; 2 Chron. 26:9; Neh. 2:13, 15: Neh. 3:13.
8. Jer. 7:31–32; 19:6; 32:35.
9. See L. Jacobs, *A Jewish Theology* (New York: Behrman House, 1973).
10. See E. Jacob, *The Interpreter's Dictionary of the Bible*, Vol. ii (New York: Abington Press, 1962), p. 689; K. Kohler, op.cit., p. 392.
11. San. 90b.
12. San. 91b.
13. Ibid.
14. This was originally a valley near Jerusalem where Moloch was worshipped. See Jer. 7:31–32; 19:6; 32:35.
15. See A. Super, *Immortality in the Babylonian Talmud* (unpublished Ph.D. Thesis, 1967), pp. 103–8.
16. Maimonides, *Mishneh Torah*, Laws of Repentence III, Sections 6, 7, 8.
17. See A. Super, op.cit.
18. Ibid., pp. 191–3.
19. Erubin 19a.
20. L. Ginzberg, *The Legends of the Jews* (Philadelphia: Jewish Publication Society, 1968), Vol. I, p. 15.
21. Ibid., pp. 57–8.
22. Ibid., Vol. II, pp. 310–13.
23. Midr. Prov., XVII, 1, 42b.
24. There were some Rabbis who proclaimed that God consigns gentiles en masse to Hell. See C.G. Montefiore and H. Loewe, *A Rabbinic Anthology* (New York: Schocken, 1974), XCIII.
25. Shabb. 31a.
26. Sanh. 74a.
27. (1) The existence of God; (2) the unity of God; (3) the incorporeality of God; (4) the eternity of God; (5) God alone is to be worshipped; (6) prophecy; (7) Moses is the greatest of the prophets; (8) the divinity of the Torah; (9) the inalterability of the Torah; (10) the omniscience of God; (11) reward and punishment; (12) the Messiah; (13) the resurrection of the dead.
28. Responsum No. 344 as quoted by L. Jacobs, *Principles of the Jewish Faith* (London: Vallentine Mitchell, 1964), p. 24.
29. S. Schechter, *Aspects of Rabbinic Theology* (New York: Schocken, 1961), p. 16.
30. L. Jacobs, *Principles of the Jewish Faith* (London: Vallentine Mitchell, 1964), pp. 388–9.
31. J.H. Hertz, *Commentary to the Prayerbook*, p. 255.
32. W.G. Plaut, *The Growth of Reform Judaism* (New York: World Union for Progressive Judaism, 1965), p. 34.
33. L. Jacobs, *Principles of the Jewish Faith*, p. 364.
34. As quoted by L. Jacobs, *Principles of the Jewish Faith*, p. 415.
35. K. Kohler, op.cit., p. 309.

Notes to Chapter 3: The Torah in Modern Judaism

1. As quoted by L. Jacobs, *Principles of the Jewish Faith* (London: Vallentine Mitchell, 1964), p. 218.

2. *Jewish Chronicle*, 2 November 1984, pp. 24–5.
3. Ibid.
4. Ibid.
5. Ibid.
6. Ibid.
7. *Jewish Chronicle*, 16 November 1984.
8. Ibid.
9. Ibid.
10. *Jewish Chronicle*, 30 November 1984, p. 19.
11. *Jewish Chronicle*, 7 December 1984, p. 23.
12. Ibid.
13. *Jewish Chronicle*, 30 November 1984, p. 19.
14. Ibid.
15. Louis Jacobs, *A Jewish Theology* (London: Darton, Longman & Todd, 1973), p. 203.

Notes to Chapter 4: Law and Freedom in Reform Judaism

1. See for example, H. Goldstein, 'Criteria for Observance in Reform Judaism' in *Torah*; S. Freehof, 'Reform Judaism and the Legal Tradition' in *Torah*; Dow Marmur, 'The Question of Ishut: Should There be Minimal Standards for Conversion in Reform Judaism', *Central Conference of American Rabbis Yearbook* (New York: Central Conference of American Rabbis, 1979); Dow Marmur; 'British Reform and Jewish Status', *Journal of Reform Judaism*, Vol. XXV: 2, Spring 1978; J. Rayner, 'Towards a Modern Halachah', *Reform Judaism* (Reform Synagogues of Great Britain, 1973).
2. See J. Rayner, 'Towards a Modern Halachah' for a clearly expressed outline of possible criteria.
3. *Debrett's Etiquette and Modern Manners* (London: Debrett's, 1981).
4. *The Times*, Summer 1981.
5. S. Freehof, *Contemporary Reform Responsa* (Cincinnati: HUC Press, 1974), p. 24.
6. D. Marmur 'British Reform and Jewish Status', p. 7.
7. Ibid., pp. 36–7.
8. D. Marmur, *British Reform and Jewish Status*, pp. 43–4.
9. See G. Plaut, *The Rise of Reform Judaism* (New York: World Union for Progressive Judaism, 1963); G. Plaut, *The Growth of Reform Judaism* (New York: World Union for Progressive Judaism, 1965).
10. As W. Jacobs notes, 'Solomon Freehof has been a lecturer in this area of Reform Jewish development. He has continued and broadened a tradition rooted in the beginnings of our movement'. W. Jacobs in an introduction to *Reform Responsa for Our Time* by S. Freehof (USA: HUC Press, 1977), p. xxvii.
11. S. Freehof *Reform Jewish Practice* (New York: Union of American Hebrew Congregations, 1963), Vol. I, p. 113.
12. Ibid., p. 65.
13. Ibid., p. 76.
14. Ibid., p. 154.

15. S. Freehof, *Contemporary Reform Responsa* (USA: HUC Press, 1974), p. 119.
16. S. Freehof, *Reform Responsa for Our Time*, pp. 204–5.
17. S. Freehof, *Reform Jewish Practice*, Vol. I, p. 116.
18. Ibid., p. 80.
19. Ibid., p. 19.
20. S. Freehof, *Current Reform Responsa* (USA: HUC Press, 1969), pp. 93–6.
21. S. Freehof, *Reform Responsa for Our Time*, 77.
22. Ibid., pp. 69–70.
23. S. Freehof, *Contemporary Reform Responsa*, pp. 146–7.
24. S. Freehof, *Reform Responsa for Our Time*, pp. 69–70.
25. S. Freehof, *Reform Jewish Practice*, Vol. I, p. 31.
26. S. Freehof, *Current Reform Responsa*, p. 105.
27. S. Freehof, *Reform Jewish Practice*, Vol. I, pp. 105–6.
28. S. Freehof, *Reform Responsa*, p. 118.
29. S. Freehof, ibid., p. 125.
30. D. Marmur, 'British Reform and Jewish Status', p. 41.
31. Ibid.
32. D. Marmur, 'The Question of Ishut: Should there be Minimal Standards for Conversion in Reform Judaism', p. 150.
33. Ibid., pp. 152–3.
34. D. Marmur, 'British Reform and Jewish Status', p. 43.
35. Ibid., p. 44.
36. S. Karff, 'The Question of Ishut: Should There be Minimal Standards in Reform Judaism', p. 157.

Notes to Chapter 5: Jewish Missionizing in Contemporary Society

1. A. Malter, 'Mixed Marriage and Reform Rabbis', *Judaism* 24 (Winter 1975), p. 39.
2. B. Martin, 'Contra Mixed Marriages', *CCAR Journal* (Volume XXIV, no. 3), p. 84.
3. J. Rosenbloom, *Conversion to Judaism* (Cincinnati: Hebrew Union College Press, 1978), p. 145.
4. There were, however, even in this period, a few rabbinic authorities who took a dim view of conversion. See, for example: Jeb. 47b 'Proselytes are as troublesome to Israel as a sore'.
5. D.M. Einhorn, *Conversion to Judaism* (USA: Ktav, 1965), p. 142.
6. Ibid.
7. Ibid., p. 144.
8. Ibid., p. 146.
9. *Rabbis Manual* (New York: Central Conference of American Rabbis, 1961), pp. 17–21.
10. It should be noted that there have been some instances of Reform rabbis requiring immersion and circumcision, but these are exceptional cases.
11. *Yearbook of the Central Conference of American Rabbis*, XLV, (1935), pp. 198–200.

12. D. Marmur (ed.) *Reform Judaism* (Oxford, Reform Synagogues of Great Britain, 1973), pp. 107–10.
13. T. Lenn, *Rabbi and Synagogue in Reform Judaism* (New York: CCAR, 1972). Since the overwhelming majority of Reform Jews live in the United States a study of American Reform Jewish belief provides the most comprehensive description.
14. S. Freehof, *Contemporary Reform Responsa* (USA: Hebrew Union College Press, 1974), pp. 139–40. 'We in the Reform movement (have) declared in *The Report of Mixed Marriage and Intermarriage*, that hereafter we fully accept a conversion made for the purpose of marriage.'

Notes to Chapter 6: Judaism and the Problems of the Inner City

1. The article appeared in the issue of 24 January 1986.
2. Ibid.
3. Ibid.
4. Ibid.
5. Ibid.
6. Ibid.
7. Subsequent citations from the Passover service that are used in this essay are from *The Union Haggadah* (New York: UAHC, 1923).
8. S. Schechter, *Aspects of Rabbinic Theology* (New York: Schocken, 1961), p. 93.
9. A.J. Heschel, *The Prophets* (New York: Harper & Row, 1953), p. 16.
10. I. Spektor, 'Nachal Yitzchak' in S. Spero, *Morality Halakha and the Jewish Tradition* (Hoboken, New Jersey: KTAV 1983), p. 134.
11. K. Kohler, *Jewish Theology* (Hoboken, New Jersey: KTAV Press, 1968), p. 326.
12. S. Spero, op.cit., p. 22.
13. Maimonides, as quoted in L. Jacobs, *Principles of the Jewish Faith* (London: Vallentine Mitchell, 1964), p. 216.
14. Ibid., p. 282.

Notes to Chapter 7: Judaism and Christian Anti-Semitism

1. Johannes Cardinal Willebrands, 'Christianity and Anti-Semitism', *Christian Jewish Relations* June 1985.
2. Ibid.
3. Ibid.
4. Ibid.
5. Ibid.
6. Origen, *Contra Celsum*, 4:23.
7. Gregory of Nyssa as quoted in Leon Poliakov, *History of Anti-Semitism*. Vol. I (London: Routledge & Kegan Paul, 1975), p. 25.
8. Quoted in ibid., Vol. II, p. 132.
9. Martin Luther, *Against the Jews and Their Lies*, 1542. As quoted in *Encyclopaedia Judaica*.
10. Martin Luther, as quoted in *Encyclopaedia Judaica*.
11. Rosemary Radford Reuther, *Faith and Fratricide* (London: SCM Press, 1975; Jerusalem: Keter, 1972), pp.227-57.

12. John Hick, *God and the Universe of Faiths* (New York: St. Martin' Press, 1973), p. 131.
13. Raimundo Panikaar, *The Unknown Christ of Hinduism* as quoted by P. Knitter *No Other Name* (New York: Orbis, 1985).
14. Stanley Samartha, *Courage for Dialogue* (Mary Knoll: 1982), pp. 151-3.
15. Paul Knitter, *No Other Name* (Mary Knoll: Orbis, 1985), pp. 201-2.
16. Johannes Cardinal Willebrands, op.cit.

Notes to Chapter 8: Obstacles to Jewish-Christian Encounter

1. Rev. C. Schoenveld in *Immanuel*, as quoted by D. Cohn-Sherbok in 'Between Christian and Jew', *Theology*, Vol. LXXXIII, 1980.
2. T.J. Shabbat, 8.
3. Origen, *Contra Celsum, 4.23.*
4. H.J. Schoeps, *The Jewish Christian Argument* (London: 1963), pp. 55-6.
5. Saadya Gaon, *Emunot ve-Deot*, trans. S. Rosenblatt (New Haven: Yale University Press, 1949).
6. Judah HaLevi, *The Kuzari*, trans. H. Hirschfield (New York: Schoken 1964).
7. Isaac Troki, *Hizzuk Emunah*, trans. M. Mocatta (New York: Schoken, 1964).
8. See H.J. Schoeps, op.cit.
9. See W. Jacobs, *Christianity Through Jewish Eyes* (Cincinnati: HUC Press, 1974), pp. 15-23.
10. Salomon Formstecher, *Religion des Geistes* (Frankfurt: 1841).
11. Salomon Ludwig Steinham, *Revelation According to the Doctrine of the Synagogue* (Leipzig: 1863).
12. See H.J. Schoeps, op.cit., pp. 55-6, 151.
13. Richard Rubenstein, *After Auschwitz* (Indianapolis: Bobbs Merrill, 1966), p. 75.
14. Ibid.
15. H.J. Schoeps, op.cit., p. 124.
16. John Hick (ed.), *The Myth of God Incarnate* (London: SCM Press, 1977).
17. Michael Green, *The Truth of God Incarnate* (London: 1977).
18. John Hick, op.cit., Preface.
19. John Hick, *God and the Universe of Faiths* (New York: St. Martin's Press, 1973).
20. Ibid.
21. Charles B. Ketcham, *A Theology of Encounter* (Pennsylvania: 1978), p. 149.
22. Walter Jacobs, op.cit., p. 231.
23. Samuel Sandmel, *We Jews and Jesus* (New York: 1965).
24. H.J. Schoeps, *Paul: The Theology of The Apostle in the Light of Jewish Religious History* (Philadelphia: Fortress Press, 1961).
25. Geza Vermes, *Jesus the Jew* (Glasgow: 1976).
26. Quoted by Walter Jacobs, op.cit., p. 126.

Notes to Chapter 9: A New Vision of Jewish-Christian Dialogue

1. Dan Cohn-Sherbok, 'Between Christian and Jew', *Theology*, Vol. LXXXIII, March 1980, No. 693.
2. Letters to the Editor, *Theology*, Vol. LXXXIII, July 1980, No. 694.
3. Ibid.
4. Ibid.
5. Valerie Hamer, 'A Hair's Breadth', *Theology*, Vol. LXXXIII, September 1980.
6. Leslie Newbigin, 'The Basis, Purpose and Manner of Inter-Faith Dialogue', quoted by C-Sh., Kings Theological Review, vol. VI, no.2.
7. Eric Sharpe, 'The Goals of Inter-Religious Dialogue', as quoted in ibid.
8. Stanley Samartha, 'Guidelines for Inter-Religious Dialogue', as quoted in ibid.
9. *Christian Jewish Relations*, Vol. 14, No. 1.
10. G.R. Dunstan, 'Law and Religion in Contemporary Society', as quoted in ibid.
11. Anthony Phillips, 'The Place of Law in Contemporary Society', as quoted in ibid.
12. C.F.D. Moule, 'A Christian Understanding of Law and Grace', as quoted in ibid.
13. W.S. Wurzburger, 'Law as a Basis of a Moral Society', as quoted in ibid.
14. U. Tal, 'Law, the Authority of the State and the Freedom of the Individual Person', as quoted in ibid.
15. C.M. Reigner, 'Review of Christian-Jewish Relations', as quoted in ibid.

Notes to Chapter 10: Judaism and the Theology of Liberation

1. S. Sandmel, *We Jews and Jesus* (New York: 1966).
2. H.J. Schoeps, *Paul* (Philadelphia: Fortress Press, 1961).
3. G. Vermes, *Jesus the Jew* (Glasgow: 1976).
4. T. Sobrino, *Christology at the Crossroads* (New York: Orbis, 1980), p. xvi.
5. Ibid., p. xvii.
6. L. Boff, *Jesus Christ Liberator* (New York: Orbis, 1981), p. 39.
7. Ibid., p. 279.
8. Ibid., p. 280.
9. J. Sobrino, op.cit., p. 9.
10. I. Ellacuria, *Freedom Made Flesh* (New York: Orbis, 1976), p. 23.
11. J. Bonino, *Doing Theology in a Revolutionary Situation* (Philadelphia: Fortress Press, 1975), p. 138.
12. P. Bigo, *The Church and Third World Revolution* (New York: Orbis, 1977), p. 131.
13. G. Gutierrez, *A Theology of Liberation* (New York: Orbis, 1983), p. 72.
14. M. Echegoyen 'Priests and Socialism in Chile', *New Blackfriars*, 52, 1971, p. 464f.
15. J. Davies, *Christian Politics and Violent Revolution* (New York: Orbis, 1976).

16. G. Gutierrez, op.cit.
17. Shabb., 119b.
18. Agadoth Shir Hashirim, pp. 18, 61.
19. Pirke Rabbi Eliezer, Ch. 3.
20. Agadoth Shir Hashirim, pp. 18, 61.
21. G. Gutierrez, op.cit., p. 159.
22. E. Tamez, *Bible of the Oppressed* (New York: Orbis, 1982).
23. J.S. Croatto, *Exodus* (New York: Orbis, 1981), p. 14.
24. Ibid., p. 15.
25. E. Dussel, *History and the Theology of Liberation* (New York: Orbis, 1976).
26. Ex. 3, 7–10.
27. E. Dussel, op.cit., p. 3.
28. Ibid., p. 7.
29. Ex. 13, 17–18.
30. Joshua 3, 9–10.
31. L. Finkelstein, *Haggadah of Passover* (New York: 1942), p. i.
32. F. Rosenzweig, *The Star of Redemption*, trans. N. Glatzer in *Franz Rosenzweig: His Life and Thought* (New York: 1953), pp. 319–21.
33. Ibid.
34. M. Lazarus, *The Ethics of Judaism* (Philadelphia: 1900), pp. 28–9.
35. K. Kohler, *Jewish Theology* (New York: Ktav, 1918), p. 462.
36. M. Joseph, *Judaism as Life and Creed* (London: Macmillan, 1903), pp. 213–15.
37. Ahad Ha-Am, *Essays, Letters, Memoirs* (Oxford: 1946), pp. 103–8.
38. G. Gutierrez, 'Liberation Praxis and Christian Faith', in *Frontiers of Theology in Latin America*, ed. R. Gibellini (London: 1975), p. 14.
39. A. Cussianovich, *Religious Life of the Poor* (New York: Orbis, 1979), p. 139.
40. G. Gutierrez, *A Theology of Liberation*, p. 84.
41. Ibid., pp. 36–7.
42. *The Union Haggadah* (USA: 1923), p. 78.
43. L. Cormie, 'Liberation and Salvation' in *The Challenge of Liberation Theology* (New York: Orbis, 1981), p. 29.
44. Ibid., p. 33.
45. D. Solle, 'Liberation in a Consumerist Society' in *The Challenge of Liberation Theology*, p. 9.
46. L. Cormie, op.cit., p. 33.
47. J. Vincent, *Into the City* (London: 1982), p. 17.
48. R.R. Reuther, *Sexism and God Talk* (London: SCM, 1983), p. 178.
49. S. Schneider, *Jewish and Female* (New York: Simon & Schuster, 1984), p. 19.
50. R. Reuther, op.cit., pp. 87–92.
51. H. Camara, *The Desert is Fertile* (New York: Orbis, 1974), p. 16.
52. Isaiah 49, 6.
53. *Singers Prayerbook*, p. 239.

Notes to Chapter 11: Judaism and the Universe of Faiths

1. Denzinger, *Enchiridion Symbolorum Definitionum et Declarationum de Rebus Fidei et Morum*, 29th ed, Freibrug, 1952, no. 714.
2. C. Hallencreutz,*Dialogue and Community* (Geneva: World Council of Churches, 1977), p. 37.
3. Ibid., p. 38.
4. *Theological Investigation*, Vol. 14, 1976, Ch. 17; Vol. 16, 1979, Ch.3.
5. J. Nuener (ed.), *Christian Revelation and World Religions*, ed. J. Neuner, Burns and Oates, 1967, pp. 52–3.
6. J. Hick, *God Has Many Names* (London: Macmillan 1980), pp. 48–9.
7. Deut. 4:19.
8. Mal. 1:11.
9. See *Encyclopaedia Talmudit*, Vol. III, pp. 348–62.
10. See. J. Katz, *Exclusiveness and Tolerance* (Oxford: Clarendon Press, 1961).
11. See L. Jacobs, *A Jewish Theology* (New York: Behrman House, 1973), p. 286.
12. Ibid., p. 287.
13. Ibid.
14. See. L. Jacobs, *A Jewish Theology*, pp. 289–91.
15. John Hick, op.cit., passim.

Notes to Chapter 12: Ranking Judaism and Other Religions

1. J. Hick, *God and the Universe of Faiths* (New York: St. Martin's Press, 1973), p. 131.
2. R. Panikaar, *The Unknown Christ of Hinduism* (New York: Orbis, 1981), pp. 24, 19.
3. S. Samartha, *Courage for Dialogue* (New York: Orbis, 1982).
4. P. Knitter, *No Other Name* (Mary Knoll: Orbis, 1985).
5. J. Hick, 'On Grading Religions', *Religious Studies*, 17.
6. Ibid., p. 451.
7. Ibid.
8. Ibid., p. 467.
9. P. Griffiths and D. Lewis, 'On Grading Religions, Seeking Truth and Being Nice to People – A Reply to Professor Hick', *Religious Studies*, 19, pp. 75–80.
10. J. Hick, 'On Grading Religions', p. 457.
11. Ibid., p. 462.
12. Ibid.
13. Ibid., p. 467.
14. Ibid., pp. 462–3.
15. Ibid., pp. 465–6.
16. Ibid., p. 459.
17. P. Knitter, op.cit., p. 231.
18. See L. Jacobs, *Principles of the Jewish Faith* (London: Vallentine Mitchell,1964), p. 219.

Bibliography

Ahad Ha-am, *Essays, Letters, Memoirs* (Oxford: 1946).

E. Berkovits, *Faith After the Holocaust* (New York: Ktav, 1973).

P. Bigo, *The Church and Third World Revolution* (New York: Orbis, 1977).

L. Boff, *Jesus Christ Liberator* (New York: Orbis, 1981).

J.M. Bonino, *Doing Theology in a Revolutionary Situation* (Philadelphia: Fortress, 1975).

H. Camara, *The Desert is Fertile* (New York: Orbis, 1974).

Central Conference of American Rabbis Yearbook (New York: Central Conference of American Rabbis, 1979).

R.H. Charles, *A Critical History of the Doctrine of a Future Life in Israel, in Judaism, and in Christianity* (London: Adam & Charles Black, 1913).

A. Cohen, *Tremendum* (New York: Crossroad, 1981).

Dan Cohn-Sherbok, *The Jewish Heritage* (Oxford: Basil Blackwell, 1988).

D. Cohn-Sherbok, *On Earth as it is in Heaven: Jews, Christians and Liberation Theology* (New York: Orbis, 1987).

Dan Cohn-Sherbok, *Holocaust Theology* (London: Marshall Pickering, 1989).

L. Cormie, 'Liberation and Salvation' in *The Challenge of Liberation Theology* (New York: Orbis, 1981).

J.S. Croatto, *Exodus* (New York: Orbis 1981).

A. Cussianovich, *Religious Life of the Poor* (New York: Orbis, 1979).

J. Davies, *Christian Politics and Violent Revolution* (New York: Orbis, 1976).

Denzinger, *Enchiridion Symbolorum Definitionum et Declarationum de Rebus Fidei et Morum*, 29th ed., Freiburg, 1952, No. 714.

G.R. Dunstan, 'Law and Religion in Contemporary Society', *Christian Jewish Relations*, Vol. 14, No. 1.

E. Dussel, *History and the Theology of Liberation* (New York: Orbis, 1976).

M. Echegoyen, 'Priests and Socialism in Chile', *New Blackfriars*, 52, 1971.

D.M. Einhorn, *Conversion to Judaism* (New York: Ktav, 1965).

I. Ellacuria, *Freedom Made Flesh* (New York: Orbis, 1976).

Encyclopaedia Judaica (Jerusalem: Keter, 1972).

E. Fackenheim, *Judaism* 16 (Summer 1967).

E. Fackenheim, *To Mend the World* (New York: Schocken, 1982).

L. Finkelstein, *Haggadah of Passover* (New York: 1942).

S. Formstecher, *Religion des Geistes* (Frankfurt: 1841).

S. Freehof, *Contemporary Reform Responsa* (Cincinnati: HUC Press, 1974).

S. Freehof, *Reform Responsa for Our Time* (USA: HUC Press, 1977).

S. Freehof, *Contemporary Reform Responsa* (USA: Hebrew Union College Press, 1974).

S. Freehof, *Reform Jewish Practice* (New York: Union of American Hebrew Congregations, 1963).

S. Freehof, *Contemporary Reform Responsa*, (USA: HUC Press, 1974).

S. Freehof, *Current Reform Responsa* (USA: HUC Press, 1969).

S. Freehof, 'Reform Judaism and the Legal Tradition', *Torah*.

Saadya Gaon, *The Book of Beliefs and Opinions*, trans. S. Rosenblatt (New Haven: Yale University Press, 1948).

R. Gibellini (ed.), *Frontiers of Theology in Latin America* (London: SCM Press,1975).

L. Ginzberg, *The Legends of the Jews* (Philadelphia: Jewish Publication Society, 1968).

H. Goldstein, 'Criteria for Observance in Reform Judaism', *Torah*.

M. Green, *The Truth of God Incarnate* (London: 1977).

F. Griffiths and D. Lewis, 'On Grading Religions, Seeking Truth and Being Nice to People – A Reply to Professor Hick', *Religious Studies*, 19.

G. Gutierrez, 'Liberation Praxis and Christian Faith' in R. Gibellini (ed.), *Frontiers of Theology in Latin America* (London: SCM Press, 1975).

G. Gutierrez, *A Theology of Liberation* (New York: Orbis, 1983).

Judah Halevi, *The Kuzari*, trans. H. Hirschfield (New York: Schocken, 1964).

C. Halbencrentz, *Dialogue and Community* (Geneva: World Council of Churches, 1977).

V. Hamer, 'A Hair's Breadth', *Theology*, Vol. LXXXIII, 1980, No. 695.

A.J. Heschel, *The Prophets* (New York: Harper & Row, 1955).

J. Hick, 'On Grading Religions', *Religious Studies*, 17.

J. Hick, *God and the Universe of Faiths* (New York: St. Martin's Press, 1973).

J. Hick, (ed.), *The Myth of God Incarnate* (London: SCM, 1977).

E. Jacob, *The Interpreter's Dictionary of the Bible*, Vol. ii, (New York: Abington Press, 1962).

L. Jacobs, 'The Origin of the Torah: A Response', *Jewish Chronicle*, 16 November 1984).

L. Jacobs, *A Jewish Theology* (New York: Behrman House, 1973).

L. Jacobs, *Principles of the Jewish Faith* (London: Vallentine Mitchell, 1964).

W. Jacobs, *Christianity Through Jewish Eyes* (Cincinnati: HUC Press, 1974).

I. Jakobovits, *Jewish Chronicle*, 24 January 1986.

M. Joseph, *Judaism as Life and Creed* (London: Macmillan, 1903).

S. Karff, 'The Question of Ishut: Should There be Minimal Standards in Reform Judaism?', *CCAR Yearbook* (New York: CCAR, 1979).

J. Katz, *Exclusiveness and Tolerance* (Oxford: Clarendon Press, 1961).

C. Ketcham, *A Theology of Encounter* (Pennsylvania: 1978).

P. Knitter, *No Other Name* (New York: Orbis, 1985).

K. Kohler, *Jewish Theology* (New York: KTAV, 1968).

M. Lazarus, *The Ethics of Judaism* (Philadelphia: Jewish Publication Society, 1900).

T. Lenn, *Rabbi and Synagogue in Reform Judaism* (New York: CCAR, 1972).

A. Malter, 'Mixed Marriage and Reform Rabbis', *Judaism* 24, (Winter 1975).

D. Marmur, 'British Reform and Jewish Status', *Journal of Reform Judaism*, Vol. XXV:2, Spring, 1978.

D. Marmur, 'The Question of Ishut: Should There be Minimal Standards for Conversion in Reform Judaism', *CCAR Yearbook* (New York: CCAR, 1979).

D. Marmur, *Reform Judaism* (Oxford: RSGB, 1973).

B. Martin, 'Contra Mixed Marriages', *CCAR Journal* (Volume XXIV, No. 3).

I. Maybaum, *The Face of God After Auschwitz* (Amsterdam: Polak & Van Gennep, 1965).

C.G. Montefiore and H. Loewe, *A Rabbinic Anthology* (New York: Schocken, 1974).

C.F.D. Moule, 'A Christian Understanding of Law and Grace',

Christian-Jewish Relations, Vol. 14, No. 1.

J. Neuner (ed.), *Christian Revelation and World's Religions* (Burns & Oates, 1967).

L. Newbigin, 'The Basis, Purpose and Manner of Inter-Faith Dialogue' in *Inter-Religious Dialogue*, Richard W. Rousseau (ed.), (Montrose, Pa: Ridge Row Press, 1981).

R. Panikaar, *The Unknown Christ of Hinduism* (New York: Orbis, 1981).

A. Phillips, 'The Place of Law in Contemporary Society', *Christian-Jewish Relations*, Vol. 14, No. 1.

G. Plaut, *The Growth of Reform Judaism* (New York: World Union for Progressive Judaism, 1965).

G. Plaut, *The Rise of Reform Judaism* (New York: World Union for Progressive Judaism, 1963).

L. Poliakov, *History of Anti-Semitism* (London: Routledge & Kegan Paul, 1975).

Rabbis Manual (New York: Central Conference of American Rabbis, 1961).

J. Rayner, 'Towards a Modern Halachah' in D. Marmur (ed.), *Reform Judaism* (Oxford: RSGB, 1973).

C.M. Reigner, 'Review of Christian-Jewish Relations', *Christian-Jewish Relations*, Vol. 14, No. 1.

R.R. Reuther, *Faith and Fratricide* (London: SCM Press, 1975).

R.R. Reuther, *Sexism and God-Talk* (London: SCM Press, 1983).

J. Rosenbloom, *Conversion to Judaism*, (Cincinnati: Hebrew Union College Press, 1978).

F. Rosenzweig, *The State of Redemption* trans. N. Glatzer in *Franz Rosenzweig: His Life and Thought* (New York: 1963).

R. Rubenstein, *After Auschwitz* (Indianapolis: Bobbs Merrill, 1966).

R. Rubenstein and J. Roth, *Approaches to Auschwitz* (London: SCM Press, 1987).

J. Sacks, 'The Origin of the Torah', *Jewish Chronicle*, 2 November 1984.

S. Samartha, 'Guidelines for Inter-Religious Dialogue'.

S. Sandmel, *We Jews and Jesus* (New York: 1965).

S. Schechter, *Aspects of Rabbinic Theology* (New York: Schocken, 1961).

S. Schneider, *Jewish and Female* (New York: Simon & Schuster, 1984).

H.J. Schoeps, *The Jewish Christian Argument* (London: 1963).

H.J. Schoeps, *Paul: The Theology of the Apostle in the Light of*

Jewish Religious History (Philadelphia: Fortress Press, 1961).

E. Sharpe, 'The Goals of Inter-Religious Dialogue' in J. Hick (ed.), *Truth and Dialogue in Word Religions: Conflicting Truth Claims* (Philadelphia: Westminster, 1974).

J. Sobrino, *Christology at the Crossroads*, (New York: Orbis, 1980).

D. Solle, 'Liberation in a Consumerist Society', in *The Challenge of Liberation Theology* (New York: Orbis, 1981).

S. Spero, *Morality, Halakha and the Jewish Tradition* (Hoboken, New Jersey: Ktav, 1983).

S.L. Steinham, *Revelation According to the Doctrine of the Synagogue* (Leipzig: 1863).

S. Samartha, *Courage for Dialogue* (New York: Orbis, 1982).

A. Super, *Immortality in the Babylonian Talmud* (Unpublished Ph.D. Thesis), 1967.

U. Tal, 'Law, the Authority of the State, and the Freedom of the Individual Person', *Christian-Jewish Relations*, Vol. 14, No. 1.

E. Tamez, *Bible of the Oppressed* (New York: Orbis, 1982).

I. Troki, *Hizzuk Emunah*, trans. M. Mocatta (New York: 1970).

The Union Haggadah (New York: UAHC, 1923).

G. Vermes, *Jesus the Jew* (Glasgow, 1976).

J. Vincent, *Into the City* (London: 1982).

E. Wiesel, *Night* (New York: Hill & Wang, 1960).

E. Wiesel, *The Trial of God* (New York: Random House, 1979).

J. Cardinal Willebrands, 'Christianity and Anti-Semitism', *Christian-Jewish Relations*, June 1985.

W.S. Wurzburger, 'Law as a Basis of Moral Society', *Christian-Jewish Relations*, Vol. 14, No. 1.

Yearbook of the Central Conference of American Rabbis, XLV (1935).

Index

Acts of the Apostles 91
aesthetic sensitivity, and the Reform
 Jew 40
After Auschwitz, R. Rubenstein 3–4,
 93–4
Afterlife
 belief in 1
 Biblical view of 19-20
 and Jewish suffering 14-17
 see also Hereafter
Against the Jews and their Lies,
 Martin Luther 87–8
agnosticism, meaning of 60
 in rabbinical students 60
 in Reform congregations 61
 in Reform Rabbis 59, 60
American Reform Rabbis,
 Central Conferences of xiii, 56–8
 *Judaism, a Manual for the
 Instruction of Proselytes* 56
 revised version of Conversion
 service 56–8
Amos, saw Israel as a sinful
 nation 70
Angel of Hell 24
Angels of Destruction 24, 25
Anglican-Jewish
 consultation (Amport)
 religious convictions
 proved an obstacle 100
 subject matter 100–1
animals, traditional
 Jewish attitude to 76
anti-Semitism ix, 2
 Christian 84–90;
 at heart of
 traditional Christology 86;
 evolution of 85–6
atheism
 in Reform congregations 61
 in Reform Rabbis 60
Auschwitz 1, 3–4, 8, 11, 14
 in the archaic religious

consciousness 4
 a hidden God 9
 not God's responsibility
 (A. Cohen) 8
 trial of God 2–3
autopsy, and Reform Judaism 44

Balfour Declaration x
Barcelona Disputation (1263) 92
being chosen, meaning of 78
beliefs, irreconcilable 103
Berg, Rabbi Charles, *Reform
 Judaism*, acceptance/non-
 acceptance of laws 58–9
Berkovits, Eliezer
 Faith after the Holocaust 9–10
 God hidden during Nazi period
 15
Bible
 containing God's revelation 38
 deeds and events involving moral
 issues 78
Biblical commandments, binding
 nature of xi–xii
Biblical criticism 33
Bigo, P., *The Church and Third
 World Revolution* 111
bitter herbs 68
black community
 advice of Chief Rabbi 64
 in the USA 121–2
Boff, Leonardo, on Jesus 109
Bonino, Jośe Miguez, on the
 Kingdom of God 110
bribery 73
Buber, Martin 95
 in discussion with
 Karl Ludwig
 Schmidt 93
Buddhism 139, 143–4
Camara, H., Jews and Christians,
 attentive to the cry of oppression
 126

Canaanites 4, 5
capitalist economy, effects of 119
caring and sharing, a wider policy
    81
Castro, Orbio de 92–3
Catholic Church, on truth in non-
    Christian religions 128
Charles, R.H. 19
Christ
    absoluteness of 108
    theoretically abstract presenta-
        tion 108
    see also Jesus
Christian Church, as the Israel of
    the New Covenant 102
Christian commitment, reference to
    Judaism 84–5
Christian witness 118
Christian-Jewish dialogue
    based on recognition of differ-
        ences between the faiths 103
    central issues for exploration
        104–5
    Judeo-centric view of revelation
        must be more tolerant 103–4
Christian-Jewish encounter,
    liberationists, and individual
    participation in creation of a new
    world 12
Christianity 132, 137, 139, 143
    mixture of Jewish and Pagan ideas
        93
    relationship with other religions
        128
    and religious pluralism 135–6
    rests on the authority of Jesus
        alone (A. Phillips) 101–2
    rise of, and cessation of Jewish
        missionizing 53
    seen as the fulfilment of God's
        revelation 102
    sees moral law as grounded in
        Jesus Christ 101
Christianity Through Jewish Eyes,
    W. Jacobs 96
Christians
    in dialogue with other faiths (L.
        Newbigin) 99
    fundamental hostility towards the

Jews 88
    little interested in plight of Jews
        96
    unjustly prejudiced against the
        Jews 85
Christology
    redefinitions of 89
    reinterpretation of 88–9
churban 10–11
circumcision 41, 43, 45, 58
    and conversion 53; and American
        Reform Judaism 55–6
    and use of anaesthetics 46
Cockerell, David, positive experi-
    ence of Jewish-Christian dialogue
    98-9
Code of Jewish Law 80, 81
Cohen, Arthur A. 6–9
    concept of deism 14–15
    on God 7–8
    *The Natural and the
        Supernatural Jew*
        6–7
    Tremendum 6
colonization 120
common sense 40–1
community life, virtues of 81
compensation, concept of 65
concentration camps, and *Kiddush
    ha-Schem* 16–17
confessional stance in dialogue 99,
    100–4
congregations, Reform, disenchant-
    ment with traditional belief
    in God 60–1
conscience, and the Reform Jew 39
conversion 48
    of a married gentile 45
    requirements for, in *Shulchan
        Aruch* 53–4
    revision of Reform service poss-
        possible 61–2
    studies of 51
    suggestion of in Old Testament
        52
    traditional vs. Reform Judaism
        58–62
conversion procedures, traditional
    and Reform Judaism 51–2

converts
    acceptance of 56
    emphasis on joining Jewish
        community 54
    motives of 53–4
    not believing in God 61–2
    positive attitude to 52–3
    question during Conversion
        service 57
    Reform Judaism, decide which
        laws they wish to observe 58
Cormie, L.
    on conditions in First World 121
    on slavery in the USA 121–2
cosmos, an expression of God 5
costume, wearing of 44
creative destructiveness *see churban*
Creed and Life, Morris Joseph,
    contemporary significance of
        Passover 117
Croatto, J.S., on meaning of
    'Exodus' 114
Crucifixion
    Jews portrayed as tormentors in
        passion plays 86–7
    as a model 10
Cussianovich, A., on the poor and
    human love 119

dead, ancient view of 19
death camps x, 9, 18
    and Jewish religious beliefs 9
    resistance to destructive logic of
        12–13
    theological dilemma of 2–3
    and the traditional believer 4
    the tremendum (A. Cohen) 7
Decalogue, centrality of moral
    praxis 79
Declaration of Principles,
    Reform Rabbis 58
deistic alternative 6–9
destruction, logic of, can be
    overcome 12–13
Deuteronomy
    final section of 33–4
    positive action against poverty 82
developed/underdeveloped
    countries, imbalance between 120

diaspora 10
discursive dialogue 100
distress and disillusionment,
    alleviation of 83
Divine encounter 129, 132
E. Dussel 114–15
Divine liberation 115
divine self-disclosure 36
divorce xii–xiv, 41, 47, 48 and
    Reform Jews 46
Dreyfus affair ix–x
Dunstan, G.R., 'Law and Religion
    in Contemporary Society' 101
Dussel, Enrique, on Moses' call to
    lead his people from captivity
        114–15

Echegoyen, M., on principle of love
    111
ecological liberation 125
ecology 125–6
economic deprivation
    Jews drawn to help suffer-
        ing groups 119
    should be addressed 82, 83
economic exploitation 119–20
ecumenism, revised 135
ego-renunciation 137
Elazar, Rabbi
    on conversion 52
    on justice and the Torah 72
    refuting Sectarians 20–1
election, defined 78
Ellacuria, I., relating to Old
    Testament prophecy to Jesus'
        mission in New Testament 110
Enlightenment ix, xiv
    and denunciation of pagans and
        idolators 130
environment, human responsibility
    for 125
equality, and Jewish ethics 74–5
eternal life 17–18
eternal salvation, belief in 17
ethical behaviour, primacy of 70,
    71–2
ethical decision-making, framework
    for absent from J. Hick
        criteria 138

ethical propriety 39–40
ethics, an area of encounter 105
Ethics of Judaism, The, Moritz
    Lazarus, moral implications of
    redemption from Egypt 116–17
Europe (Medieval), Judaism,
    Christianity and Islam 130
euthanasia, and Reform Jews 46
Exodus experience 67–70
    Jewish understanding of 69–70
Exodus, the 113–18
exploitation and oppression, struggle
    against 113

Face of God after Auschwitz, The,
    Ignaz Maybaum 10
Fackenheim, Emil 12–14
    and the new Commandment 12,
    15
Faith after the Holocaust, Berkovits,
    E. 9–10
Faith in the city 63
    Chief Rabbi's response 63–6
faith in God, obligations of 72
faith of Israel, response to God's
    will 118
faiths, universe of 89–90, 128–34,
    140, 145
family, and regeneration of inner
    cities 66
feminist theology 124
festivals, length of observance of 44
Finkelstein, A.L., on the importance
    of the Passover celebration
    115–16
First World
    inequalities between rich and
    poor 121
    nature of exploitation 121–2
Formstecher, Alomon, *Religion des
    Geistes* 93
freedom from oppression 67–8
Freehof, Rabbi Solomon
    attempting to systematize law
    within Reform Judaism 42–7
    on conversion for marriage
    150(n)
    customs not necessarily observed
    43–4

elimination of laws on humane
    grounds 46
inconsistency of 45, 46–7
traditional laws: abandoned if
    discriminating against women 45;
    abandoned if not adapted to
    modern life 45–6; to be followed
    43–4
fundamentalism, Islamic 143
    L. Jacobs disputes J. Sacks under-
    standing of the concept 34
    neo-Orthodox 31–3
    Orthodox, and critical research
    34–5
    and the Torah 32
future world, notion of 20

Gan Eden *see* Heaven
gentiles
    and entry into world to come 25–6
    wishing to marry Jews 61
German anti-Semitism ix
God
    according to Cohen 7
    acting in the future 8
    belief in: despite obstacles 9–10;
    no longer necessary for Reform
    Jews 62
    covenantal relationship with
    Israel 10
    disclosing himself xiv–xv, 36,
    103–4
    hidden 9–10
    intervening in history 8
    in Jesus 102
    Jewish understanding of 17
    as leader of the people 115
    as a loving father 133
    Maybaum's conception of 12
    as a moral being demanded
    righteous living 78
    nature of, A. Cohen's redefinition
    8–9
    permitting nations to serve own
    deities 129
    requiring obedience to his ways
    112–13
    revelation of himself may become
    confused and distorted 133

role as a teacher 8
the saviour of the enslaved 119
seen as revealing himself: to Jews
    and others 132; only to the Jews
    131–2; a serious theological
    defect 132
the supreme ruler 70–1
traditional beliefs and the Holo-
    caust 1–3
transcendent and immanent 8–9
trial of at Auschwitz 2–3
true nature of, in Pentateuchal
    revelation 103
true understanding of 91
ultimate nothing (R. Rubenstein)
    4, 6
God and the Universe of Faith,
    Professor John Hick 95
God-man relationship 71
God's love 133
good of the community 41
gospel message, subversive 111
Gregory of Nyssa, castigation of Jews
    86
Griffiths, Paul 136
Gutierrez, G.
    on the capitalist economy 119
    on the Exodus experience 113
    on human beings assuming
        responsibility for own
        destinies 120
    on shift away from past values
        111–12

Ha-Am, Ahad, on Moses the libera-
    tor 117–18
Habbakuk, denouncing sin 73–4
Haggadah 67, 68
halachah
    divine teaching 8
    non-fundamentalist 34
halachic observance, dilemma of
    xi–xiii
halachic system xv
halachists
    a better knowledge of the past
        34–5
    modern, role of, L. Jacobs vs.
        J. Sacks 33

Hamer, Valerie, 'A Hair's Breadth',
    dialogue and mutual understand-
    ing 99
Heaven
    described 22–3
    qualification for entrance to 21
Hell
    confinement to, result of
        disobeying God's Torah 23–4
    described in Jewish literature 23
    eternal punishment in 21
    rabbinic view of repugnant 28–9
Hereafter
    concept of in rabbinic Judaism
        29
    nature of 21–6
    no appeal to 15
    in rabbinic thought 20–1
    see also Afterlife
Hertz, Dr J.H. (late Chief Rabbi)
    doctrine of immortality of the
        soul 28
    rejected doctrine of eternal
        damnation 29
Hick, Professor John 129
    on assessment of religious phe-
        nomena 136
    evaluative framework open to
        criticism 136–8
    God discloses himself in numer-
        ous ways in all generations
        133–4
    God and the Universe of Faith 95
    on radical transformation of
        Christian view of religious
        pluralism 88
    on a revolution in theology 135
    seen as a non-judgemental
        inclusivist 136
    on validity of religious concepts
        and practices 136
Hinduism 137, 143
    seen as idolatrous 130
historical criticism, importance of
    35–6
Holocaust x, 1
    a *churban* 11; explanation may
        seem offensive 11–12
    difficulties for classical theism 7

Fackenheim's view 12–14
and the founding of the Jewish
state 14
a human *tremendum* 7
not forgotten 96
part of God's plan 9
result of God's intervention (I.
Maybaum) 10
and revelation 12–14
theological dilemma of xi
Hoshiah, Rabbi, on conversion 52
human beings
assuming responsibility for own
destinies 120
responding to God 7
human dignity, Jewish ethical
concern for 76–7
human freedom 7
within Jewish law 8
human life, positive affirmation of
value of 4
human motivation, and Jewish
morality 75–6
human spiritual quest 133
Hurwitz, Phineas Elijah, on
Jeremiah's injunction 130
immortal soul 28
immortality
in Biblical period 29
promise of 18
imperialism 120
Incarnation, doctrine of 97
disagreement in Christianity
concerning 94–6
an internal Christian issue 99
liberal interpretation of 98
indifference and secularism,
challenge of to Jews and
Christians 97
Ingram, Rev. Chaim, and
fundamentalism 35
injustice, incompatible with the
Kingdom of God 111
inner cities, help from more affluent
sectors of society 66
inner-city deprivation, a new
awareness
needed 122
inner-city problems, modern, Jewish

response to 81–3
Inquisition 16
interfaith dialogue 100, 103
possibility for 106
interfaith encounter 134
interfaith relations 129
intermarriage 43
Isaiah 126
saw Israel as a sinful nation 70
Islam 130, 132, 137, 139, 143, 145
Islamic fundamentalism 143
Israel, people of, historical mission
to be a light to the nations 77–8
Israel, State of 27
doubts about the viability of 8
state as a source of salvation xi
Israeli-Arab wars x

Jacobs, Rabbi Dr Louis
conflict with Rabbi Dr Jonathan
Sacks 31–7
and halachic authority 33
and halachic change 32
interpretation of Messianic hope
27–8
revelation a matter of faith 32
sees the Bible as record of God
confronting the Jews 36–7
sees Judaism as a developing faith
36
The Origin of the Torah; a
Response, answering J. Sacks
33–5
The Tree of Life, reviewed by
Rabbi Sacks 31–3
on value of punishment as deterrent 28
Jacobs, W.,*Christianity Through
Jewish Eyes* 96
on Solomon Freehof 148(n)
Jakobovits, Lord (Chief Rabbi) 81
advice to the black community 64
recommendations forget richness
and fullness of Jewish heritage 81–2
response to *Faith in the city* 63–6
Jeremiah, sacrifice of children 20
Jerusalem
destruction of 10
rebuilding of 22

Roman devastation of second Temple 10–11
Jerusalem Talmud 91–2
Jesus 138
    centrality of 101
    as the climax of human history 102
    human figure obscured by traditional theology 108
    a Jewish figure 96, 107
    nature of (C. Ketcham) 95
    a new understanding of 108–10
    not seen as absolute (R.R. Reuther) 88
    as a Palestine Jew 109–10
    seen by Christians as Christ and Lord 85
    understanding and defining 108–9
    understood as God Incarnate 102
    see also Christ
Jewish community
    awareness of discrimination against women 124
    belief in divine reward 16
    in crisis xv
    divisions of ix
    and ecological responsibility 125–6
    importance of liberation and emancipation themes 120
    and liberation theology 126
    and the poor 122
    selectively tolerant attitude to other religions 131
    transmitting Jewish heritage 64–5
    wider 41–2
Jewish ethics 116–17
Jewish faith
    belief in World to Come 15
    centrality of 133
    intersecting with Christian liberation theology 113
Jewish history, contemporary explanations for 26–7
Jewish homeland x
Jewish hope for the future 77
Jewish identity, confusion concerning xiii–xiv
Jewish law 53–4
    need for transformation xii
    pre-Enlightenment xv
    and Reform Judaism 58
    and self-respect 65–6
Jewish mission to convert, belief in 54–5
Jewish morality 71–3
Jewish nationalism x
Jewish Organization Association x
Jewish people
    Exodus and self-understanding 115–16
    exploited and oppressed 67
    fragmentation of ix, xv
    should identify with today's poor 82
Jewish religion 118
Jewish religious groupings, problems of xiv
Jewish social ethics, distinctive nature of 73–7
Jewish State
    focus of Jewish religious and cultural identity 29
    founding of 14
    need for x
Jewish status xiii–xiv
Jewish suffering, and the Afterlife 14–17
Jewish teachings, comitment to the downtrodden 82
Jewish theology
    contemporary, in a state of crisis 14–15
    post-Holocaust 7
    traditional 4, 9–12
Jewish thinkers
    progressive, seeing God as providential Lord of history xiv–xv
    unable to believe in a traditional God after the Holocaust 3–6
Jewish thought, and Holocaust theologians 17
Jewish tradition, and morality 73–7
Jewish work ethic 65
Jewish world, divisions in xi

Jewish worship, modernization of
sought ix
Jewish-Christian dialogue
at the deepest level, seeking religious insight and understanding 100
confrontation of differences between faiths 98–9
critique of a liberal approach to 98–9
a new vision 98–106
on a personal level 96–7
positive 107
positive signs in 94–6
significance of historical Jesus 109–10
Jewish-Christian encounter, obstacles to 91–8
conflict between Christian and Jew 91–4
contemporary encounter 96–7
positive signs in dialogue 94–6
Jewish-Christian relations, in the light of the Holocaust 93–4
Jewry, world, shift of focus 11
Jews
binding authority of law contained in the Torah xi–xii
bound together by feelings of community and peoplehood 37
British, no demand for multiethnic society 64
chosen by God as a sacrifice (I. Maybaum) 10
feel suspicion and distaste for Christians and Christianity 96
hatred of 86–8
historical experience different from Christians 63–4
hope lies in God's rule on earth 118
hostility of Christians 91–2
individual approach to Jewish laws xii
and inner city restoration and reconstruction 83, 123
modern, no belief in Torah MiSinai xii
must accept Divine origin of the Law 26
need not accept theories and concepts of the rabbis 26
a new orientation to Jesus through liberation theology 109
no longer found in inner cities 66
not divinely chosen (R. Rubenstein) 4–5
Orthodox
lapsed 141
modern, failure to live up to halachic requirements xii
and problem of humiliation 65
rejection of Christ as Saviour, Christian view of 85–6
and relief for the poor 65
reluctant to seek converts 62
should sympathize with underprivileged in First World 122
should take steps to eradicate poverty and suffering 119
and the Third World 120–1
see also Reform Jews
Joseph, Morris, *Creed and Life*, contemporary significance of Passover 117
Josephus, *Against Apion*, on Judaism and converts 52–3
joy and fulfilment 4
Judaism ix
according to Hillel 27
according to R. Rubenstein 5
act of sanctification (*Kiddush ha-Shem*) 15–17
at centre of universe of faiths 131
belief in God as supreme ruler 112
Biblical, on early life 19
and the building up of self-respect 66
and Christian anti-Semitism 84–90
and fundamental issue of assimilation xv
gap between traditional and contemporary views xii
and liberation theology 107–27
mainstream, confusion over central beliefs 26–9

major problems in modern age
29–30
modern: in grading of religions
140–2;
the Torah in 31–7; theology of
(A.Cohen) 6–9
non-Orthodox, religious chaos xiii
Orthodox 145; and Pentateuchal
infallibility 140–1; no longer seen
as a viable religion 141; rejecting
Reform converts 47; view of Reform
Judaism 47–8
and other faiths 129–30
post-Enlightenment, and
the Passover Festival 116
presents conception of God-idea
55
and the problems of the Inner
City 63–83
progressive, in confusion 49
reconciling with feminism 124
relationship with other faiths xiv
religion not separated from life
78
scientific study of ix
seen as an authentic and true religious expression 90
sees charity as form of self-help
66
sees no fundamental difference
between Jew and non-Jew 74–5
should seek plurality in dialogue
(V. Tal) 102–3
theological impasse separating
Orthodox from non-Orthodox 37
traditional, conversion to 52–4
and the universe of faiths 128–34
work and family life important
66
and world religions, models of
131–4
see also Reform Judaism
justice
concept unclear 40
importance of 72

Ketcham, Charles B., *A Theology
of Encounter* 95
Kiddush ha-Shem 15–17

Kimche, Rabbi Alan, on total
acceptance of authenticity
of the Torah 35
Kingdom of God 110–13
and rabbinic ethics 70–1
as seen by Jewish people 73
Knitter, Professor Paul 136
guidelines for grading religious
faiths 138–9
on the theocentric model 89
Kohler, Rabbi K.
on ancient Jewish view of the
dead 19
Jewish Theology 29
Passover as a symbol of thanksgiving 117
Kung, Hans, and salvation 128–9

Last Supper 104
Latin America, in context of the
capitalist economy 119–20
Lavater, Johann Caspar 93
Law, divine origin of 17
Lazarus, Moritz, *The Ethics of
Judaism*,
moral implications of redemption
from Egypt 116–17
legislation (Leviticus and Deuteronomy), to prevent abuse of the
poor 119
Lenn, T., *Rabbi and Synagogue in
Reform Judaism* 59–61, 150(n)
Levinska, Pelgia, on resistance 13
Leviticus
bribery 73
positive action against poverty 82
Lewis, Delmas 136
liberation 67–8, 70
of the oppressed 110–11
liberation theologians
development requires withdrawal
of capitalistic countries 120
explaining how God guides
destiny of the persecuted 115
focus on plight of Third World
poor 119-21
and oppressed of First World 121
stress Moses' role in liberation

process 114–15
liberation theology
    Christian 69; a new direction to
        Christian thought 109
    historical Jesus, a starting point
        for reflection 108–10
    and life in the inner-city 122–3
    use of Marxist social criticism
        107–8
liberation theology, and Judaism
    107–27
    areas of social concern 118–23
    ecology 125–6
    the Exodus 113–18
    the Kingdom of God 110–13
    a new understanding of Jesus
        108–10
    women's emancipation 123–4
liberty 116–17
Life after Death, doctrine of 15
Limborch, Phillip van 92–3
liturgy
    features of 104
    revision of ix
love, principle of 111
Lowental, Dr Tali, Torah supra-
        rational in life of Jewish
        people 35
Luther, Martin, *Against the Jews and
        their Lies* 87–8

Maimonides
    on avoidance of embarrassment
        to others 76–7
    Guide to the Perplexed 21
    principles of the Jewish faith 27
Malter, Rabbi Allen, study of mixed
        marriages 51
man, as centre of creation 71, 112
Marmur, Rabbi Dow
    arguing for ritual immersion 41
    and conservatism of British syna-
        gogues 47
    unconcerned with reaction of
        Orthodox community 48
marriage, and Reform Jews 44
Martin, Rabbi B., a study of
        conversion 51
Mascall, E.L., on Jewish-Christian

dialogue 98
Maybaum, Ignaz 10–12
    churban in Jewish history 10–11
    conception of God 12
    God making use of Hitler 15
    The Face of God after Auschwitz
        10
medical ethics 101
Meir, Rabbi, on resurrection in the
        Torah 21
Mendelssohn, Moses, irrationality of
        Christian doctrines 93
Messiah 23, 112
    coming of 71
Messianic Age 21–2
Messianic hope, fulfilled by Jesus
        85
Messianic redemption 21–2, 26,
        29–30, 71, 112
    doctrine modified 27
Messiahship, Christian reinterpreta-
        tion of 85
Middle Ages, Jewish suicides 16
Milson, Michael, on God and lan-
        guage 35
Minz, Rabbi Judah 44
misery and exploitation, elimination
        of 112
Mishnah, and traditions 80
mixed marriages 51
modern world, brought about by the
        Holocaust 11
moral action, focus on 77–81
moral assessment (J. Hick criterion)
        137–8
moral evils, engendered by religious
        faith 138
moral implications of redemption
        from Egypt 116–17
moral issues, no general concensus
        39–40
moral law 105
moral life
    emphasis on 79
    and God's plan for humanity 13
    seen as foundation of Jewish faith
        79
moral precepts, grounded in the will
        of God 72–3

moral transgression 79
morality
  obedience to God's love in Jesus 101
  primacy of 79, 80
Moses
  journey through Hell 24–5
  and liberation process 114–15
  seen as the liberator 117–18
Moses, Rabbi A., belief in Jewish mission to convert 55
Moule, C., 'A Christian Understanding of Law and Grace' 102
muselmann 13
Mysterious Other 89
mystery within religions 135
mystical religion 4, 6
Myth of God Incarnate, The 94–5
  Preface to 95

Nahmanides, Rabbi Moses, answering in Barcelona disputation 92
Natural and the Supernatural Jew, The, Arthur A. Cohen 6–7
nature paganism 5, 6
nazism, rise of x
neo-Orthodox fundamentalism 31–3
neo-Orthodoxy ix
New Testament 107
  anti-Semitic perspective explained 97
  Jesus' teaching in 110
  Jewishness of 84
  scholarly exploration as basis for dialogue 96
New Testament writers 84–5
Newbigin, L., 'The Basis, Purpose and Manner of Inter-Faith Dialogue' 99
Newman, Isaac, importance of historical criticism 35–6
Noachide Laws 25–6

Old Testament, and the Hereafter 19–20
Old Testament roots 108
oppressed, liberation of 111
oppression, freedom from 126

oppression and persecution, against the Divine plan 109
Origen
  Contra Celsum, God's punishment of the Jews 92
  on the 'deserved suffering' of the Jews 86
Orthodox movement
  and Jewish status xiii
  see also Jews, Orthodox; Judaism, Orthodox
Orthodox opinion, inhibiting nature of 34

pagan worship, condemnation of 129
paganism 5, 6, 8
Palestine
  migration to x
  partitioning of (by UN) x
Panikaar, Raimundo, on mystery within all religions 88–9, 135
pantheism, reversion to 5
Passion plays, writers' view of the Jews 86–8
Passover
  at the heart of Jewish aspirations for humanity 120–1
  contemporary significance of 117
  Jews at one with redeemed ancestors 117
  sustaining the Jews in their tribulations 117
  as a symbol of thanksgiving 117
Passover ceremony, unites Jewish people with their ancestors 69–70
Passover, Festival of 67–9, 115–16
Passover meal
  significance of 116
  symbolism of 68–9
Passover Seder 67
  Divine pledge 68
  and the Last Supper 104
Passover service, lesson of 69
Paul, Saint
  criticism of the Law 84
  a Jewish figure 96, 107
  teacher of New Testament ethics 101

Pentateuch 31
assumption that every word was transmitted by God to Moses 20–1
and human dignity 76
Jewish attitude to animals 76
legal codes, moral guidelines as specific rules 78–9
view of Reform Jews 142
Pentateuchal infallibility, challenges to 140–1
Pentateuchal Law, expansion of 80
pesticides 125
Pharisees 84
Phillips, A., 'The Place of Law in Contemporary Society' 101–2
pogroms x, 2
pollution, a modern problem 125
polytheism 131
seen as fallacious 132
poor, the
and the Jewish community 122
rights of upheld 111
situation of 83
solidarity with 119
the starting point of theological reflection 118–19
poverty
eradication of 111
to be fought against 119
prophetic books
link Jesus to his Jewish past 110
repeating ethical standards 79
prophetic message 70
prophets
condemning abuse 119
the conscience of the nation 70
proselytes *see* converts
Proverbs, Book of, reinforcing Torah teachings 79
Psalms 104
psychological considerations, and the Reform Jew 40
punishment, eternal, discarded belief 28
Purim, Festival of 2

Rabbi and Synagogue in Reform Judaism, T. Lenn 59–61, 150(n)

rabbinic attitudes to animals 76
rabbinic eschatology, decline of 26–9
rabbinic ethics, and the Kingdom of God 70–1
rabbinic literature
amplified biblical law 79–80
later, man's role in bringing about God's Kingdom 112–13
views not binding 17
rabbinic period, conversions during 52–3
rabbinic teaching, emphasised primacy of morality 80
rabbinic thought, and the Hereafter 20–1
rabbinic tradition, and the Oral Law 32
rabbinic writings, Medieval 92
rabbinical career, motivation for 59–60
rabbinical students, movement away from traditional beliefs 60
rabbis
concern for human hearts, Mishnah 75
explaining God's ways to man 26
morality and religion forming a single whole 72
see Kingdom of god as taking place in this world 112
struggling against idolatry 129–30
unable to compel congregation to follow Jewish law 48
upholding God's moral precepts 72
see also American Rabbis
racist policies, of nazis x
Rahner, Karl, on salvation and other faiths 128
realm of the dead, references to 19–20
reasonableness, as a criterion 41
redemption from Egypt, moral implications of 116–17
Reform code of law, criteria for 38–42
Reform Jews
distinguishing between ritual and moral law 38–9

English, and the good of the community 41
and Messianic dream 27
must be free to make up own minds 49, 50
unable to decide which traditional laws to retain 38–42
Reform Judaism
American, reform practice in 42–7
beliefs of 28
conversion to 54–8; problem of conversion 58–62
English, and Jewish law 47–9
impossible to frame new code of laws 49
individual should have freedom to practice meaningful observances 49
and Jewish Law 58
law and freedom in 38–50
more in tune with needs and expectations of followers 141–2
a prophetic faith 142
and traditional observances 41
unlikely to be influenced by English movement 49
Reform movement, and Jewish status xiii
Reform Rabbinical Conferences, encouraging conversion to Judaism 55, 56
Reform rabbis 149(n)
active search for converts 51
American: attitude to conversion 54–8; Central Conferences of xiii, 56–8
inform about Jewish law 49–50
role of 142
refusal to die, a holy act 13
Reigner, C.M., 'Review of Christian-Jewish Relations' 103
relevance, notion of problematic 39
Religion des Geistes, Salomon Formstecher 93
religions
evaluation of not judgemental 142–3
grading of: criteria for 136–9; a

sociological process 143
ranking of 135–45
seen in relation to the world 105
validity of 136
religious belief
difference between traditional and Reform conversion 59
problem of xi
religions claims, central obstacle to Jewish-Christian dialogue 94
religious commitment
necessary for conversion 57–8
and Reform conversion 59, 61
religious leaders, moral character of (J. Hick) 138
religious pluralism xiv–xv, 88, 89, 135–6
religious symbols, nature of 104
resistance, importance of acts of 13
resurrection 22, 29–30
a Biblical doctrine 20–1
doctrine of replaced in modern times 28
in the Torah 21
Reuther, Rosemary Radford
on ecological responsibility 125
reorientation of Christology 88
on women's work 123
revelation
as the basis of morality 102
disagreement over constitution of 38–9
fundamentally differing conceptions of 36
non-propositional view of 33–5
not complete and absolute in any religion 103–4
traditional concept and act of faith 36
Revelation According to the Doctrine of the Synagogue, S. L. Steinham 93
revolution, advocation of 111
reward and punishment 20
rich and poor
gap needs to be bridged 122
inequalities between 121
right intention 75
right-mindedness 75

right speech 75-6
righteous
    future compensation for their ills
        20
    sharing in a divine life 17–18
    vindication of 29–30
ritual
    and area of encounter 104–5
    and symbolism in religion 48
ritual immersion 40, 41, 53, 55, 58
ritualism 40
Rosenbloom, Rabbi J., study of
    conversion 51
Rosenzweig, Franz 7
    on the connection between
        Passover and the Sabbath 116
    a real understanding of
        Christianity 97
Rozenzwieg-Ehrenberg
    correspondence 96–7
Rubenstein, Richard 3–6, 14
    After Auschwitz 4; Jewish-
        Christian relations in the light
        of the Holocaust 93–4
    redefinition of God's nature 6

Sabbath Observance 40
Sabbath-Passover connection 116
Sacks, Rabbi Dr Jonathan
    conflict with Rabbi Dr Louis
        Jacobs 31–7
    criticizes Jacobs' use of
        'fundamentalist' 32
    laws as rules governing the
        community 32
J. Sacks vs. L. Jacobs, irreconcilable
    differences 35–7
salvation, open to non-Jews
    observing precepts of sons
        of Noah 130
salvation and liberation, and reli-
    gious ideas (J. Hick criterion) 137
Samartha, Dr Stanley 135–6
    belief in the Mysterious Other
        89
    'Guidelines for Inter-Religious
        Dialogue' 100
sanctification, act of *see Kiddush ha-
    Shem*

Sandmel, Samuel 107
Schechter, Solomon, and the King-
    dom of God 71
Schneider, S., and liberation of
    Jewish women 124
Schmidt, Karl Ludwig, in discussion
    with Martin Buber 93
Schoeneveld, Rev. C., on impossibil-
    ity of Jewish-Christian religious
    dialogue 91
Schoeps, H.J. 107
    on lack of Jewish-Christian
        dialogue 94
secularism, modern 105
self-help 65
    in the Jewish community 65–6
self-improvement policy 64
self-respect 65–6, 66
shank-bone 68
Sharpe, Eric, 'Goals of Inter-
    Religious Dialogue' 100
Shulchan Aruch, code of Jewish law
    53–4
sin, denunciation of 73–4
Sinaitic revelation xiv, 31, 103, 131
sinners
    categories of (in Mishnah) 21
    in hell 24–5
slander, an evil 75–6
social concern
    areas of 118–23
    and the Jewish people 67
social deprivation, and Judaism 66
social divide between rich and poor
    82–3
social justice, and Hebrew prophets
    70
society
    more just, building of 122
    and religions 105
    sexist structure of 123
soul
    evening visit to Hell 23–4
    immortality of 28
spiritual demands, satisfaction of 140
Steinham, Salomon Ludwig, *Revela-
    tion According to the Doctrine
    of the Synagogue* 93
suffering, and the Jewish people 1

symbols, logic of 104
synagogue, place in Jewish life 10–11

Tal, U., 'Law, the Authority of the
    State, and the Freedom of the
    Individual Person' 102–3
Talmud
    Babylonian 21, 23
    and concept of compensation 65
    concept of Hell 23
    Jerusalem 91–2
    and the righteous non-Jew 74–5
    and tradition 80
    and work ethic 65
Theocentrism 89–90
theological coherence (J. Hick
    criterion) 137
theological difficulties, evasion of
    9–10
Theology of Encounter, A, Charles
    B. Ketcham 95
theology of protest 1–3
Third World theologians, and the
    Exodus 114
tikkun (restoration) 12
    post-Holocaust 14
tolerance, needed of Jews 103
Torah 79
    collaboration between God and
        man (L. Jacobs) 32
    concern for human dignity
        includes thieves 77
    confusion over status of xii
    and equality 74
    a halachic consitution 32
    heaviness of yoke of 54
    interpretations and Pentateuch
        80–1
    in modern Judaism 31–7
    negative commands 75
    Oral 34, 80
    Orthodox rigid fundamentalist
        understanding of origin of 34
    resurrection in 21
    seen by Reform Jews as open
        and developing 142
    slow growth of 31
    as a unified text xii
    which elements are of divine

    origin xiii
    written 80, 103, 131; validity of
        not questioned xii
tradition, and moral behaviour 80
traditional laws, retention of by
    Reform Jews 41–2
Tree of Life 22
Tree of Life, Rabbi Dr Louis Jacobs,
    reviewed 31–3
tremendum, as used by A. Cohen 7
Tremendum, Arthur A. Cohen 6
Trial of God, The, E. Wiesel 2–3
Truth of God Incarnate 94–5

unemployed, are unfulfilled 83
universe of faiths 89–90
    and Judaism 128–34
    relativistic conception of 140
    theocentric conception of 133–4,
        145
unleavened bread 67, 68–9
urban mission 122–3
    discovering Jesus' message in city
        life 122–3

verbal inspiration 36
    and revelation 33–4
Vermes, Geza 107
viability, criterion of 139–42
    application of 142–4
    evaluates religions on basis of
        effectiveness 144
Vincent, John, on inner-city people
    122

Werblowsky, Zwi, on verbal
    inspiration in Jewish
    Orthodoxy 31
Wiesel, Elie
    case for and against God 3
    and the Spanish Jewish family 3
    struggle with religious doubt 15
    The Trial of God 23
    theological implications of the
        Holocaust 1–3
will of God, and moral precepts 72–3
Willebrands, Cardinal Johannes,
    arguing that Christianity is
    not anti-Semitic 84–90

Wise, Rabbi T.M., belief in Jewish
     mission to convert 54–5
women, within Church structures 124
women's emancipation 123-4
women's self-respect, restoration of
     123-4
world religions
     modern approach to 132–4
     not all today play major role in

lives of adherents 144–5
World to Come, divisions of 21–3
worship, an area of encounter 104
Wurzburger, W.S., 'Law as the Basis
     of a Moral Society' 102

Zionism, and Jewishness 29
Zionists, secular, and the return
     to Israel 27